Praise for *Productive Learning*

"Fans and disciples of Seymour Sarason (and I am one) all know that education reform needs a change in course. Indeed, the daily practices of schools, education research, and U.S. educational policy all need such a change. Neither Professors Głazek and Sarason, nor anyone else, can give yet a complete description of what these changes would involve. But when the change happens, the leaders of the change will all acknowledge their considerable debt to this book. The reason is that the needed change in school classrooms will be very hard to recognize as such unless these leaders are thoroughly familiar with the concept of 'a context of productive learning.' In this book, Głazek and Sarason collaborated on an extraordinarily daunting attempt to create and analyze a context of productive learning in which, simultaneously, Sarason was the student and Głazek the teacher and vice versa. They attempted what must surely be a 'Mt. Everest' example of the concept: explanation of Einstein's famous formula $E = mc^2$. The result should be of intense interest to a broad audience concerned with the present problems of science education as well as the nature of a context of productive learning."

—*Kenneth G. Wilson, H. C. Youngberg Trustees Distinguished Professor*
Nobel Laureate for Physics, 1982
The Ohio State University

"Professors Głazek and Sarason have written a creative and instructive book that will be read for years to come. Drawing upon their backgrounds in physics and psychology, they, like C. P. Snow in his book *Two Cultures and a Second Look,* support Einstein's recommendation as to the importance of the humanities. The authors' purpose is to help readers acquire a substantive grasp of how Einstein accomplished what he did and the implications of this for educational reform. The reader's view of teaching and learning will be forever changed by the authors' insights."

—*Dale L. Brubaker, Professor Emeritus of Education*
University of North Carolina

"This is an interesting and provocative book, written by a psychologist with several thousands of hours of observation and analysis of classroom teaching in public schools and a physicist. The book starts with a critique of teaching in our schools and explains why educational reform has been so minimal in its effects. The movie *Mr. Holland's Opus* is used as a distinguisher between good and bad teaching methodology. These chapters are followed by physics chapters on the foundation of Einstein's $E = mc^2$. The authors follow Einstein's thinking and use the features of light as a vehicle for their discussion. They fold in stories and shy away from formulas, which they leave for Appendices. The book ends with a chapter on the philosophy of teaching. The book is well written and eminently readable;

the arguments are easy to follow. I recommend the book to anyone interested in the basis of modern physics and Einstein's role in it."
—*Ernest M. Henley, Professor Emeritus of Physics*
University of Washington

"By making accessible and intelligible Einstein's theory of relativity, this remarkable book reveals to its readers the power and possibility of their own learning, and, in doing so, brilliantly demonstrates the power and necessity of productive learning for everyone."
—*Andy Hargreaves, Thomas More Brennan Chair in Education*
Lynch School of Education, Boston College

PRODUCTIVE LEARNING

Science, Art, and
Einstein's Relativity
in Educational Reform

Stanisław D. Głazek   Seymour B. Sarason

CORWIN PRESS
A SAGE Publications Company
Thousand Oaks, California

KH

Author photo of Stanisław D. Głazek by Piotr M. Jeżewski.
Author photo of Seymour B. Sarason by Stanisław D. Głazek.

For information:

Corwin Press
A Sage Publications Company
2455 Teller Road
Thousand Oaks, California 91320
www.corwinpress.com

Sage Publications Ltd.
1 Oliver's Yard
55 City Road
London EC1Y 1SP
United Kingdom

Sage Publications India Pvt. Ltd.
B–42, Panchsheel Enclave
Post Box 4109
New Delhi 110 017 India

Printed in the United States of America

Library of Congress Cataloging-in-Publication Data

Głazek, Stanisław D.
Productive learning: Science, art, and Einstein's relativity in educational reform / Stanisław D. Głazek, Seymour B. Sarason.
     p. cm.
Includes bibliographical references and index.
ISBN 1-4129-4059-1; 978-1-4129-4059-7 (cloth) — ISBN 1-4129-4060-5; 978-1-4129-4060-3 (pbk.)
    1. Learning. 2. Educational change—United States. 3. Science—Study and teaching—United States. I. Sarason, Seymour Bernard, 1919- II. Title.
LB1060.G557 2007
370.'973—dc22

                                            2006008165

This book is printed on acid-free paper.

06   07   08   09   10   10 9 8 7 6 5 4 3 2 1

Acquisitions Editor:	Elizabeth Brenkus
Editorial Assistant:	Desirée Enayati
Production Editor:	Melanie Birdsall
Typesetter:	C&M Digitals (P) Ltd.
Indexer:	Sheila Bodell
Cover Designer:	Rose Storey

2/7/08

*To Dominika and Kuba
and
To Lisa Pagliaro*

It is not enough to teach man a specialty. Through it he may become a kind of useful machine but not a harmoniously developed personality. It is essential that the student acquire an understanding of and a lively feeling for values. He must acquire a vivid sense of the beautiful and of the morally good. Otherwise he—with his specialized knowledge—more closely resembles a well-trained dog than a harmoniously developed person. He must learn to understand the motives of human beings, their illusions, and their sufferings in order to acquire a proper relationship to individual fellow-men and to the community.

These precious things are conveyed to the younger generation through personal contact with those who teach, not—or at least not in the main—through textbooks. It is this that primarily constitutes and preserves culture. This is what I have in mind when I recommend the "humanities" as important, not just dry specialized knowledge in the fields of history and philosophy.

Overemphasis on the competitive system and premature specialization on the ground of immediate usefulness kill the spirit on which all cultural life depends, specialized knowledge included.

It is also vital to a valuable education that independent critical thinking be developed in the young human being, a development that is greatly jeopardized by overburdening him with too much and with too varied subjects (point system). Overburdening necessarily leads to superficiality. Teaching should be such that what is offered is perceived as a valuable gift and not as a hard duty.

—A. Einstein, *New York Times*, October 5, 1952

SOURCE: This is an excerpt from "Einstein Stresses Critical Thinking" by Benjamin Fine in the *New York Times*, October 5, 1952, found using the online archives ProQuest Historical Newspapers, *New York Times* (1851–2002).

Contents

About the Authors

Stanisław D. Głazek is a professor in the Institute of Theoretical Physics at Warsaw University and the author of over 50 original articles in leading professional journals, mainly about theory of the subatomic structure of matter. During sabbatical leaves, he worked in German and American universities including Regensburg University, City University of New York, The Ohio State University, and Indiana University. He also was a Fulbright Scholar and a recipient of a grant from The MacArthur Foundation.

Seymour B. Sarason is Professor Emeritus of Psychology, Yale University. During his distinguished 48-year career, he has been one of the most astute observers and incisive critics of efforts to reform our schools. Among his more than 45 published books are *The Predictable Failure of Educational Reform* (1990), *Schooling in America: Scapegoat or Salvation* (1983), *The Culture of the School and the Problem of Change* (1972, 1996), *Charter Schools: Another Flawed Educational Reform* (1998), and *And What Do You Mean by Learning?* (2004).

Acknowledgments

We want to express our gratitude to Drs. Robert Perry and Alan Towbin who read our drafts and reacted helpfully to us. We are grateful to The MacArthur Foundation for a small grant, which made it possible for the two authors living in two different countries on two different continents to meet and finally finish the book that had occupied them over a period of years. It goes without saying that Lisa Pagliaro's efforts to be helpful were predictable and essential. We want to acknowledge our gratitude to the following people in Poland for their contribution to our understanding of what happens between the minds of a student and a teacher: Drs. Konrad Bajer, Maria Ekiel-Jeżewska, Piotr Goldstein, Piotr Rączka, Magdalena Skompska, and Adam Smólski. We would like to thank Prof. A. Trautman of Warsaw University for bringing the existence of Lenard's textbook and the comments in Miller's work to our attention. Finally, and very important, we acknowledge with deep gratitude the help that Ania Głazek ceaselessly provided us during the entire course of work on this book.

1

Structure of the Book

This book is intended for several overlapping audiences: students and teachers in science courses in high schools; students and teachers in science courses in college; and a much larger group of people who already have a college education, which convinced them that they wanted nothing to do with math, sciences, and especially physics. At the same time, the book is addressed to the educators and reformers who are deeply interested in creating opportunities for productive learning by generations of students. About a century has passed since Einstein's work was done, and it is not an exaggeration to say that 99.9% of the American population has not the faintest idea of the meaning and consequences of his contribution, and we include here many scientists who are not physicists. But our goal is not to popularize science. We aim to explain what is missing in the educational system and what reformers need to think through in order to become able to begin a process of meaningful change. Our goal is not to provide a ready-to-follow instruction how to do it, an instruction that everybody will be able to follow without effort, but to point out what needs to be achieved for those who are interested in the heart of educational matters. We make our point by first describing many examples of what is involved, including what happens in classrooms and what $E = mc^2$ means. Having analyzed these examples, we will come to basic conclusions concerning reform toward the end of the book. The reader is asked to remember, as we indicated above, that this book is in no way meant as a popularization of Einstein's work, *but rather as an attempt to help readers acquire far more than a superficial grasp of how Einstein accomplished what he did and what this implies for the future of educational reform.*

In deciding to write this book, we knew we had to confront several problems. The first problem is that teaching subject matter requires that you make as explicit as you can what you mean by learning. As we make clear in this book, we have concluded that one basic reason for the failure of educational reform movements is a superficial and fuzzy conception of learning. More specifically, the criteria for distinguishing between contexts of productive and unproductive learning do not exist in any readily available form and go undiscussed.

The second problem is that the teaching of science in our high schools and in introductory science courses in college is scandalously poor. If that statement represents a consensus, it has the effect of glossing over the fact that the quality of teaching non-science subject matters does not come up smelling like roses.

The third problem is that we have developed a conception of a context of productive learning in which the teacher-student interpersonal relationship is center stage. But in writing a book, we and the readers are not in an interpersonal relationship. The readers cannot ask us a question, nor can we ask them or see their body language. In a context of productive learning the interpersonal relationship is, among other things, one of mutual safety and trust.

There was, however, one feature of our audience that we felt was unquestionably valid: They would approach the book with feelings of insecurity, even anxiety. And yet they were curious about what they had heard or experienced about science, math, or Einstein. This was not our imagination; such feelings are precisely what students told us they had. For us, their curiosity had to be nurtured, encouraged, and developed. That meant to us that our starting point had to be that curiosity.

In our experience, this curiosity—curiosity about any subject matter— about what made the subject matter both interesting and important was no small issue. In our case, we decided that the starting point was, How come issues surrounding the measurement of the speed of light ultimately led to $E = mc^2$? In other words, the worst starting point would be to plunge into the details of the formula $E = mc^2$ itself. It was exactly this kind of decision making that explains why we devote two chapters to four Hollywood films that show the viewer the differences between contexts of productive and unproductive learning in the lives of young people and their teachers.

This sensitivity to where students are psychologically coming from is reflected in the fact that in this book there are very few equations, and the ones that are included in the main text only involve addition, subtraction, multiplication, and division. One of the goals of this book is to help readers grasp the basic problems Einstein was confronting, how he solved them, and the consequences of his solution. And perhaps the most difficult problem for people to understand is that Einstein pulled the rug, so to speak, from under the millennia-old idea that time was absolute, which means that it is the same for all observers regardless of where they are and how fast or slow they move with respect to each other. As we emphasize in these pages, the millennia-old conception of time works well for us earthlings in our daily existence. It does not work at all as soon as we start to deal with large speeds on Earth or large distances in outer space.

Before going directly to $E = mc^2$, would learners be interested to know that long before Einstein came on the scene, nations had a vital practical interest in and competed in discovering more accurate methods for the measurement of time at a distance? That it was vital for military purposes, transportation, and communication? That Einstein spent about five years in a Swiss patent office in Bern reading and judging patent applications on improving measurements of time by clocks? Would students find it interesting to be told how and why not only nations but individual scientists were occupied with the measurement of time? We answered all of these questions in the affirmative, and our experience supported that answer.

There was another part of the story we felt had to be included if the reader was not to be left with the impression that Einstein was a young physicist working alone on a problem that he was able to solve because of his brilliance and creativity. That he was brilliant and creative the reader would accept. But that "alone" leaves out history and its contexts. It leaves out, for example, the very high correlation between war and scientific and technological advances. That was true, in the case of physics, before Einstein and after him. The atomic bomb and nuclear reactors for generating useable energy employed results of Einstein's work. Nor should it go unnoticed that almost immediately after World War II ended the American military was the first agency to publicly express its concern about two things: how the teaching of science in schools extinguished interest in a career in science, and why it was in the public interest to begin to reform schools. In fact, it was the military that began to fund projects by scientists to develop new, more accurate curricula. That this curriculum reform movement was, for all practical purposes, a failure was a consequence of the lack of a firsthand experience of school culture, as well as a total avoidance of any meaningful discussion of the distinguishing features of contexts of productive and unproductive learning. In the half-century since, it is as if no one has learned anything, and in our concluding chapter we discuss our discouragement (to indulge in understatement) about the educational reform initiative of President George W. Bush.

This book has gone through several stages, each of which had to be abandoned as not appropriate for the book format. In the first stage, we prepared a syllabus for teaching $E = mc^2$ to a self-selected group of high school students and one of us (Głazek) spent about four months teaching at one of the best Warsaw high schools. The experience told us that what was intended could not be achieved within a school environment where students have many duties and the system does not allow for extended analysis of issues that students want and need to think about in order to gain confidence in their own reasoning about the issues. Despite these difficulties, when at the end of the experience the students were asked to evaluate what they had learned, without exception they wrote that it was "new, new, new." More specifically, they felt that they grasped some important new points about Einstein's work, especially about the concept of time. But it was also clear that the environmental pressures to attend to homework and many other school activities did not allow them to study according to our syllabus. The lesson we drew was that the predetermined syllabus was not appropriate for the contemporary classroom. Candor requires that we say that the "teacher" (Głazek) fell into the predictable and understandable trap of bending under the pressure to cover the subject matter, thinking that he had to adhere to the specially designed sequence of topics the syllabus contained.

However, it was not clear to him at that time that the problem was elsewhere than in the syllabus. So, he redesigned the syllabus and went through it over a period of about a year with a group of three self-selected, college-educated adults (two scientists and a teacher of science). The shocking result was that the adults had even greater barriers to overcome in the classroom-like environment than had the high school students. Namely, the adults were constantly concerned about their image in the eyes of others, about how much they appeared to understand. Głazek often observed that adults were not prepared to easily admit to difficulties they had with the subject matter and, primarily, with the interpersonal relationships. These relationships were difficult because the course concerned basic notions such as time and space and, most important, how one thinks about them. An adult running into a basic conceptual difficulty in public feels very unsafe and endangered; in order to preserve status, he or she may choose not to ask questions when a serious difficulty is blocking his or her mind. It became clear to Głazek that the interpersonal relationship between a teacher and a student is essential for the discussion concerning relativity and $E = mc^2$. The experience allowed us, a physicist and a psychologist, to begin talking about issues of education that were no longer focused on the subject matter as much as they typically are. Of course, the same issues were very important between the two of us: one virtually ignorant about psychology and the other about physics.

It turned out that the more we studied the subject from the standpoint of how two minds can or cannot communicate, what are the barriers, and what is required to overcome them, the more we saw how different our frames of reference were concerning almost every issue that came up—far beyond any specific element of the subject matter. Bit by bit, we uncovered to each other—and together—how dramatically different were our starting points and how much we had to go through to overcome the disparity between our frames of reference. The nature of our relationship in writing this book is described in some detail in Chapter 2.

From the initial images of what needs to be done in order to explain $E = mc^2$ and how it should be done—greatly underestimating the magnitude and type of difficulties one has to overcome—we went a long way, to the point where we understood that the first goal of productive teaching is to create and sustain a relationship of safety and trust in which any and all questions can be articulated. Initially, the subject matter is far less important than a thorough understanding of the relationship between the minds of a teacher and a student.

The question then emerged, How can one explain what matters most in the process of teaching using the book format? A book is not a classroom or a place to meet and talk, ask, respond, ponder, take time to solve a problem, and come up with a solution. The only possibility we found was to tell a sequence of stories.

Speaking very personally and honestly, we were forced to the conclusion that unless and until the distinguishing features of contexts of productive and unproductive learning are understood, evaluated, revised, and the appropriate process of teaching continuously redesigned, educational reform will never see light at the end of the tunnel. One of us made that prediction, orally and in print, in 1965 and in 1990 said the same thing in a book titled *The Predictable Failure of Educational Reform.*[1] Our experience in schools and colleges teaching $E = mc^2$ has not changed our minds about the future. This conclusion is elaborated at length in the last chapter of this book.

Nothing in this book is intended to blame anyone or any group for the failure of the educational reform movement. Educational reformers are well-intentioned individuals who want to improve the outcomes of schooling. And the same is true for teachers, the teachers of teachers, parents, and public officials who feel obligated to do something, almost anything, to improve matters. But all of them are locked into a conception of learning that is self-defeating. The situation resembles attempts to explain the properties of light using pre-Einstein theories of time.

There are a handful of instances where the reformers have employed a conception of learning very similar to what we have written, and they have done this with at-risk urban high school students with inspiring consequences. But these exceptions simply have not and will not spread beyond the confines of their demonstrations for which there is credible evidence, not mere opinions.

Finally, if at the point of a gun we were forced to say in one or two sentences what this book is about, it would go as follows: Just as Einstein destroyed the notion that mass was one thing and energy was another, entirely unrelated, subject matter and the interpersonal context are inevitably and indissolubly intertwined. But the magnitude of difficulties associated with comprehending this statement exceeds the magnitude of difficulties that people usually have with comprehending Einstein's relativity. Our book attempts to explain what this statement is supposed to mean.

The structure of the book is as follows. Chapter 2 explains in an introductory way why and how a physicist and a psychologist came to write a book on the implications for educational reform of Einstein's revolutionary scientific contributions. In order to explain what we have to say, we need two basic items of input. One item is a story about the content and meaning of the formula $E = mc^2$, which we tell in this book in a way that we think is most helpful to a person who never had a chance to appreciate what Einstein did. We have studied the problem of how to explain Einstein to high school students, to adults, and between the two of us. On this basis, we attempt to guess what may be going on in the reader's head, and we start from there. This particular motivation does not stem from our assumption, which we do not make, that we know better what the readers do or should think, but it does mean that we cannot be truly helpful by reporting what we have understood without beginning a discussion from issues familiar to the intended readers. As far as a book format allows, we try to build an interpersonal relationship with a reader and use this relationship to create a context of productive learning. However, our main goal is neither explanation of $E = mc^2$ itself nor popularization of science in general. We want to discuss and explain the role of the context of productive learning in educational reform. The example of $E = mc^2$ helps us explain what we mean. But in order to begin from a familiar starting point, we need to show first how an application of the concept of context of productive learning may look in the practice of a school. We need to begin by showing examples of a relationship between a teacher and a student that we have in mind when we speak about the context of productive learning.

Therefore, we begin in Chapter 3, "Mr. Holland's Opus," with a description of the career of a music teacher in a contemporary school. This story is based on a film with the same title, and it illustrates with a number of examples what is involved in a context of productive learning in which the teacher understands the way of thinking of a student and uses this understanding to communicate with the student in a meaningful way, building a context of productive learning in the environment of a classroom, a school, or home. *Our bigger point is that the concept of a context of productive learning is not specific to music.*

Chapter 4 then makes a transition from art to science. We invoke examples from mathematics, astronomy, rocket science, and dancing. Although it is commonly believed that principles of teaching in the case of music must be completely different from principles of teaching in physics, we argue to the contrary and illustrate what we mean with examples. The common assumption that art and science are vastly different, and the related belief that productive learning in art is or should be based on different principles than in science, are most probably a result of the school practice that inculcates such opinions rather than the actual state of the matter. As soon as we make the point about the context of productive learning having basically the same nature in art and in science, we are ready to begin the story of $E = mc^2$.

Chapters 5 to 16 form a carefully arranged sequence of interrelated stories that culminate in the explanation of how the formula $E = mc^2$ comes about. We attempt to build a collection of images that we consider relevant to the concept of productive learning in the case of $E = mc^2$. The imagery is related to the experiences that we deem familiar to almost every intended reader. One can think that the images and our stories about them form pieces of a puzzle. The reader needs to put the pieces together with our help. We foresee a number of difficulties that a reasonable person may have when trying to imagine and think about the host of problems that Einstein had to grapple with, such as how fast a beam of light moves or what light is made of and how it is seen by different observers.

We hope that by reading the sequence of chapters the reader will eventually become the owner of a set of interrelated, comprehensible, and historically plausible images that facilitate understanding of how a concept of a frame of reference emerges from the need of a human being to precisely describe what happens around him or her. Basically, a carefully built frame of reference is a practical tool for learning about the world, and learning is largely related to a process of building and improving one's own mental frame of reference. By using the story of $E = mc^2$, we can introduce a precisely defined concept of a frame of reference that is used in physics. Then, a concept of a relationship between two frames of reference of two different observers, in physics called a theory of relativity, is discussed. This relationship is used by one of the observers to interpret in his frame of reference the results of measurements that are made and described by the other observer in his own and different frame of reference. Thus, the two observers learn about the same events using their own frames of reference, and they need to understand the relationship between their frames in order to exchange information in a meaningful way. A comparison of their findings in an imagined, tabletop experiment leads to the formula $E = mc^2$. The two observers are called Max and Ming, and it is explained in Chapter 11 why we chose those names.

The key Chapter 17, "Toward a Conception of Learning," takes advantage of the story of Mr. Holland and the story of $E = mc^2$. The chapter combines information from the two stories in order to explain the concept of a context of productive learning as a process that is based on a meaningful exchange of information between a teacher and a student. We use the two stories, what happens in Holland's school and what happens in Einstein's relativity, to show an analogy between them that illuminates the problem of the failure of educational reform.

The formula $E = mc^2$ means that there exists a necessary relationship between the energy E of a piece of matter and the mass m of this piece of matter. The relationship reflects the relationship between frames of reference of two observers in physics. The concept of a context of productive learning means that productive learning of any subject matter is necessarily connected with the interpersonal relationship between a teacher and a student. As the energy E of a body cannot be separated from its mass m, productive learning of any subject matter cannot be separated from the interpersonal relationship between a teacher and a student. Our understanding of how $E = mc^2$ comes about originates in the understanding of how frames of reference of two observers are related. The key issue of education is the interpersonal relationship between a teacher and a student, why it needs to be built, how it is built, and how it is used in a process of productive teaching and learning.

The meaning of this analogy requires study for two reasons. One reason is that Einstein's relationship between frames of reference of two different observers of one and the same world of events is not easy to grasp. Einstein discovered the relationship more than a century ago, and the public is still unaware of the content and meaning of his discovery because it is hard to figure out, given the teaching practices adopted in the current educational system. The other reason is that the relationship between frames of mind of a teacher and a student is harder to comprehend than Einstein's theory because the interpersonal relationship between human minds is much more complex than Einstein's relationship between frames of reference of observers in physics. Nobody can tackle outstanding problems of educational reform with lasting success without being prepared for a much greater conceptual effort than Einstein's relativity requires. This is why educational reforms fail, and why they will continue to fail until the relationship between the minds of a teacher and a student is properly recognized and judiciously employed in the process of design and redesign of a self-correcting reform.

The context of learning in a classroom is embedded in the bigger contexts of the educational system and society. The last part of Chapter 17 draws on the stories we tell in the earlier chapters and discusses what reformers need to think about before they engage in attempts to solve the real problem. We explain why the intellectual caliber of the challenges of educational reform vastly surpasses common perception. The challenge is much greater than Einstein ever faced because his considerations were limited to the physics of matter that is not alive and cannot think, feel, or respond to stimuli in the context of its own existence, all these factors determining the result of the teaching that a human being is exposed to. But knowing the magnitude of implications of the formula $E = mc^2$ that followed from a proper understanding of how different observers see the same world in physics, we draw by analogy the conclusion that a proper understanding of the context of productive learning, based on understanding of the interpersonal relationship between the minds of a teacher and a student and on how they see the world and each other, will most probably lead to unimaginable improvement in our educational practice and, hence, also in the quality of our lives.

2

And What Do You Mean by Learning?

From the outset of the authors' collaboration on this book, it was agreed that Sarason would write this chapter in order to represent, in a preliminary way, why and how a Yale professor of psychology (Emeritus) and a much younger professor of physics at the University of Warsaw came to collaborate on a book about the implications of Einstein's revolutionary scientific contributions for educational reform. That question can be asked in another and more general way: Why do most highly educated people regard $E = mc^2$ as a total mystery impossible for "ordinary mortals" to understand?

By way of answering this question, I (Sarason) ask the reader to ponder the following question: What if before World War II people were asked if and when women would be flying airplanes in battle, reach the highest levels in corporate America, or be serious candidates for the presidency of the country as well as of major universities? A very small number of people would have said that only in some very distant future, perhaps in a century or more, could they envision these changes. What the bulk of people would have said is that the minds and talents of women were, to use current jargon, not "wired" to make them adequate to what those activities demanded. In brief, women were not up to coping with those demands. Two decades after World War II, changes in the roles of women would begin to give different results, and if you repeated the same question today, people would wonder on what planet you had been living.

Another example. For millennia before the late eighteenth century, it was considered self-evident that the masses of a nation were incapable of ruling themselves and needed a ruler who unilaterally would make all decisions and would direct the masses and protect them from the consequences of their incapabilities and cognitive immaturity. And except for a very occasional revolt, the masses truly believed they were not capable or worthy to be other than dutiful peons at the bottom of the mountain, at the top of which were the all-powerful, all-knowing exalted rulers. That is why the American and the soon-to-follow French revolutions are signal events in human history. Capability was redefined.

What can people become? What are the contexts that determine how this question should be explicitly posed and answered and relevant action implemented? In this book, the focus will be on the classroom, a site intended to achieve goals deemed essential for students. It is a site for learning embedded in a larger context called "a school," which in turn is part of "a school system," which in turn is not comprehensible apart from its relationship to other external "groups and agencies" with vested interests in how educational pedagogy and practice contribute to meeting stated goals. The list is quite long: parents; local, state, and federal governments; preparatory programs in colleges and universities for teachers and administrators; unions; and the courts.

The classroom is a small, circumscribed place, but it bears the imprimatur, in formal and informal ways, of the external groups and agencies. When people talk about "our school system," they refer to their city or town's schools, although since and because of World War II they increasingly have come to see that what they call "their" school system is a part of a larger system, the parts of which are frequently in an adversarial relation to each other. This larger system of vested interests is uncoordinated and regarded by people generally as malfunctioning, by which it is meant that students are not being helped to learn what they should and can learn.

This dispiriting state of affairs has over the past six decades led, predictably, to blaming a variety of factors that have been feckless and/or counterproductive in their consequences. I have discussed these issues in all of my writings, beginning in 1965 when, orally and in print, I predicted the current state of affairs. Today, I make the same dysphoric conclusion about the initiative of President George W. Bush. Most relevant here is my recent book, *And What Do You Mean by Learning?* This chapter has the same title.

The origins of my position go back to my 1954 book, *The Clinical Interaction.* I described and discussed there the variables that are omnipresent in the act of a clinical psychologist administering a test to a person for the purpose of obtaining information to serve as a basis for a therapeutic course of action. Clinical interactions, if filmed, will vary considerably to a viewer. Nevertheless, regardless of these surface variations, they all reflect the role of variables essential for comprehending any one of those interactions. The variables are not arcane; indeed, once stated they are obvious. The problem is that identifying and taking them seriously is a complicated and demanding affair.

My 1971 book, *The Culture of the School and the Problem of Change* (reprinted in 1996), builds up to the conclusion that the context of learning in the classroom far more often than not blatantly ignores the variables I discussed in *The Clinical Interaction* (1954). And that is why, in 1990, I wrote *The Predictable Failure of Educational Reform.* I berate myself that it took me much too long to recognize, if I was right, that continuing to ignore all these omnipresent variables truly doomed educational reform.

Pessimist I was, but I did not want to be a messenger of doom. However, as the years went on, I could not avoid the conclusion that unless those variables were taken seriously, the American social fabric would deteriorate, as would the values and goals that are distinctively American. You can write two histories of America. One would emphasize hypocrisy, sleaze, rampant materialism, and misguided self-interest. The other would be a history of struggles to protect individual rights, an independent judiciary, a free press, and, as in the case of World War II, to oppose inhuman tyrannies which, if they were successful, would be the end of America as we knew it then and as we know it today.

The effort to change and improve our schools—an effort that since World War II has cost trillions of dollars from local, state, federal, and foundation sources—has been fueled by constitutional obligations centering not on equality of outcomes but on equal opportunity to learn, change, and grow. An inadequate school system is America's Achilles' heel in an increasingly dangerous world.

THE CLASSROOM AND THE ATOM

Physicists had long known that atoms had a structure, dynamics, a nucleus, and that atoms were not of a piece; they varied in weight, number of constituent particles, volatility, and size of the nucleus. (It is more complicated than that, but it need not detain us here.) They knew that the nucleus contained, relatively speaking, a large amount of energy and that if that concentrated nuclear mass was split, it would release energy sufficient to split nuclei in other atoms. If they were correct, it would explain or be relevant to an explanation of many phenomena in the universe. It also meant that in the distant future, humans would acquire all the energy they needed.

Around the time that World War II broke out in Europe, two refugee physicists demonstrated that they had split the atom with predictable consequences. It also meant that an atomic bomb could be developed that when dropped would have incalculable consequences for an enemy. The danger was that Germany would develop a bomb first, in which case the

War would soon be over. That is why physicists in this country asked Einstein to write a letter to President Franklin Roosevelt stating that knowledge existed that made it possible to develop such a bomb.

Three problems had to be solved: first, to perfect a way to ensure that the atomic nucleus would split; second, to be able to harness and control the released energy; third, how best to construct and deliver the bomb. You could say that for physicists, the splitting of the nucleus and releasing its energy was tantamount to finding their scientific Holy Grail. And this was accomplished by a laser-like concentration on the invisible atomic nucleus, which split.

So what does splitting the nucleus have to do with educational reform? What is analogous to the nucleus of an atom in educational reform? My answer, which will be elaborated later, is the classroom, and the igniting force is the teacher. There are four parts to my answer.

1. All educational reforms, regardless of how they vary in theory or in the details of implementation, explicitly intend to alter behavioral, programmatic, and interpersonal regularities in existing classrooms. To alter these regularities in desired ways can only be achieved through a teacher as the igniting force.

2. The existing regularities are deemed inadequate and ineffective for the goal of capitalizing on and exploiting the interests and abilities of students' learning and cognitive growth. The purpose of the reform is to unlock students' energy, which will fuel the motivation to learn and do more than before the reform started. For example, the reformer may be aware of studies or draw on personal experiences and classroom observation, which all tell us that as students go from elementary to middle to high school, their interest in and respect for school learning steadily decrease. The reformer seeks to unlock student energy and motivation that will alter that state of existing affairs; if successful, independent observers will agree that a marked change has occurred and the change is measurable.

3. Every reformer knows that changes in students are impossible unless an organizing nuclear force in the classroom also changes. That nuclear force is the teacher (as it is the parents in the home). Unless appropriate changes in teachers occur, the reform will fail. The reform requires the teacher to be a different and better igniting force.

4. The reformer knows that the classroom is a complicated social situation composed of students varying in all sorts of ways and teachers who vary in all sorts of ways. Students and teachers are not particles whose features can be tracked in a cloud chamber or nuclear reactor. The reformer also knows that the individual classroom is embedded in a larger system of classrooms, which can and will be barriers to his or her efforts.

Unfortunately, the above four points have, for all practical purposes, been given short shrift by almost all educational reformers. In the analogy with nuclear forces, to ignite a productive reform would require serious understanding of what the four points say and what would have to happen outside of and concomitant with school in order for the expected changes to occur over time.

There is one word in the above that requires special consideration. It is a word that probably has the highest word frequency count in the educational literature. And I know of no reformer or teacher who will deny that the word is of bedrock importance—self-evidently, they will say—because it is the glue that suffuses everything in the classroom. It refers to visible and invisible phenomena. Indeed, the regularities we discern in a classroom, pre- or post-reform, are not comprehensible without knowing or flushing out what the reformer or teacher understands by that word. The word is *learning.* When I ask people generally (and educators in particular) what they mean by learning, they are initially silent; a puzzled expression appears on their faces. It is as if they feel they should have no difficulty defining the word. They usually proceed to articulate broad generalizations about changes over time. With no exceptions, they are dissatisfied with what they said, a reaction I had years ago when I asked it of myself.

A PROVISIONAL DEFINITION OF LEARNING

The word or concept of learning is not like the words "sticks and stones," which refer to visible and palpable objects. I use the word learning to refer to a process that takes place in an interpersonal context (student and teacher) and, in the case of the student, comprises internal features to which we conventionally apply such labels as "motivation," "cognitive," "affective," "emotional," and "attitudinal." These features are omnipresent and seamlessly interrelated, and their strength is never zero. In the teacher-student interaction, it is not only the student who "learns" but also the teacher, a fact that too often is glossed over or ignored. In the case of the teacher, whose obligation is to understand the process going on in the student, the strength of the features comprising the learning process will be of a different order and pattern than in the case of the student.

What I am emphasizing here is that in the context of productive learning both teacher and student are learning. What a student learns in the interactions with the teacher always stands in some relationship to what the teacher learns about the student. Teacher and student have different frames of reference, which can vary from no overlap in mutual understanding to a productive mutual understanding.

It is obvious that this definition implies that teachers should have a level of sophistication far beyond what preparatory programs help them acquire today. It is no less obvious that even if they acquire such a level of sophistication, it requires time with students as *individuals* that teachers of a class of more than about 15 students do not have, especially today when teachers are judged solely by the degree to which students can regurgitate on tests the subject matter they have been taught.

Of course, subject matter is important, but not if its contents are soon forgotten and relegated to the file-and-forget category or experienced as medicine given by uncomprehending adults. Yeats is often quoted as having said that the purpose of education is to light fires, not to fill empty vessels. We are told that curiosity kills the cat. From the earliest days to its death, the human organism is the most curious, exploring, question-asking organism on Earth. You would never know that if you observed the modal classroom, especially in middle and high schools.

PRODUCTIVE AND UNPRODUCTIVE CONTEXTS OF LEARNING

By what criteria can we distinguish between productive and unproductive contexts? The question is unanswerable—if by an answer you mean test scores and graduation or going on to college, all of which are important but none of which tells us anything about how the individual has assimilated, judges, values, and utilizes subject matter. Risking oversimplification for the sake of brevity, let me just say that what I would want to know about a student is the strength of his or her wanting to learn, to learn more about self and others and the world the student lives in. From the standpoint of most students, that world is dramatically and unfortunately different from the world of schooling.

I know of no school system that seriously and systematically determines the substance and strength of students' wanting to learn as I have described it. Some schools will seek to determine unsigned responses to questions about use of drugs and alcohol, sexual activity, smoking, or cheating. A good deal has been learned about how to obtain these and other confidential data, including ways of determining when an individual's responses may not be truthful. The point is that methods exist, or can be developed, for measuring a variable like "wanting." No one has ever denied that this variable is revelatory and important, not only for the individual but also for those whose professional obligation is to create and sustain a context of productive learning.

Students are not atoms or puppets; they are not empty vessels to be filled with knowledge and routinized cognitive skills. Students begin schooling wanting to become more than they are. They want to "grow up." And although they cannot put into clear language what growing up means, they expect they will be engaged in a process that will give them a sense of growth, of personal agency, of competence, of being someone whose individuality is recognized and fertilized.

However vague, those expectations refer to a context of productive learning in which teachers will play a central role. Teachers sincerely and deeply want to play that role; they are not villains intent on squelching those expectations. They are, rather, victims of preparatory programs in which they acquire a conception of learning conducive to a context of unproductive learning. What they acquire in these preparatory programs is in no way antithetical to the culture of a modal school today with their undergirding assumptions for how they should be organized and structured. Schools are not unique institutions but different, sharing characteristics of all complicated institutions such as universities, corporations, religious and political institutions, and so on.

An argument can be made that in the post-World War II era schools have responded to mounting external criticisms by introducing a number of changes in their effort to improve the quality of educational outcomes. The assertion is true if by it is meant that there has been a long list of fads and fashions that were adopted: new curricula, the open classroom, site-based management, increased parental participation in decision making, staff development, entry into the profession only after a college education, computers as a form of educational salvation, raising standards, charter schools, magnet schools, vouchers, sanctions on ailing schools, and more. Aside from a school here and a school there (the usual exceptions), the overall picture nationally has not changed. There is, of course, no single variable or explanation for these failures. There is no one starting point for educational reform. But wherever you start, it will take decades before the reform under optimal conditions will be able to claim to have brought about a general change. That optimal conditions cannot be counted on is a realistic assumption. However and wherever you begin, there are, in my view, two inextricably related starting points. The first is clarifying what is meant by learning. The second is mounting a research program to judge how any conception of learning will distinguish between contexts of productive and unproductive learning. Until those interrelated steps are taken, 50 years from now there will be moaning and wailing about an ineffective system of schools. The fruitless game of blame assignment will go on. Is physics really different?

For hundreds of years, physicists unreflectively assumed what they considered self-evident: Time is absolute. But Einstein, by what he termed "thought experiments," demonstrated the invalidity of that assumption.

For hundreds of years, really millennia, people assumed that they knew what learning was. I am suggesting (I have proved nothing) that that assumption is wrong and has had self-defeating consequences.

GŁAZEK VERSUS SARASON AND VICE VERSA

The idea to collaborate to write this book was Stan's. He had read what I had written on educational reform and was especially taken with what

I wrote about contexts of productive and unproductive learning. Several things powered his interest. First, he was appalled at what passed for science education. He was no less critical of the lack of interest of some of his scientific brethren in public education, including physics. He also did not agree with the assumption that it was an exercise in futility and an indulgence of masochism to expect that even college-educated people, let alone high school seniors, could grasp the substance and significance of Einstein's theory of relativity in any meaningful way. It was an assumption with which—in the ways of the self-fulfilling prophecy—the educated public came to agree. For Stan, the problem was not what ordinary mortals are but what they can become, not what they have learned but what they could learn. He thought that it was an obligation—a socially responsible obligation—to seek and develop ways to make the Einsteinian revolution understandable at an intellectually respectable level, to remove the mystery surrounding $E = mc^2$.

I was intrigued by his suggestion for several reasons. First, throughout my life and writings and professional roles (plural) there is one theme: Human history is about many things, but the most fateful one has been how conventional wisdom has been a barrier to ideas that challenge the existing relationship between what people are and what they can learn to be. Second, I never had a course in physics and my attempts to read numerous books about Einstein were, to indulge in understatement, totally unsatisfying and led me to conclude that I did not have the kind of brain that could comprehend the theory of relativity. From my point of view, I was the problem, not the authors of the books I read. Third, in high school I had math, geometry, and algebra, which ensured that I would never willingly take such courses in the future, a conclusion at which all other students in these classes had arrived, a fact I did not find consoling. I had the mental marbles to memorize the subject matter but not those special marbles to understand what I was memorizing.

When I was ill and my mother gave me a bitter-tasting medicine, I took it because I knew I was sick. I needed the medicine. Why did I need algebra and geometry? They had no personal meaning for me, I had no motivating reason to embrace them.

I had reservations about collaborating with Stan. Although I told him that my knowledge of relativity was a smidgen above zero, I sensed that he could not believe that I was as ignorant as I said. One thing I have learned about teaching, teachers (myself included), and the curricula they use or are required to use is that they do not start where the students are coming from, psychologically and substantively, and they also do not adopt an appropriate time perspective.

That is why I told Stan that if he could teach me to understand the logic and content of Einstein's contribution, I would confer upon him something akin to a Nobel Prize. If he could teach that to me, he could teach it to any biologically intent high school senior or college student, regardless of his or her major interest. He could count on me to want to learn, to give it my time and effort. And I said that in unvarnished language several times before we began. I also said that if it became clear to me or him that in the collaboration either of us felt our individual purposes were not or could not be met, we would say so and remain friends. I had already determined that I wanted him as a friend because I regarded him as a bright, decent, likeable person. I felt totally safe to trust him to be gentle and forthright when he would soon find out the dimensions of my ignorance.

What worried me was that Stan is a mountain climber who has reached the top of the usual high mountains—with the exception of Mount Everest, on and around which too many climbers are resting forever. My reservation about collaborating was that although we had discussed at length what I considered the features of a classroom context of productive learning, he had primarily taught university students in physics. His experience in schools and classrooms was next to nil. He had never attempted, in the courses he taught for undergraduates not majoring in physics, to teach them the significances of $E = mc^2$. I thought that Stan did not have the required grasp of the context of productive learning that he would need in order to teach me.

I did not dream up my conception of the context of productive learning. It developed over years of observing many hundreds of classrooms and talking to teachers and students. And although the absolute number of teachers who create and sustain a context of productive learning is scandalously low in schools, when you do observe such teachers, you are brought up short and the flow of adrenalin increases. It is like what former Supreme Court Justice Potter Stewart said about pornography, "I have trouble defining it, but I know when I see it." Stan was going to teach me relativity. Would I be able to help him grasp what was involved in creating and sustaining a context of productive learning?

I knew it would not be easy because it requires major changes in your thinking and practices. My reservations took on a complexity for one obvious additional reason: We were not and could not create a context of productive learning between us and readers of the proposed book because there could be no interpersonal relationship between us and the readers. That meant we would have to be extraordinarily sensitive and creative in how we used language and examples to convey with minimal distortion the story of $E = mc^2$. The audience for whom we would be writing is, for the most part, composed of educated people who "know" nothing about Einstein, or who know that he is not their cup of tea. As in my case, their eyes glaze over when they peruse a book on relativity which, by the end of the first chapter or two, convinces them that their brain is not wired to comprehend its contents.

It was easy to say we must be extraordinarily diligent and creative, which, like the ideal qualities of motherhood, are desirable virtues imperfect people can only approximate in action. But we would not be able to see and be with readers with whom we have no interpersonal relationship, who cannot stop reading to ask us a question, and who cannot show us their faces and body language.

I knew all that from the start, although I had not said to Stan that we would fall short of the mark, albeit less than others who made an effort intended to be read by a general audience. I have long consoled myself that it is no sin to fall short of the mark; it is a sin to have no mark that may be attainable by you. So we began.

And so did the predictable problems, just as they do in marriage—in our case, a sought-after intellectual wedding. It is literally the case that if we were to describe the problems we encountered, it would be the size of a modest book. I shall discuss a few problems most directly illustrative of the questions that arise when you adopt the conception of learning I presented earlier.

One problem was the use of equations. It was Stan's position that equations would automatically convey their importance for purposes of precision, which physicists require for their findings. If the key equation was not in our story, we would be robbing the reader of an understanding of what Einstein's theory and predictions were. It was my position that the goal of the book was to help the reader grasp the logic, nature, and history of concepts. Why was Einstein intent to explain why the speed of light is always the same, 186,000 or so miles per second? Why is it constant for observers regardless of how fast they are moving in relation to each other? Why did Einstein come to question the validity of the way we think about and measure time? The formula $E = mc^2$ says that the energy of all bodies depends on their mass times the square of the speed of light. It is not that energy is one variable, mass is another, and the speed of light a third one; that was the pre-Einstein conception. In the real world, the formula says, it is one dynamic process in all bodies everywhere. These and kindred concepts could be grasped without equations by the readers of our book, I assumed. I understood, reported, and applauded Stan's desire for readers to get a more complex understanding. Stan is, among other things, a mathematical physicist; he thinks in the language of mathematics. My language consists of words and concrete imagery. Our differing points of view had enormous relevance for a context of productive learning. Who was our intended audience? How well do we know that audience in regard to our pedagogy and time perspective? Where do we start? How do we avoid boring them or overwhelming them with what they cannot assimilate? How do we prevent reaching the conclusion that the operation was a success but the patient died?

Stan was like the stereotype of the Jewish parent (he is not Jewish) who wants only the best for her child, and "best" is correlated with the amount of knowledge the child must or is expected to learn, the more the better. Stan was reluctant to accept my opinion that science education in American secondary schools, and in most colleges, was blatantly poor and counterproductive. He could not believe that this state of affairs was probably worse than it was in Poland, perhaps a good deal worse. It is understandable that he did not know, as educators and the general public do not know, that a major stimulus of the post-World War II reform movement came from the military agencies. Almost immediately after the war ended, these agencies asserted that the sciences, which had been crucial in winning the war and were essential for the future of the country, would not be able themselves to attract enough students and increase the quality of education programs for scientists and engineers. The military had learned that by the time students finished high school, their interest in a scientific career had been largely extinguished. The reform of school science curricula was initially supported by the military agencies. But the seeds of that support neither sprouted nor blossomed. (We will have much more to say about science and math education in the final chapter, where we suggest the situation has gotten worse.)

I was adamant about my reluctance to be an author of a book targeted for an audience that long experience had taught me, rightly or wrongly, would come to the book with attitudes of incompetence toward math and the presumed unfathomability of Einstein's ideas. Yes, we would be delighted if they bought the book, but we would be crushed if it had the fate of Steven Hawking's best seller about the new conception of time, a book that I and almost every other reader could never understand or finish; a case where the operation was a success but the patient died.

Bear in mind that Stan was in the role of my teacher, which quickly sensitized him and was a source of enormous frustration and puzzlement for him. I told him I may be an extreme case of ignorance compounded by embarrassment, but that was what he and I were up against. I also told him that even without using equations, it would be the opposite of easy to forge language that would convey the spirit and truths of what Einstein discovered.

At an early point in the collaboration, Stan set to teach relativity to a small sample of high school students in Warsaw. He did so with six high school students who volunteered to work. They wanted to learn, obviously a self-selected sample. He worked with them over a combined period of about four months once a week after school. On two occasions, there were long intervals between meetings. These students had a good deal of homework for their regular school classes. It was not an ideal situation for teaching and learning. From Stan's expectations, he told me in a letter, it did not go well. Only one student "got it all," and by "all" he did not mean or know that he was confident that the student's understanding was secure. The other students did not get very far. Stan was disappointed. But he asked the students to write a page about their reactions to the experience. When I read the papers, I was forcefully struck by how much the students enjoyed and were stimulated by their experience, even though it was apparent that they knew they had difficulty comprehending some of the concepts. Their eyes had been opened to concepts heretofore a total mystery to them. If Stan was disappointed, I was not. Even if what I learned from the students' letters was incomplete, it was not wrong. If it had been a very new and challenging experience, it increased and did not extinguish their interest in relativity. But Stan had never taught high school students, and he readily told me that he did not feel he had done a good job of teaching.

So what would he consider a good job? I told him that it was understandable—and I use that word advisedly and sincerely—that he had violated some features of a context of productive learning. One was that he had started with a predetermined conception of what he wanted them to learn in a predetermined unrealistic time period, which did not allow him to take seriously his understanding of and relationship with students as individuals who obviously and inevitably vary in attitudes, assets, and vulnerabilities. There is nothing more subversive of a context of productive learning than a rigid, predetermined "curriculum" according to a classroom clock. You may have to do just that in a factory, but a classroom is not a factory. A factory makes things. A classroom purports to be in the business of nurturing, fertilizing, and expanding human minds.

Stan was my teacher and I was his student. It was, for me, one of the most intellectually and interpersonally rewarding experiences ever. Not the least rewarding is that it illuminated for me why people have difficulty understanding (really accepting) what a context of productive learning requires of a teacher, any kind of teacher. It was as a result of my collaboration with Stan that I wrote *And What Do You Mean By Learning?*

Why is it easy for people to readily agree with what I have termed a context of productive learning and then implement it in action in ***inappropriate*** ways, or, worse yet, consider the context really utopian in its implications for educational reform?

One reason is that people are socialized in ways, and to a degree unreflectively, to accept what, for the sake of brevity, I will say is the conventionally vague conception of learning that sounds virtuous and self-evidently valid. People, for example, do not recognize that learning, any type of learning in any context, involves unlearning previous aspects of knowledge, habits, skills, and attitudes. What you have to unlearn is never emotionally neutral in regard to the features constituting the learning process. That is the major reason for people to conclude that understanding Einstein's theory at some meaningful level is a task they do not want to confront. And they are right, in the sense that what they have been told and tried to read (or have seen lectures or videotapes) about Einstein's theory quickly reveals that their accustomed ways of thinking about mass, energy, light, space, and time will have to be unlearned and that the process is by no means captured by terms like "trial and error" or "you can do it."

I and many other people have seen and interacted with children of bilingual parents who could, by age two or three, speak and understand two languages, as if they were "born" that way. An adult learning a new language is understandably mystified why he or she is having so much trouble learning the new language. After countless hours of discussion and of reading draft after draft of the chapter on relativity, we resolved our differences by largely eliminating equations and discussing them in Appendices. That resolution was possible because Stan came to see that we were not writing a book merely to superficially acquaint readers with the basic concepts of relativity, but rather to help the reader grasp how those features were interrelated and how they ultimately allowed Einstein to change our accustomed view of the world, from atoms to the entire universe.

We would not talk down to the readers, we would not require them to become competent physicists, but to take seriously that they chose to read the book because they are people with a curiosity about relativity. Our task was to avoid blunting or extinguishing that curiosity, that wanting, which would stimulate them to expend intellectual energy to comprehend why what Einstein did was literally revolutionary, no less so than the Copernican demonstration that the Earth revolved around the Sun and not vice versa. And it was no less revolutionary than the physical laws that Newton discovered.

It is not generally known that those earlier revolutions did not take hold, even in the scientific community, for almost a century after their discoverer had died. It is now a century since Einstein published his papers. His fate has, in some ways, been worse because (again) even though in the broad scientific community a majority of its members know that Einstein made remarkable discoveries, they are hard put to explain the logic and substance of what he did. It is different, of course, in the community of physicists who regard what they know as beyond the ken of other types of scientists. The consequence has been that the educated public knows nothing about relativity except that what Einstein did cannot be comprehended at any meaningful level by the general public. I will have more to say about this at the end of the chapter.

Let me now turn to a set of problems that tempted me to title the following paragraphs "Famous Last Words."

THE PROCESS OF TRANSLATION

In deciding to collaborate, I knew there would be writing problems, by which I mean that writing is a form of translation in which the ideas and imagery in your head have to be translated into words and sentences that capture what is in your head. You are like a sculptor who is seized by an idea or image you want to render in a solid block of limestone. You may know the properties of the stone, and you have the tools by which the stone can be made to reflect the image in your head, a concrete, complex image that you will sculpt out of the stone. You would think that writing would be less difficult than sculpting because your tools are very familiar to you: language, pen, pencil, paper, or computer. It is not less difficult than sculpting; it is just different.

From the time I was in high school, I knew I would be a writer, regardless of my choice of career. I quickly learned that writing was easy as long as you overlooked the distance between your imagery and the words you put on paper. It is next to impossible to maintain the distinction between words you write and imagery in your mind, unless you have some standards and you care about what people understand about what you have written. Writing is a back and forth between the internal and external, a constant war that never ceases, even with a peace treaty or a truce. This is not a problem for a writer who wants only to satisfy himself or herself and is not concerned to have the book published and read. I assume there are such people. I have never known one. The writers I know are intent to reach an audience who will say that what the writer has written is understood by them as the writer had hoped.

I knew this book would be difficult to write, more difficult than anything I had written. Much of this book would be about ideas, concepts, and procedures about which I knew little or nothing but which Stan, my teacher, would help me understand. Far more than he, I knew it would not be easy, which is why I stated clearly that I could put my name on the book only as a junior author and only if I understood its contents the way I wanted our audience to understand it. If our intended audience did not gain such understanding, we could not blame the reader. What we owed the reader was more than a superficial grasp of the logic and substance of Einstein's contribution. It was our responsibility to help them grasp those by clear step-by-step instructions in language that was as clear as we were capable of.

In the course of teaching me, Stan came to see that eschewing equations was not an instance of throwing the baby out with the bathwater. But I underestimated the difficulty of our task of translation. It was by no means unusual that we would spend a morning on one paragraph (stopping occasionally for bagels, cream cheese, and coffee). What I found particularly helpful is how Stan would come up with examples—often taken from the history of pre-Einstein physics, which set the stage for Einstein's revolutionary contribution. For example, why European governments and their scientists were aggressively competing to come up with a precise way to synchronize clocks separated by varying distances. Or why paradoxes in pre-Einstein conceptions of relativity led Einstein to the most searching description and analysis of time and position of moving bodies. Or how tiny differences in measurement have enormous significance for what we think about the nature of the world. And it was Stan who selected four well-known movies that portrayed the differences between context of productive and unproductive learning.

Translation from the mind of an author to that of the reader is not just communication, although in many instances they overlap. Translation is conventionally understood as an attempt to render in one language what someone wrote in another language without distortions that do an injustice to the ideas, imagery, and style of the original writer. Somewhere in one of her remarkable books, Edith Hamilton presents translations over the centuries of an excerpt from a play of one of the great Greek dramatists of Periclean Athens. Hamilton does not have to tell the English-speaking readers that these translations seem awkward and often mystifying to the reader, who finds them dull, opaque, and is puzzled by the heights of acclaim given to the author. And then Hamilton presents her translation, and (for me) the clouds parted, the bright sun appeared, and the beauty and power of the excerpt hit me square in the face.

Stan and I are not in Hamilton's league. If the two of us always knew that, it was no excuse for not trying to translate Einstein in a way that would help readers come to appreciate—a word that refers to increase in value—what Einstein did. It is apparent that we were dissatisfied with (but respectful of) what others have accomplished in confronting the same task for a comparable audience to ours. Whether we have done this better or worse than others will be judged by our readers.

THE READER'S OBLIGATION

I am sure you have read a novel and come to a passage or page about which you are not sure you are getting the point the author is making. So you think that perhaps you are dense, you read it again, and you may decide to read on, or go back to the previous chapter, or plunge ahead in the hope that what puzzles you will be clarified. Or, the author refers to a character or place or event that is vaguely familiar, but you cannot remember where earlier in the book the author refers to what is puzzling you now. (These are the kinds of instances that drive me nuts when I read Tolstoy.) Writers of detective stories are particular masters in casually dropping a hint on page 20 and not referring to it again until page 200, by which time your memory of page 20 is unrecognizable and you have no desire to search for the hint.

There are no hints in this book; there are places where the readers will, we hope, feel obliged to read and re-read, motivated by the certain knowledge that no one can understand Einstein without struggle precisely because he challenges one's accustomed ways of thinking about such familiar concepts as light, time, space, energy, and mass. Humans live on Earth dealing with the practical routines of daily existence. But, as Einstein demonstrated, those familiar concepts are totally ineffective and misleading for understanding the laws of the universe. Life on Earth is not exempt from these laws. Our accustomed concepts serve us well; they "work" for us as long as the gravity of the Earth keeps us on it and tiny differences in measurements only have tiny consequences.

It's another story when you seek to comprehend how the universe is structured and works. There is absolutely nothing in the conception of a context of productive learning that implies that learning is easy, unaccompanied by struggle, a ladder of success easy to climb, exempt from the dictum that the more you know the more you have to and want to know.

EDUCATIONAL REFORM

I am aware that I have devoted much of this chapter to Einstein's relativity contributions. What the reader needs to know is that our collaboration was made possible by total agreement on several things.

First, that which we call an educational system has been, is, and will continue to be deplorable if truly radical changes are not initiated. That is most flagrantly obvious and egregious in the case of science education.

Second, unless and until contexts of unproductive learning are replaced by productive ones, educational reform will continue its sorry record.

Third, we were challenged by the thought that we should discuss productive learning in regard to a subject matter not represented in any meaningful way in high schools, a subject matter that challenges traditional, overlearned concepts of time, space, and energy.

Fourth, we justified our choice of the subject matter by our belief that people should come to appreciate Einstein's relativity and are capable of acquiring such knowledge at a nonsuperficial level that would increase the number of people who might seek more knowledge in a scientific career. At the present time, as in the past, a large fraction of those entering college avoid courses in science, especially in math and physics.

The final reason was very decisive. Both Stan and I were in agreement that as a theoretical, practical, and research problem, educational reform is far more complex and daunting than what Einstein was up against. Einstein knew the history of his discipline, and theories of light had been around for some time. The substance of his theory did not have to do with changing attitudes of people, complex organizations, cultural-political traditions, or people embedded in an economic system where issues of power and vested interests, differing conceptions of what people are and could become, and of course a self-defeatingly unarticulated conception of human learning are all omnipresent.

Put it this way: We can do without Einstein's work, but we cannot do without a transformed educational system. Many people know in a vague way that a failing educational system will slowly and steadily transform our society in ways not to their liking. The ongoing reform initiative of President George W. Bush will, we predict, confirm the maxim that the more things change the more they remain the same, or get worse.

Nothing was more confirming about my conception of learning than what occurred in the relationship between Stan and me. As I indicated earlier, we are different kinds of people and we come from very different countries and family backgrounds. I knew little or nothing about physics (let alone Einstein). I have spent decades in and around schools. Stan had little or no experience in schools. I was eager, but much less than Stan, to collaborate. I knew that Stan vastly underestimated the issues and problems that would arise. I knew that both of us were not shrinking violets who would resort to superficialities at the expense of standards and goals, and we both knew that we would have a rough time because we would only work together for a week or two, four to six times a year.

It may seem unusual to the reader that the second chapter of this book is largely about the nature and course of the collaboration. Such matters are usually discussed briefly in a preface. It deserved a special place in this book because the story of the collaboration is paradigmatic of a context of productive learning. I said that Stan was my teacher and I was his. I was his pupil as he was mine. It was an unusual interpersonal context, one whose potential for unproductive learning was high because in our role of teacher each had a lot to unlearn and learn, inevitably frustrating, requiring a bottomless reservoir of patience, always keeping in mind that we had to understand each other as a student and pupil. We each were obliged not to forget that as teacher and pupil we were not God's gift to perfection and that our desire to pull it off must never waver or decrease.

Two factors deserve special emphasis: personal safety and interpersonal trust, two sides of the same psychological coin. I quickly was at ease in exposing my ignorance of physics and relativity, without worrying that by his language, facial expression, and other forms of body language Stan thought I was beyond rescue or I was unteachable. Similarly, Stan did not flinch or feel resentment when I would say that although he had read everything I had written about productive learning, he had nevertheless written paragraphs and pages based on the assumption, an invalid one, that our intended audience could understand what he was trying to say. I knew from the outset something that Stan could not appreciate when we started: Someone who had not spent time in our schools, like the professor of physics he was, could not know what an unproductive context of learning the bulk of our classrooms are. And since our intended audience would also be college-educated people who had avoided taking physics and math courses, we could not afford to write on the basis of a vague hope they would grasp what Stan had written. "I may be," I said frequently, "an extreme example of what it took for you to get me to see some light at the end of the tunnel, but experience has forced me to conclude that I am not that extreme." Stan never took what I said with resentment or an unkind putdown.

I have no doubt that if each of us was on the psychoanalytic couch freely associating about our relationship, the picture I have painted would not be one of sweetness and light. But one thing would not change: We very quickly developed feelings of safety and trust with each other. Without such features, a context of learning is an impoverished one.

The reader may contend that it is unwarranted to generalize from a one-on-one context to a classroom where teachers may have, say, 25 students. Our conception of learning will require many changes. A teacher whose pedagogy rests on a conventional conception of learning is not likely to be a "better" teacher with a class of 15 students than one with 25. Of course class size is important, but the hope for consequences will depend on one's conception of a context of productive learning. I have seen teachers of classes with 20 or 25 students approximate and sustain a context of productive learning. We will have much more to say about these matters in the final chapter of this book, where it will become apparent, we hope, that our conception of learning will require radical changes in our schools and the selection and training of educators.

There have been numerous occasions when I have presented my views and in the question and answer period I have gotten this response: "I agree with much of your critique of the existing state of affairs and the past failures of attempts to reform it. But you are a utopian [one person said I was as unrealistic as Don Quixote] asking citizens to support changes that at the present time only potentially may bear edible educational fruit." My answer, then and now, is that the criticism was, in all respects, precisely that directed in 1787 to those who forged the American Constitution. And there were more than a few among the members of the constitutional convention who worried that their critics might be right.

The controversy about what people are and what they can become has a very long history. It is a controversy documenting that the human mind is our greatest ally and foe.

3

Mr. Holland's Opus

Features of the context of productive learning are equally important in all disciplines because they are required for educating a person. This task is not specific to any discipline. In order to illustrate these statements, we shall discuss two apparently very different disciplines: art and science. Our goal is to show how similar they are with respect to the context of productive learning.

This chapter describes the case of music. We take advantage of the movie *Mr. Holland's Opus.* The main character of the movie, Glenn Holland, was a musician who became a teacher of music in a high school.

Initially, he was ignorant about the school environment and he did not know how to teach. All he knew about teaching was what he was taught during his own schooling, and, presumably, in a preparatory program in college. What he learned had little to do with the concept of productive learning. When he tried to repeat for his students what he went through in his education, he could not win the students' attention, exactly as his teachers did not win his attention. Consequently, he did not communicate with his students on the issues that truly mattered to him in music. And being in a typical school environment, he was alone and without help when he was miserably failing with his students. But he was a talented man, curious and passionate, and eventually he had an awakening: He discovered the meaning of a context of productive learning. His understanding of how to teach effectively then developed in a lifelong learning process. In that process, Holland influenced the lives of hundreds of students. They were grateful to him for his helping them to find their desired paths into the future. In the same process, Holland also learned how to live his own life.

However, Mr. Holland's teaching career abruptly ended when he was fired at the age of 60. His accumulated experience in teaching was expendable in the system he worked in. His knowledge and skills were considered irrelevant in areas other than music, such as mathematics or science. When the budget had to be cut, the music program was terminated, and he was let go.

We describe Mr. Holland's story here not only to better explain what we mean by the context of productive learning, but also to prepare our demonstration in the next chapters: If the educational system Holland worked in were based on the recognition of the context of productive learning as the key factor in the education of a person, then firing Mr. Holland would be considered a crime against the system. Letting him go would be viewed as fundamentally contradictory to the system's principles. And in the system we propose, the one that would be based on the context of productive learning as the underlying and overarching principle, there would exist a great desire and multiple options for utilizing Holland's knowledge and skills for the benefit of many more students, teachers, and other participants in the system.

Before you read this whole chapter, however, we suggest that you see the film *Mr. Holland's Opus*. The film is available on video or DVD. The running time is 143 minutes.

When watching the film, you can observe that from very early on it forces us to consider how an experienced teacher would prepare to teach students. To be effective, we expect, she or he would first try to determine what students knew and what their skills were. To gain this insight, a teacher would need to spend some time with the students, observe their reactions to various questions and situations, and understand their way of thinking on the pertinent issues. Only then would the teacher be able to adjust the teaching process to the students' interests and abilities, predicting areas where they would have difficulties. The skillful teacher would thus first interact with the students, find out where they were in regard to the goal the teacher wanted them to reach, and only then start the teaching process precisely from that point.

Similarly, if we, as writers of this book, wanted to find out where you, as a reader, are coming from, we would have to meet and talk with you. But writers of books cannot talk with all readers they want to reach before writing their text. This is why we want you to see the movie.

As a side remark, we are obliged to give justice to all filmmakers and their audiences and say that there is nothing truly new about this idea. The concept of presenting vivid images for initiation of meaningful dialogues was used already in ancient theaters.

FEATURE 1. MR. HOLLAND'S
FIRST DAY IN SCHOOL

The story of Mr. Glenn Holland starts on the first day of his work at the John F. Kennedy High School, where he was hired as a music teacher. Holland applied for the job because he needed money to pursue his goal: He was a musician and wanted to write music. His wife, Iris, encouraged him to take the job. She described the job as "just a gig." After four years of working as a schoolteacher, he would have enough money to compose at will, become famous and rich. If it didn't work, Holland could always try something else, she said.

Mr. Holland woke up very early on that day after another night of working on his symphony, and he drove to school to begin his career as a teacher. At 7:30 A.M. he parked his car in front of the school building. He did not have the slightest conscious understanding of the dynamics of the world he was about to enter.

When he met Vice Principal Wolters in the parking lot, he immediately discovered that he would have to put up with having Wolters as his boss. Much worse, he would have to put up with having a boss, something that a freelancing composer was not used to having in any form, and certainly not in the form of Wolters. Holland immediately learned that Mr. Wolters was not a kind or sensitive person; Wolters made a nasty comment about Holland's car as soon as Holland introduced himself.

Confused, Holland walked into the building. The school was crowded like a beehive and he was lost. Mrs. Jacobs, the principal, caught him in the crowd and took him to his classroom, explaining on the way what she expected from him as the music teacher.

Holland was too self-absorbed to remember that it was Principal Jacobs who hired him. We can immediately infer from their very brief dialogue (Mrs. Jacobs did almost all of the talking) that there was no meaningful contact between the two of them before Holland came in to teach.

The hallway conversation was the entire and only preparation Holland received before he faced a class of students and started "teaching" music in a school that, for all practical purposes, was visually and spatially a mystery to him. The hallway instruction by Mrs. Jacobs also tells us that Holland's experience with teaching was limited to courses he took in college to "have something to fall back on." Mrs. Jacobs did not like this attitude. It was clear that Holland's remark was insulting to her as a teacher and a principal. But we know that the attitudes Holland brought with him on that first day were in part a consequence of his being entirely unprepared for people like Wolters and Jacobs, who wrongly assumed that Holland knew what he was supposed to do in his classroom. There was nothing in his interaction with Wolters and Jacobs that in any way indicated that they understood what a teacher thinks and feels on the first day he or she becomes an independent teacher.

Mrs. Jacobs spoke swiftly. She told Holland that he was expected to advise some students. Holland had no idea what that could mean. He imagined that Mrs. Jacobs spoke about students who were unusually talented in music and who required his attention as a musician. But he was not sure, so he asked if they were good. "They are trying hard," she explained, and Holland remained puzzled. Mrs. Jacobs also told Holland she expected in a few days his lesson plans for the first two months.

All the talking happened in a crowd of hurrying students. Holland entered his classroom unprepared for what he was to face. His mindset was a guarantee that he would have trouble, and he truly did not know what to expect of his students or himself. This is how Mr. Holland's socialization began on his first day as a teacher.

From what he did in class, it is not a great leap to conclude that he considered it his duty to teach students the essence of music in some abstract way, using highly technical terms, and on a factory-like schedule. Most probably, he thought that such a plan for teaching could lead to learning because he had received the same treatment when he was in school. He forgot that it had not been a successful strategy from the students' point of view. Something happened to him over the years, at school and later, so that as an adult he was already on the other side, willing to force students to do things he hated to do when he was young. He did not realize at that time that students were not interested in what he was trying to teach them. As a result of this disparity, he was soon to discover that not only students but also teachers wished to be somewhere else rather than in school.

He came to school to earn money and have free time for working on his music every day. The actual purpose of teaching was not particularly important to him. He was surprised that his vision of the job as easy and not time consuming was laughable to a gym teacher, Bill Maister. Holland met him at his first lunch. Maister laughed because he could not remember when he had any free time. Holland probably imagined that a football coach had even less work to do at school than a music teacher had. If this was not the case, what would he be faced with himself?

At the same first lunch at school, Holland saw that the place was not a democracy of teachers and students, not a union that could even remotely resemble the concept of school known already to Socrates. The students were treated as inferior beings. Holland did not like this practice, and he attempted to address students with some courtesy.

But the students were used to the unequal treatment. Mr. Holland addressing them as Mister or Miss was probably raising suspicion in their minds that he was unprepared, weak, or did not really know what he was doing. In contrast, Vice Principal Wolters treated students badly with no hesitation, as if he was confident of some bigger power being on his side. Holland's courtesy could be considered by students as a sign of his inadequacy in a world where standards were set by people like Wolters.

Holland might also appear to the students to be lacking the ability to maintain discipline, as if there were no comparable power behind him to the power that stood behind Wolters. Such weak appearance could stimulate students to demonstrate against the mindless rules of the school, using his classroom as a stage for exhibiting their disappointments and frustrations. They would not dare to do so in Wolters's class.

FEATURE 2. POST-DAY ONE: FAILING WITH STUDENTS

Holland started with an encyclopedic definition of music, by which he meant classical music, not the popular music the students knew and loved and listened to endlessly. The film depicts well the passivity, disinterest, and sullenness of students. Holland gave them reading assignments, which they would have to memorize and thus become able to pass a test. This is how he thought he could teach the students the language of music that would enable them to appreciate "real music." When he wanted to illustrate various concepts, such as a musical scale or a key, he would play a line or two from Bach or Beethoven on the piano. No wonder that a barrier was increasing in strength between Holland and his students. It could never occur to Holland to use illustrations from popular music. To Mr. Holland, appreciation of music meant appreciation of classical music.

Holland tried hard to break through the growing barrier between him and his students. For example, he offered to come before the first period in the morning to help a red-haired girl to learn to play the clarinet. As a result, his understanding of how little time he would have left for writing his music, if he wanted to be available to students in this fashion, was slowly sinking in.

It took him quite some time to understand also that students did not know and understand music as well as he did, and that they were not interested in the aspects of music that he was trying to teach them. They were lacking any basis for such interest. This may look like an obvious mistake on his part, but it is a very common phenomenon among new teachers regardless of their discipline.

Students perceived his lessons as a necessity, something they had to put up with, while he was trying to teach them according to his plan, the best way he could. The paradox of the situation was that Holland loved music and he wanted students to love it too, but all he could do according to the curriculum led only to mutual disappointment. In this unnatural curriculum setting, when the students' orchestra continued to perform quite awkwardly, Holland was so desperate for some kind of success that he felt obliged to praise their playing as "good." His face, however, was saying that something was clearly very wrong. He did not know what it was, and nobody was there to help him out. He was alone with this problem.

He was forcing himself to continue working because he needed the money. This motivation had nothing to do with educating young people.

He became conscious of the need to make choices, perhaps cynical ones. For example, he could take advantage of the system instead of remaining loyal to his idea of the music appreciation class. But the problem was compounded by the brute fact that by the end of the year, the students should have learned an instrument and their orchestra would have to perform.

Finally, Holland went over students' tests at home and saw how poorly they did. The results angered him. He got the idea that he would go back to class and force students to learn. And when he had a problem with a disobedient student, he threw him out of the classroom and ordered him to report to the commonly hated Mr. Wolters. Then, he demanded that the students repeat the material with him until they got it right.

And here came a surprise: The school bell rang and made a fool of him. Students were walking out of the classroom, and he could do nothing but watch them leaving, indifferent to his attempts. The school system began to show him how little his own personal struggle counted in the real-life circumstances of mass schooling.

Although the process of Mr. Holland's alienation from the school could have started at that point and could have subsequently taken him entirely out of the domain where authentic learning and teaching could materialize, concrete experiences did not allow this to happen. We will review these experiences, recalling how they occurred in the school environment and outside of it.

Holland knew that the red-haired schoolgirl, Ms. Lang, struggled with playing the clarinet. He was sorry that she could not play as well as she wanted. But he was so preoccupied with his own unfulfilled musical ambitions that he could not care much about the student as a person. And her attempts appeared hopeless to him. Eventually, he was getting tired of his fruitless efforts to help her and all others in the school. He was burning out.

When he was leaving the classroom at the end of the day while Ms. Lang was still practicing, he said "Give it up, Ms. Lang." A moment of silence that followed his remark made him understand what he had just said, and he stopped short in the doorway. Probably, he suddenly imagined what such words would mean if his teacher said something like that to him. And he had to return to the room and say, "I meant, give it up for today." But it was too late to correct the error. Ms. Lang heard Holland well. It was clear that she practiced so hard not because she enjoyed playing the clarinet. In fact, her ability to play a note was near zero. Instead, she wanted to be good at something.

Why? She told Holland that everybody in her family was good at something. Her sister had a ballet scholarship at Juilliard. Her brother was going to Notre Dame on a football scholarship. Her mother was a great watercolor painter and her father had a beautiful voice. She was good at nothing. She had dreamed that the clarinet could be her specialty, and she was failing. His telling her to give up was killing her last hope for fulfilling her expectations of herself.

Holland knew what it meant to be in such a situation. His efforts to compose music were not rewarded with a great career. This was why he ended up in teaching in the first place. What Ms. Lang said almost certainly reverberated in his thoughts.

Holland's stress grew to the limits of his ability to endure it when Mrs. Jacobs told him he was not giving his students any useful direction. She defined teaching as filling students with knowledge and giving them a compass so that this knowledge would not go to waste. And she told him that he was stuck as a compass. Holland was enraged and he was ready to leave the school. But Iris, his wife, told him at home they were expecting a baby. Holland had to continue earning money. Because he was not able to stand the nonsense of teaching that had nothing to do with music as he knew it, he had to find a solution to his problem of failing with students. Note, however, that he did not think about his problem as a failure of the system he worked in. He thought about his failing with students as a problem specific to his classes, solely the result of his own inability to teach.

Let us look for a moment at the definition of the teacher's job that Mrs. Jacobs gave to Mr. Holland. On the one hand, her definition sounded reasonable because she did not reduce teaching to loading students' minds with information, which was exactly what he initially tried to do. She said that students should be instructed how to use their knowledge so that it would not go to waste in the future. Therefore, we could intuitively agree that her definition was valuable and Holland should have appreciated its meaning.

On the other hand, the metaphor of giving students "a compass" was not clear enough to distinguish between good and bad teaching. For example, one could suspect that "the compass" might mean a set of directives of the sort she gave Holland when she ordered him to prepare a detailed schedule of lessons for two months. She did it as if she assumed that Holland was able to predict the rate and depth of learning by his students. He was certainly not able to do so. Therefore, her directives were actually misleading Holland.

Also, too often people say that after they left school and started to work, things turned out to be different from what they heard at school. In other words, they had to unlearn illusions built into their minds at school. They discover that some "knowledge" should be unlearned, instead of being kept and used. And too often we have to admit that we prefer to forget "knowledge" that we had at the time of passing finals, knowledge that we considered useful only for the purpose of passing the exams. Therefore, Mrs. Jacobs's description of the goal of education was susceptible to many interpretations. Unfortunately, such imprecise definitions are often accepted as sufficient for inventing and running school programs. In view of the ambiguity contained in the principal's approach to teaching, how could Holland's attitude toward students change?

FEATURE 3. BREAKING THROUGH THE BARRIERS

The awakening happened to Holland when he learned that he was going to become a father. He suddenly understood that he would teach his child about music quite differently from how he was teaching his students at school. His child would learn the truth about music, while at school Holland was only earning his money at great personal expense.

After this realization, Holland came to the classroom as a completely changed person, rejuvenated, relaxed, and confident. He beamed with certainty that he knew what he should be doing. And one thing was obvious: He came into the classroom with a crystal clear idea about what was wrong about his music lessons so far—they were not fun; there was no truth in them about music as he knew it.

He asked the class if anyone remembered the difference between the Ionic and Doric scales. They gave no answer. This only confirmed Holland's belief that so far his teaching had no real impact on the students. At this point, however, he no longer thought that "nobody could teach these kids," which he had earlier told Iris. Now he blamed himself for not being effective because he now knew he should not have been doing what he was doing before. Now he had the understanding that he should show his students why he himself loved music, why he wanted to write music, and what music could become for them if they learned about it his way. The value of music itself, and his understanding that he could explain to students what this value was, gave him the strength he needed.

Holland could easily play whatever he wanted to and he could let students hear the power of sound as he knew it. Instead of engaging himself in some empty activity that cluttered students' minds with abstract notions of scales, he asked what kind of music the students liked to listen to. They were surprised by the question. They did not know what to say. They might even think that Holland did not feel quite well that day and they had to be careful about saying anything.

The same student whom Holland sent to Vice Principal Wolters some weeks earlier was particularly frightened when Holland looked at him, awaiting an answer. Mr. Holland said, "Do not be afraid," when he noticed that the student was afraid. Earlier, in the despair of his failure, it might please him that he commanded such fear, but not anymore. Now, he knew that his goal was not to keep order in the classroom, discharge information, and check tests. The classroom was no longer a purposeless place for him. It was going to be a stage on which he would perform music for students and with students.

So, when the student cautiously said, "Rock and roll?" Mr. Holland knew what to do next. He was so sure he was on the right track that he asked more students what they liked most to listen to. Another girl also said rock and roll. Only one student in front said, "Classical." And what did Mr. Holland say in response? He said something rude and inappropriate for a teacher who tried to make sure that his manners never offended his students: He said, "Brownnoser." But he was so confident about his line of action that he allowed himself to be so blunt. He added a smile to sweeten the words a bit, and he punched his way through by asking, "Does any one of you like to listen to Bach?" Only the brownnoser was sure to say "Yes." But at this point, Holland did not allow the student to interfere, and he continued with unusual vigor, a surprise for all students. He said, "I bet that all of you, whether you know it or not, already like Johann Sebastian Bach."

He walked to the piano and played a rock and roll melody. Students liked it very much. They smiled. Holland asked what this was called. All students knew. Who wrote it? Students gave the name of the band, "The Toys." "Wrong," said Holland. He stopped playing and he said that it was Minuet in G by Johann Sebastian Bach. And he played it again a bit differently, in the original form, so that the students could immediately recognize the change. They saw that the old music, which they would initially consider dead and uninteresting, was very much alive in their present day. Bach wrote it in 1725, and both versions, the old one and the new, were prime examples of the Ionic scale.

Students gulped the lesson like juice. The "Ionic scale" was no longer two empty words naming a useless notion. They knew what it was and they were interested in learning more about it.

Holland saw at this point that his approach was working. He went on to the next step and asked students to listen again. He told them to try to recognize the connective tissue between what he played before and what he was playing now with full speed—a big rock and roll hit.

Students were excited. They loved to listen to him playing. Hands were up in the air with tons of questions. And Holland was so excited that when he described it all later at home to his wife his excitement rose again, and she got excited too.

The whole attitude of Mr. and Mrs. Holland toward the school job changed at this point. The work was no longer separated from music—it was a part of what Holland wanted to do. Mr. Holland understood in concrete terms what he could do well. It became clear that he was to spend a long time doing this, and they decided to buy a house.

The next day, when the red-haired Ms. Lang came in the morning to the music room only to tell Holland that she wanted to give up the clarinet, he was prepared to respond differently than usual.

He let her listen to a record of some famous rock and roll band for a moment, and he asked whether she liked it. Yes, it certainly was fun. Was the clarinet fun? She wanted it to be. He asked her to play again, but this time he took away her notes and asked her to play without them. But how could one play without notes?

This was the key point: Music was not notes. Notes were only for writing it down. Music was the thrill of performing, playing it straight from your heart. And he asked her what she liked most about herself when she looked into a mirror. She liked her hair. Her father used to say it was like a sunset. Holland asked her to close her eyes and play the sunset. She attempted, struggled, and eventually went through the hard places. From that moment on, she and Holland could play together, she on the clarinet and he on the piano. For the first time, she was satisfied with her performance; perhaps she was satisfied with herself for the first time in her life. Therefore, it could have been one of the most important moments in her life. She felt her own ability. And Holland's approach was affirmed. He was no longer teaching music. He was teaching students, using music.

With Holland's help, Ms. Lang changed her attitude toward music completely. Music changed for her from the collection of notes she would force herself to practice without understanding, and without pleasure, to something she could perform with closed eyes, as an expression of her feelings and thoughts, with the full and complete satisfaction that such an act was bringing to her. She understood the secret of music in one tiny example, thanks to Holland's assistance, and she, from this starting point, was prepared to travel into the world of music as far as she wanted to. From a person who did not believe in her ability to achieve anything, she became a person who was aware of her inner strength and desire to learn new things. Mr. Holland opened her eyes to the fact that learning could produce results she desired as soon as she stopped pretending, stopped mechanically repeating meaningless motions, and instead engaged herself in the process.

At this point, in addition to what Mrs. Jacobs said about the goals of education, two new definitions of the goal begin to take concrete form in the film. One originates in the fact that music, in Holland's words, "is fun." One has to be careful, however, not to get an impression that "fun" could be understood as "no effort." It was certainly easy to listen to a record. But the rock band had to practice for a long time to produce the recording. In the same way, a sportsman could say that running a marathon was fun, although he had to more than break a sweat over the hundreds of miles that he had to run in preparation for the event. The sportsman could say he had "fun" training, and the rock band members could say they had "fun" practicing. One could also say that learning music is "fun."

Effort is always required to effect the change from the condition one is in before one learned something to the condition one is in after one learned it. This process of gaining new knowledge, understanding, and skill, never happens without effort—no pain, no gain. But it is fun to make the effort, even if it is a great effort. In general terms, learning is fun as soon as one really learns. Thus, quite generally, the goal of teaching could be described as letting students understand in concrete cases that learning brings satisfaction. One can help them practice learning to exhaustion, which happens when one learns to dance and gets tired, or when one plays tennis and must take a break, or when one plays a guitar and fingertips become painful from pressing on the strings. With time, the fingertips harden so much that one stops feeling the pain.

The other definition of the goal of education that begins to emerge at this point is that a student learns how to reach the limits of her or his abilities and how to push these limits further out. Teachers' goal could be, then, to open students' conscious eyes to the fact that these limits exist and can be changed. This way, the teacher could help students see the prospects of going on a path of conscious learning and thus embarking on the expedition of their life. The students could be shown that they can explore territories they never saw before, and in one way or the other they will operate at the limits of their ability all the time, with the great fun and satisfaction this can bring to them.

These two ways of defining the goal of education are quite different from what Mrs. Jacobs described. She said that Holland should provide students with knowledge and give them a compass. But recall how Holland introduced the notion of music to his class on the first day of school. His students had no idea how to define music at that time and they did not answer any of his questions. So, convinced they knew nothing and needed to acquire new knowledge, he read to them from the textbook that "music is sound, in melodic or harmonic combinations, whether produced by voice or instruments." Since nobody reacted, he asked whether anybody had questions. Nobody had any, and no real learning occurred. The information was provided and the students could recite it. Still, they learned nothing in this abstract way, the way that was entirely outside the context of their experience. Providing knowledge so ineffectively rendered a compass useless because students did not know the goal.

Deep from inside, it came to Holland that it was not right to read such definitions to his students. He became a musician because music fascinated him, not because he heard the definition of music. Therefore, putting the pieces of the puzzle together, he discovered that he should make the same kind of fascination available to his students.

As a musician, a composer, he knew something of immense value to him, and he wanted to share it with students. And he could use music in innovative ways as soon as he understood that he needed to start from where the students were—they did not have experience with music as he did.

Thus, Holland made a leap of putting himself in the students' shoes and asking himself what he would need to understand music if he were a beginning student in the music appreciation class. Figuring this out allowed Holland to do what was required for the students to mentally engage in the lessons. In this aspect, Holland's approach resembled how Stanislavsky taught actors in his theater in Moscow at the beginning of the twentieth century. His methods became a foundation of the modern school of acting, and his textbook in three volumes, the first one called *An Actor Prepares*, had more than 30 editions over 60 years, in numerous languages worldwide. Teachers in all areas must see the teaching process from the learner's point of view.

An actor, such as Stanislavsky, could explain to his students from where his acting drew strength. He used his skills to put himself in his students' minds, and he created contexts of productive learning for them using this insight. Similarly, Mr. Holland was a musician and he used music to teach his students. He understood that he needed to look at music as his students did. Their view was not the mature view he had. He had to understand the difference. Once he understood that, he played rock and roll to his students as an invitation to learn more about music. And he was able to take them on the path to subjects as difficult as Bach's music. Note, however, that not everybody welcomed Holland's approach.

Rock and roll was perceived as a grave mistake by Vice Principal Wolters. He had no comprehension that rock and roll was a trailhead for the students' learning path to music appreciation. Rock and roll itself probably did not sound as awkward to him as he pretended. But he was afraid of the opinion of the Board of Education and the parents who considered rock and roll improper.

By the same token, if only Wolters were against the rock and roll lesson, it would not be a big problem. He, by himself, could not do much harm to how Holland was teaching, especially under Mrs. Jacobs as principal. The truly unfortunate circumstance was that Wolters represented a way of thinking about education that was characteristic of a large and influential group of people.

This thinking was dangerous not only to what Mr. Holland was trying to do. It also questioned whether art was essential for education. Wolters most probably did not understand art, as people whose opinions he shared didn't, and he was afraid that he would lose control over the school if he allowed rock and roll in the classrooms. In Stanislavsky's book, he could be portrayed as an advocate of mechanical acting, like a puppet.

But Wolters, or his supervisors, cannot be blindly blamed for the troubles Mr. Holland encountered after he had played rock and roll in his class. We have to appreciate that Holland shifted to a new approach to teaching that was unknown to his supervisors. We stress "unknown." These people believed in teaching in the way they were taught by their teachers. We all teach the way we were taught. The mammoth consequences of this dominant correlation for the society go far beyond music or one high school story. And although so far we were speaking only about music, the same concerns all areas. And if it does, the whole educational system structure and function were responsible for what Wolters, his supervisors, and parents were thinking. These issues will be addressed later.

Note, however, that the notions of the overarching goal of education and how the whole system supports or disintegrates processes that serve that goal are visible in the story of Mr. Holland's teaching career. All teachers, including teachers of teachers, must understand that Stanislavsky could teach his students how to become good actors because he understood what it meant to his students to study acting with him.

FEATURE 4. LIFELONG LEARNING OF TEACHING

Once Holland's learning how to teach ignited, it never stopped. When he learned, he changed. The changes created the desire and capacity to learn more, and this process had no end. But it was not an orderly process. His life and career unfolded in a way that could not be predicted. For example, he could not predict that his son would be deaf and he could not foresee how this fact would influence his life and work.

Many more factors contributed to his learning in important ways, and they often were in conflict with each other. For example, he encountered prominent time-sharing conflicts between writing music, teaching at school, and being a father and a husband. In the middle of these overlapping relations, he was learning how to resolve the trajectory of his life and become an effective teacher. But the element of surprise was never absent, and he was entirely not expecting that he would be fired at the age of 60 and that he would be unable to do anything about it. Life being unpredictable, Holland needed to learn and to adapt to new situations all his life.

His lifelong learning was a very complex process that no one can fully understand. But it is possible to name and describe some aspects that one can partly explain. Our point is that learning how to be a good teacher takes years of hard work and hands-on experience with students.

This is not to say that the colleges should provide something that they do not or cannot provide. Our point is that teachers need systematic, institutionalized opportunities for intellectual growth during their whole careers. If teachers do not have such opportunities, they are not able to honestly encourage students to grow themselves. This intellectual and emotional growth process must continue throughout life. Think about how much time Holland needed to eventually tackle the problem of his relationship with his son. The way Holland was educated at schools and university did not help him in reaching that point.

FEATURE 5. SCHOOL AND HOME

When Mrs. Jacobs and Mr. Wolters asked Holland to direct a marching band that would play at football games at school, Holland was shocked. As a musician, he thought himself to be above this kind of music. He thought it was inappropriate for a music appreciation class teacher to help cheer up crowds at football games. Nevertheless, this assignment became a source of major lessons for him, an opportunity to perform with his students in front of many people outside of school, and a source of personal satisfaction. We are not saying that Jacobs and Wolters predicted this. They wanted the football games to look better. So, if the band was a success, it was Holland's and his students' achievement, far beyond the understanding of the matter by his principals.

When Mr. Holland worked on the marching band preparation for the town parade, he heard for the first time that "if he could not teach a kid how to play, he was a lousy teacher." This was an important moment in Holland's learning about the essence of teaching. The comment concerned student Louis Russ, whom Holland was to teach how to play a drum. The football coach, Bill Maister, wanted Russ, one of the best players on the school team, to continue to play. But Russ had bad grades and Mrs. Jacobs suspended his participation in the games. The team needed him, and the coach knew that football was everything to Russ. If he were forbidden to play, Russ would not be able to believe in himself again. Throwing the ball was the only thing he was good at and studying was very hard for him.

Maister figured that if Russ got a credit in music, he could come back on the team and continue in school. So, when Maister saw Holland hopelessly trying to get students to march in the band, he offered his help with the marching lessons if Holland would teach Russ how to play an instrument, any instrument, and if Holland gave him a passing grade. Initially, Holland hesitated, but he later changed his mind and started to work with Russ.

Russ did not know anything about playing any instrument. After a discussion, they chose the drum and Louis Russ started to work on it with great hope and energy, ready to do all it would take to earn the credit. But his approach was similar to Ms. Lang's attempts to play clarinet, which we already described. Russ did not feel the rhythm and banged his big drum, often falling out of rhythm with the band.

Although Holland should have immediately seen the similarity between Russ and Lang, he treated Mr. Russ almost as he treated Ms. Lang at the beginning. As a teacher, Holland was certainly patient with Russ. But he was irritated when he had to stop the orchestra because of Russ losing rhythm. Since Russ did not make progress for a long time, Holland concluded that Russ could not pass. When Maister asked him how the kid was doing and Holland said that Russ would fail, Maister told Holland that if Holland was a music teacher and could not teach a kid, any kid, how to play a drum, then he was a lousy teacher, period.

Holland needed the harsh remark to see the problem anew and to start working on a solution. Perhaps he saw it as a personal challenge. The problem probably also challenged his belief that everybody should be able to actively enjoy music. Holland had identified the problem and was ready to tackle it. He stopped dismissing it as unsolvable. They had spent hours together, sometimes long after school. Holland would put his hands on

Russ's feet to help him move them with the rhythm, and he banged the football helmet on Russ's head with a drumstick while Russ tried to reproduce the rhythm on the drum.

When Russ began catching the rhythm, Holland stopped the orchestra and he pointed at Russ. Whenever Holland stopped the orchestra before, he did it to point out a mistake. Russ waited for criticism. After a moment of suspended silence, Mr. Holland said, "Mr. Russ, you made it." It was a critical moment for Russ, indeed. A real triumph. But the observation we want to make here goes somewhat further. We want to focus your attention on the short period of silence in the orchestra. Russ was playing on a big and loud drum. This made him responsible for the rhythm for the orchestra. No one could play comfortably if Russ did not perform well. So, everybody was aware of errors that Russ was making. Everybody would have noticed a mistake if Russ made it. But when Holland pointed his baton at Russ and paused, he made them uncertain. Then they all burst out with joy.

At this point, successful learning was no longer an abstract notion for Holland and his students. They felt in their hearts what Russ had accomplished. It was real. They understood what it meant to him. They knew that Russ's success spoke well for their performance as a band. They achieved a harmony of music and of the team. Everybody laughed. They could almost touch the fact that successful learning was a source of unforgettable joy, for the students and for the teacher.

Note, however, the huge difference between Holland's approach to teaching students at school and how he approached the problems in educating his deaf son, Cole. He devoted a lot of effort to teach Russ, he learned from that process a great deal, and still he did not make much effort to understand how to teach Cole. It would be an oversimplification to parallel the relation between a father and a son with a relation between a teacher and a student at school. However, it is hard not to observe that Holland did not pay much attention to learning sign language, which was the only means of meaningful communication with his son.

Most probably, Holland did not see a possibility of teaching Cole about music. Cole felt rejected by Holland, and he could not come forward. Holland did not understand at that time how important it was for Cole to have his father's approval.

In a way, Russ was as deaf to rhythm as Cole was to sound. We know from later scenes that if Cole had ability to understand music, it was mainly through the rhythm; he could feel vibrations of the loudspeakers. As a teacher, Holland undertook the task of teaching Russ how to play the drum, while as a father, he neglected Cole. We can safely conclude that it was hard for Holland to make connections between these two cases. The film shows that he had to do a lot of work and to accumulate considerable experience before he could begin to pay conscious attention to the difficulties that prevented him and Cole from understanding each other.

And only after he discovered that Cole felt rejected could Holland think about how to overcome the difficulty. As a result of improving the father-son relationship, the processes of communication between Holland and Cole greatly improved and productive learning from each other began. This example shows how much time and experience a teacher needs in order to grasp the truths that are essential for productive teaching and learning. All students need to feel their teacher's approval, approval they earned.

People need many opportunities and a lot of time to see the generalizations and to become able to take what they learn in one area of their lives and apply it in another. It would be naive to expect that a few years of college education could make a teacher. The lifelong opportunity for learning is essential for teachers to develop their ability to create contexts of productive learning for their students and transfer their experiences from case to case with ease of skillful application.

Holland's relationship with Cole was a source of many lessons for him. For example, Holland had difficulties in learning about his son's abilities. One day Iris brought Cole to the music class. Holland was in the middle of conducting and the class was playing well. Holland smiled when he saw his son coming in the door. Cole started to move his hands, mimicking the moves of his father. He closed his eyes. The piece ended and the class went quiet. But Cole continued to wave his hands with his eyes closed because he did not hear that the music had stopped. His waving looked odd in the silence of the room. Iris touched Cole's shoulder to let him know he should stop. Holland was looking at Cole. The boy smiled. He finally saw his father at work, which was so important. But Holland could not genuinely smile back. Possibly, the deafness of Cole was the reason that Holland did not believe he could find a way to communicate with Cole as he wished to, in music. The scene was clearly showing that Holland could not accept that Cole would never be a musician, and he could not smile back.

So far, we have discussed three prominent examples of how Holland learned to teach. The examples of Ms. Lang and Mr. Russ concerned his students at school. In these cases, one could claim that teachers' education is or can be limited to the school floor. The third example, of Cole, happened entirely outside any college or school. And while Holland was able to see that he was failing with teaching students, he was hardly recognizing that he was failing with his son. Holland needed help to see the point. His wife, Iris, had helped him understand it in the context of his home. What we need to see now is that Holland needed the help of Iris, somebody who was very close to him, in order to learn something important that concerned his own life.

One day Holland was sitting at the piano and working when Cole and Iris returned from a science fair in Cole's school. Holland had decided not to go with them because he was busy with preparation of a music program for his students. Cole walked in, still very excited by the fair, and he was signing so quickly that Holland could not understand. Iris helped: Cole discovered astronomy and wanted to be an astronaut. Holland gave him the sign "Good"; Cole turned around and went upstairs. As soon as he left, Holland asked, "Who put that stuff in his head?" "As a matter of fact, his teachers," answered Iris.

We should recall that she spoke with Holland about the fair that morning and she hoped very much that Holland would join them at the fair. But Holland had to finish the orchestrations for his kids at school and he did not find the time. She was upset that it was always so. If it was not the school play, it would be a band practice, grading of papers, or some student committee would need an adviser. Iris spoke quietly and slowly, but Holland sensed she was upset. She could no longer tolerate the fact that he was busy with the school and neglected their son. The tension grew because Holland was also getting angry that he could not continue working on the orchestration. Perhaps he thought that Iris did not appreciate what a challenge it was for him to do it well.

He snapped, "A science fair is not the end of the world." Iris understood that Holland had not really listened to her in the morning. Holland objected and assured her that he had heard her, he always did. Iris did not believe that Holland truly heard what she was saying. She explained again that Cole wanted Holland to be there very, very much and it was awful that Holland did not have time to come. He said, "You know what's really amazing? No matter what I do, no matter how hard I try, sooner or later anything I try turns out to be wrong." Did he mean that Iris always complained? Or could he mean that his son was not as "good" as he wanted him to be? He might think that Cole was his failure.

Iris felt the anger rising in her, an unusual feeling for her because she was always trying to understand Holland, and she asked, "Why is every other child more important to you than your child?" Holland exhaled, "I am a teacher, Iris." She cried, "You are his father." Holland was already losing control of himself and shouted, "I am both. I do one thing, I let him down. I do the other thing, I let the school down. How the hell am I to be everything for everybody? Huh?" Iris had a ready answer: "You have to make priorities." "I am," said Holland, "He is my son and I love him. And I do the best I goddamn can, okay?" Iris responded, "You know what? Your best is not good enough. So, go on. Write your music." And she left the room. Holland certainly had something to think about.

It is clear from the film that the events at home influenced Holland's approach to teaching. There is also no question that Holland was continuously learning how to be a better teacher in the contexts that were completely different from formal college or usual school contexts. In particular, Holland discovered what he could do to improve his relationship with Cole in the unfortunate context of John Lennon's death.

John Lennon, a great musician and a member of The Beatles, was an outspoken proponent of peace. When Lennon was shot, Holland felt as if his own life and music were ultimately questioned. He left school and walked home very slowly that day. His car was so old that he did not drive it any more. He gave it to Cole, who took care of it as his hobby.

Cole was working on the car engine in the garage when Holland came in and touched Cole's hand to say hello. They looked at each other. Cole had a black eye and Holland asked him what had happened. Cole had had a fight. Then Cole asked Holland why he was so sad. Holland did not want to talk about it because he thought that Cole, being deaf, could not understand who John Lennon was. But Cole insisted, so Holland told him that John Lennon had been killed. Going into the house, Holland said, "You wouldn't understand."

Iris met Holland halfway inside. She heard the news and she was very sad, too. A moment later Cole came rapidly into the house, slamming the garage door behind him. He was angry with Holland and wanted Holland to listen to him. Iris helped translate Cole's signing to Holland to make sure he could understand what his son was saying. Cole said, "Why do you assume that John Lennon's death would mean nothing to me? Do you think I am stupid? I know who John Lennon is."

Holland was very surprised by the determination and aggressive tone with which Cole spoke to him. He tried to turn to Iris, saying, "I never said he was stupid." But he did not finish because Cole forced Holland's face to turn back and said, "You must think so if you think that I don't know who The Beatles are, or any music at all. You think I don't care what it is that you do or what you love? You're my father! I know what music is. You could help me to know it better. But no, you care more about teaching other people than you do about me." And Cole stepped back, made one more sign, and left the house.

Iris wanted to follow him, but Holland stopped her and asked, "Iris, what does this mean?" and he repeated the last sign Cole made before he left. Iris answered, "It means asshole."

Late in the night, Holland could not sleep, he was sitting downstairs and thinking about his relationship with his son. He wanted to protect him, make sure Cole would not be hurt, or disappointed. He realized now that he did not understand Cole.

The next morning, Holland saw through a window how Cole was working on the car engine. Since Cole could not hear how the engine worked, he would press his head against a long screwdriver that touched the engine block. He was checking whether the engine was working correctly by feeling the vibrations of the screwdriver. Holland certainly thought about an analogy with the deaf Beethoven, who pounded keys of his piano to feel the vibrations of sounds instead of hearing them. This event helped Holland understand that he had to find a way to teach his son more about music.

The major task was to figure out a way to communicate with Cole in his language. Holland knew that Beethoven used vibrations, but before he saw Cole working on the engine he had not realized that Cole could comprehend music that way, too.

Holland visited the school for deaf children and asked a teacher how he could make music more understandable for deaf "listeners." Two ideas came up. He could invite a sign language interpreter, who would describe what was happening at the orchestra and what the music was like. There also could be lights changing with the rhythm and tone, to enable deaf people to visualize the music.

Holland and his class prepared a concert for the deaf. It was a very successful, uplifting event. The deaf audience signed excitedly during the performance. They noticed changes in the lights and contemplated movements of people playing, almost as if they heard the music. This was a clear example of the fact that in order to communicate with students, the teacher had to adjust the means of communication to what the students were prepared to receive.

Holland took the opportunity of the concert to create a bridge between Cole and him, the bridge of love, understanding, trust, and mutual respect. After the main performance, Holland thanked the audience for applause, asked for silence, and said that he would now sing for his son, Cole. He sang John Lennon's song "Beautiful Boy." The song says something about education: Care and trust are essential in the growth of a man.

At the end of the song, Holland changed the name Sean (Lennon's son) to Cole. This whole event assured Cole of his father's true interest in him. The next day, Holland and Iris found Cole sitting on the loudspeaker in the living room, trying to feel the music. Oh, how happy they were to see this. Cole smiled. Holland turned the amplifier to maximum power. Finally, the father and son could begin talking about music.

FEATURE 6. TEACHING IN THE CONTEXTS OF LIFE

We stressed the importance of concrete contexts in which Mr. Holland learned how to be a good teacher. This section discusses some important examples of how Holland used contexts of life in his work.

Let us start with the basic issue of the goal of a music appreciation class. It was meant to introduce students to classical music. When Holland understood that students were not interested, he completely changed his approach and played rock and roll for them. This was discussed before. But one could argue that this was inappropriate because rock and roll was too primitive a music and would distort students' perception of music. If this were true, rock and roll would be in contradiction with the goal of the curriculum of the music appreciation class.

However, rock and roll was the actual level of familiarity with music that the students experienced in the course of their lives. Holland used rock and roll as a starting point precisely for this reason. But he wanted to build students' education up from that level to more and more sophisticated melody and harmony. He, as a musician, recognized that he should provide students with an example that would be understandable for them and, therefore, could be, and was, attractive. His plan apparently worked because at the next graduation the school orchestra performed very well. We repeat this example here because rock and roll was an element of students' lives, and Holland put his lesson of music in this context. There was no contradiction with classical music because Holland built a path for the students from rock and roll to the classical music whose appreciation was, indeed, the goal of the curriculum.

The marching band project provided Holland with an opportunity to teach Mr. Russ. Although we already have discussed this example from the point of view of what Holland learned from it, the case of teaching Mr. Russ also deserves a comment about how Holland used the context of the band performance to motivate Mr. Russ. We need to compare the case of Mr. Russ to the earlier case of Ms. Lang.

In the case of Ms. Lang, the issue of learning what music was about was similar, but there was no pressing deadline of public performance. In contrast, Mr. Russ knew very well that his drum was important for the band to keep the rhythm, and he had to learn quickly to be ready on the day of the parade. So, it was natural for him to practice and try to get it right.

If he and Holland were meeting after school and struggling with learning rhythm just to get Russ to pass a grade, it would be an act of devotion to teaching with no bigger purpose than pushing a kid to the next class. In the context they were working in, there was a bigger purpose: Mr. Russ wanted to be a part of the marching band that needed him.

In this setting, Mr. Russ had a clear goal to achieve: to play the drum correctly. The grade he would get for success was an obvious reward to think about, but the motivation came from playing music in the band and not from the grade alone. In fact, when he got it right, his biggest rewards were quite different from obtaining the passing grade. He learned how to play the drum, and he could then be a full member of the band. We suggest that he also achieved something much more important. Namely, he felt competent, able to rise to the challenges he was confronted with in his life. He earned a place in a real marching band. He also learned through this experience that he could go on with his life beyond football. He could now try to shape his future as he saw fit. Mr. Russ's parents were proud of their son, not so much because he brought home a good mark from school, but because they saw him marching and playing very well on the parade day, a happy man. Are any of these productive learning outcomes specific to music? Certainly not.

Holland's ability to teach his students in the contexts of real life was illustrated with particular strength in another case that happened several years later. He had a student, Mr. Stadler, who was very smart and who easily memorized all dates, scales, and names. But he was rude to the rest of the class. Stadler once insulted another student, and the two almost started to fight at the end of the period. After the bell rang, Holland ordered Stadler to stay. Stadler openly declared that it was improper for Holland to hold him and that Holland could not do anything to him because he knew everything Holland was supposed to teach in that class, and he did not need Holland's "bullshit."

Holland got mad. He told Stadler that he only appeared so smart and needed to prove it because the title of the class was "Music Appreciation," and Holland did not see Stadler's appreciation of anything. Holland told Stadler that he was an inch from being suspended and ordered him to write a paper on the subject "Music—A Language of Emotion." Stadler objected, "You cannot make me do it," but Holland snapped, "Watch me." He warned Stadler that it was not for an extra credit and promised to flunk him if the report was not on Holland's desk at the end of the term.

That would be all if not that a girl entered the room and handed Holland a note. He read it quickly, looked at Stadler, and ordered him to come to the room next Saturday at 10:00 A.M. Stadler asked, "Why?" Holland responded, "Research," and left the room.

Stadler did not learn "why" until Saturday. He would remember that day his whole life. That day was the day of funeral of Mr. Russ, the drummer. He had been was killed in Vietnam. When Stadler and Holland arrived at the cemetery, it was still not clear to Stadler why he was there. But he sensed the sorrow in Holland and other people from the school who also came, and he asked who the dead person was.

Holland was very brief. He told Stadler it was a kid whom he taught to bang a drum, Louis Russ. Russ made the state wrestling finals for three years running. Holland told Stadler, "He was never as smart as you are. He had to work real hard to even graduate. Maybe it's why it meant so much to him." Holland did not say anything more. Soldiers fired three times. Russ's father was handed the American flag. A boy from Kennedy High played a trumpet, and the ceremony was over. "You can go now," said Mr. Holland, and Stadler went away. He understood how selfish his attitude was toward other students, and why.

The value of teaching in contexts that matter to students was particularly transparent in the case of Ms. Rowena Morgan. She was singing the lead part in "The Gershwin Review" that Holland orchestrated and conducted in his school. During a rehearsal, Rowena was singing the following part:

> Won't you tell him,
>
> Please put on some speed,
>
> Follow my lead,
>
> Oh, how I need
>
> Someone to watch over me.

She was singing so well that Sarah, Holland's colleague, exclaimed to Rowena, "It was perfect, darling. Mr. Holland?" Holland listened to Rowena's singing very carefully, one could say intensely. When Sarah asked what he thought, he said, "It was good. Can I talk to her for a moment?" Sarah nodded and Holland ordered a short break.

He came up on the stage where Rowena waited. She was a little bit confused. She said she tried to do her best. As he was coming near her, Holland assured her it was fine. And when he came up on the stage and stood next to her, he said he just wanted to ask her a question. He stood close enough so that only she could hear what he was saying. And he asked, "What do you think the girl is really feeling here?" Rowena wasn't sure and she admitted, "I don't know." Holland lowered his voice, saying, "You have to know, or you can't sing. This song is wistful, Ms. Morgan. It is about a woman who is alone in a very, very cold world. And all she wants more than anything is to have someone to hold her close and tell her that everything will be all right." Holland's voice went to a whisper, but Rowena could hear it very, very well. "It's about a need for love in your gut." Rowena looked into his eyes and nodded. He said, "Okay? Let's try again from the very top." The rehearsal went on and Holland remained focused on Rowena's performance.

Holland never had an opportunity before to work with a student as talented as Rowena, and he wanted her talent to shine. But he did not try to talk her into singing. Instead, he helped her understand what singing was about. It is important to recognize that Sarah, also a music teacher, was enthusiastic about Rowena's singing but did not take the opportunity to teach Rowena as Holland did. He showed the student that learning to sing was something relevant to her own life in ways that she would never underestimate.

Let us also point out that the episode with Rowena occurred in a real-life setting in a different sense. Holland wanted the production of "The Gershwin Review" to succeed, and in the budget situation the school was in, the success was important for multiple reasons for many people. We can safely assume that Holland felt motivated to explain to Rowena what she needed to convey through her singing because he himself wanted the audience to be moved by the music of the performance, and he knew what was required to achieve that.

Let us also observe that the Gershwin production went on practically against the will of Wolters, who had become the principal of the high school after Mrs. Jacobs. He had reluctantly agreed to "The Gershwin Review" going forward only if there was a strong chance that it would pay for itself. Teachers and students knew that they had to attract a considerable audience to the show and collect for the tickets. This was the only way for them to earn the funds they needed to stage the show. But given the chance, teachers and students worked very hard together. Eventually, the show was a great success. This experience certainly helped all students appreciate values and skills required for success in life, more than any rote study for a grade could ever do.

FEATURE 7. CHANGE

Although it may appear obvious, we should say here that the processes of learning that Holland went through influenced him far beyond what one would usually describe as merely learning. He changed. The change was the important aspect of his learning, and we should never overlook the fact that learning and change always occur together.

When learning is not productive, it induces little change. When it is productive, it invariably changes a person. One can even suggest that productive learning is recognizable through the changes it causes, the changes it is associated with, and the changes it results from.

For example, look at the change in the attitude of Holland toward his principal, Mrs. Jacobs. When he was a beginner in teaching, he had no particular respect for her. But over several years, he changed so much that he eventually appreciated Mrs. Jacobs a lot. Let us point out just one example of how the contexts of school life induced this change.

After Mr. Wolters found out that Mr. Holland played rock and roll in class, the school Board of Education had concerns about the music program at Kennedy. Mr. Wolters and the Board perceived rock and roll as undermining school discipline, which they considered to be a pillar of proper education. We add that when Wolters attacked Holland in Mrs. Jacobs's presence, in his impulsive speech against rock and roll Wolters had to correct himself from "We do not think it is right" to "I do not think it is right." We can infer that Wolters aspired to become a principal so much that sometimes he already saw himself as one, even before Mrs. Jacobs retired. He was also desperate to gain more respect for his point of view. If people would not give it to him voluntarily, he was ready to force them using whatever power he could summon for this purpose. But he knew to correct himself when he overstepped the level of his authority in the presence of Mrs. Jacobs, as long as she was the principal.

About his own appreciation of music and learning, one should note that Wolters invoked Stravinsky as an ideal of disciplined music that students should study, instead of being exposed to rock and roll. Holland could not resist pointing out that the suggestion lacked consistency because Stravinsky's music carried the spirit of the Russian revolution, which was known for overthrowing virtually all discipline of the Western world at that time.

It was clear that Holland and Wolters did not like each other for deep reasons, and one of the reasons was that Wolters appeared in the role of instructor with no qualifications for that role. But he was Mrs. Jacobs's right hand. This fact had to cast deep shadows on the image of Mrs. Jacobs in Holland's mind.

Assuming that Holland did not like the fact that Mrs. Jacobs worked with Wolters, we should also note that Holland did appreciate differences between Jacobs and Wolters. We know that she was afraid that the school Board might request cancellation of the whole music program, and she wanted to defend what Mr. Holland was doing if the issue came up at the next meeting of the Board. She needed to know what to tell the Board. Holland suggested that she tell them that "he teaches music and he will use anything, from Beethoven to Billie Holiday to rock and roll, if he thinks it will help him to teach a student to love music." "That's a reasonable answer," said Mrs. Jacobs.

It is not hard to guess that there were many situations in which Holland was effectively learning about the circumstances that Mrs. Jacobs had to work in. In the long run, Holland began to appreciate Mrs. Jacobs's work more and more. He eventually came to admire her. We can safely say so because he felt deeply rewarded when she gave him a compass, a symbol of recognition for his style and achievements in teaching.

She waited with this gesture until she was retiring. The words of her recognition of his work made him speechless for a moment. This demonstrates that he went a long way in his understanding of the principal's role in school, from the time when he was a new teacher and did not pay much attention to Mrs. Jacobs to the moment when he felt honored by her gift. It took him several years to gradually change his mind about her.

A sequence of deep changes of Holland's ideals and goals was most clearly visible in the example of his relationship with his son. His attitude toward Cole was changing in parallel with his learning how to be a good teacher. The changes required many years to happen. When Cole was to be born, Holland decided to teach school to have a stable income. He wanted to take good care of Cole and share with him his love for music. At that time, teaching at school was for him a means to earn money. Then, Cole's deafness was a shock.

Later, when Holland was teaching about Beethoven's music, he let students listen to his Seventh Symphony. An important aspect of the lesson was that Beethoven was deaf. The idea that Beethoven could direct an orchestra, let alone compose a symphony, was pathetic to most people. In response, Beethoven composed and conducted the Seventh Symphony. Holland told students to imagine how the perfect orchestra was playing in Beethoven's mind and how the real orchestra desperately tried to catch up. Beethoven's ability to write music was incomparably greater than anyone could expect.

The inner forces in Beethoven were much stronger than his deafness. Holland told his students that Beethoven cut the legs off his piano and, lying on the floor next to it, pressed his head to the ground and pounded the keys to hear his music through the vibrations of the floor. All the students in the classroom were mentally engaged in Holland's story and Beethoven's music. At that moment, the music appreciation class achieved a quality that rarely occurs in any kind of school. Holland was focused on the subject so much, and the class was so intense, that when Holland stopped talking, nobody moved for a while. A student raised his hand, but Holland did not see it right away. The boy asked how Beethoven could know that he wanted to play a sound, say C, if he was deaf. And Holland could not fully control tears coming to his eyes when he was saying that "Beethoven wasn't born deaf." Holland's son was. Although we have already described some aspects of this fact, we need to explore it further here to describe changes in Holland caused by his learning how to teach his son.

Holland thought that his son would never become a musician, would never appreciate music, and could never understand Holland's passion for music. But over time, as he learned more and more about how to teach his students, Holland's attitude toward his son changed completely. From the lack of interest in Cole so vast that Holland was not even learning sign language, he moved over time to deep appreciation of the inner world of Cole. Eventually, Holland understood "where his son was coming from" and how to interact with him. It was one of the biggest triumphs of his life.

We stress that this great change was parallel to changes that Holland experienced as a result of learning what it meant to be a teacher. This is worth reiteration: When people learn, they change, and the true changes have profound meaning in their lives. The essence of productive learning is that the changes help people to become more conscious beings.

Holland's attitude toward his career in music underwent a big change, too. The magnitude of this change became clear when he was teaching Ms. Rowena Morgan. He was so much impressed by her talent that he advised her to be a singer. Rowena came to Holland after the first performance of "The Gershwin Review" to ask how well she was doing, and he assured her she was doing very well. She then told him that she had decided to quit school and go to Broadway theaters in New York right after the show closed.

In a stunning move, Rowena also proposed that Holland would go with her. He could compose beautiful music and she could sing. They would be happy. He was surprised, but he had to admit that as a musician, 20 years earlier he might have considered such a step the right thing to do. Working with her made him happy, and he saw in her a woman he could love. However, when Rowena met him, he already was a husband and a father. Music was still very important to him, but differently. This was the big change.

He realized that his mission was to be a partner to young people in their learning, but his goal was to see them succeed in music independently of him. As a husband and father, he could not go with her, but his response to Rowena's proposal reflected also the change in his attitudes toward music and teaching. He would not go with her, but he gave her the address of his friend who could take care of her in New York.

The last change we wish to elaborate on here, but certainly one of the most important changes in Holland's way of looking at his mission as a teacher, was the change in his attitude toward the Board of Education. When he came to school to teach, he was an employee who wanted to earn money and have time for writing music. He was not concerned about key questions of education, such as what was its overarching goal. He also did not think or worry about who set such goals and in what manner, who ruled the system, how, and why it was done this or that way.

However, as he learned how hard it was for him to do his job well, and how having Wolters as his principal was making it still harder, he became aware of the fact that Wolters would not be able to govern the school without the support of the Board of Education.

After Mrs. Jacobs retired, the school culture changed a lot with Wolters as the next principal. On the critical day we have in mind, Holland was asked to come to Mr. Wolters's office. A secretary suggested he should wait because Mr. Wolters was busy. When Holland was still standing there, Sarah, his fellow music teacher, left Wolters's office, crying. She didn't want to talk to Holland and she went away. Holland got angry with Wolters because there was no legitimate reason to make her cry. He walked into the principal's office to clarify the situation and defend her.

He did not expect what Wolters was about to tell him. We quote here some excerpts from the dialogue between the two men, the great teacher and his principal.

When Holland was let into Wolters's office and asked what was wrong with Sarah, Wolters avoided answering the direct question by inviting Holland to sit down.

Holland: "I'd rather stand, thanks. Why is Sarah crying, Jim?"

Wolters: "All right, I'll come right to the point. You know how acrimonious the budget meeting was, the Board of Education meeting last Tuesday. Be that as it may, each school in the district has been asked to submit proposals on ways of reducing cost by 10 percent, for September. This is what I decided."

Wolters handed Holland his proposal, in which the music program was removed from the curriculum.

H: "The entire music program."

W: "And art, and drama."

H: "Well, congratulations, Jim. You've been looking for a way to get rid of me for 30 years and they finally gave you an excuse."

W: "You know, I'm not as popular as you. I'm not anybody's favored anything."

H: "That's because you are the enemy, Jim. You just don't know it."

W: "What? I care about these kids just as much as you do. And when I am forced to choose between Mozart and reading and writing and long division, I choose long division."

H: "Well, I guess you can cut the arts as much as you want, Jim. Sooner
       or later these kids won't have anything to read or write about."

Holland was leaving. Wolters suggested he could write him a recommendation. Holland snapped, "I'm 60 years old, Jim." When he was passing through the door on his way out, he noticed the portrait of Jacobs on
the wall next to the door and pointed out that Jacobs would have fought
it. Wolters retorted that she would have lost. But Holland knew that she
would have fought it and so would he.

Holland's fight led to a hearing by the Board of Education. At that
hearing, he tried to explain what teaching is about. But he was accused of
making arguments for the sake of keeping his job. He could not explain to
the Board members that he was speaking for the benefit of students, not
himself. He told the Board they made wrong choices because they did not
work hard enough on key problems they had to solve. The Board president
was irritated and said, "Mr. Holland, I don't think you have any real
appreciation of our financial problems." Holland knew well that the Board
was missing the point. Money was important, but the problem was elsewhere. He said, "You know, the big problem here is that you people are
willing to create a generation of children who will not have the ability to
think, or create, or listen."

The president wanted to close the session by saying, "Mr. Holland, as
I said, we've done the best we can." But Holland responded, "Your best
isn't good enough," and he and Iris walked together to the exit.

This scene reflects how much Holland changed. He became a conscious defender of the ideals of his work as a teacher. He understood that
he was competent and that he was ruled by people who had no understanding of what teaching is about. He also understood that he could not
do much about the course of events of which his life was a part. He had
grown up to say that the knowledge and skills necessary for productive
teaching were not sufficiently appreciated by the Board members, and he
implied that important people in the system were not sufficiently prepared
and were not working hard enough to be able to improve the situation. It
takes time for teachers to realize that they are part of a bigger setting in
which they have very little say, while the performance of the system
hinges on their work.

FEATURE 8. WHAT PASSES FOR COLLEGIALITY

It took Holland a long time to comprehend what his work was about. The
education he received at schools misled him about it. Working as a teacher,
he had to unlearn many illusions and figure out how to deal with the challenges he faced. The history of his learning process suggests that it would
help him a lot in solving professional problems if a system existed for
working teachers to share their experiences and discuss solutions. Such a

system or tradition did not exist in his school, and it does not exist in the great bulk of schools. When Holland was 60, potentially he could have provided invaluable assistance to other teachers, if only the desired structure and the appropriate motivations existed. But they did not exist in Holland's school. Instead, what passed for collegiality was limited to the struggles of the kind illustrated by the faculty meeting, when teachers and Principal Wolters were deciding about a production of "The Gershwin Review."

Wolters was against the production and wanted to cut the senior year music program altogether. Teachers were outraged. He said, "People, people, please, let's keep in mind why we are here. We look for things that will keep money in the school coffers, not take it away." Holland asked, "At the expense of what?" Wolters responded, "I have a responsibility to the Board of Education, and there just isn't the money to fund such projects, not any more." Teachers were dismayed. Holland reacted angrily and said to his colleagues, "So what am I doing here? And why are we teaching anything? This is the kind of thing that's important to me." To the hot debate that followed, Mr. Wolters could only say, "Let's move on, please, let's move on."

This scene is so familiar. Mr. Wolters appeared in a role that one could see as analogous to the role of a detached and incompetent teacher who was forcing students to follow an unrealistic curriculum. He felt entitled to disregard the issue of whether they were interested in the matter and whether they had any intrinsic motivation to offer alternative solutions. Wolters also entirely ignored the issues that were most important for the teachers. He played the role of their superior because he wanted to, and he did it in a way that made them hate him. His arguments had nothing to do with how the teachers perceived the situation.

He had three spurious arguments to offer: higher authority, limited money, and shortage of time. None of these arguments had anything to do with students' learning. Teachers of little experience and without understanding of the system would not be able to resist such pressure. All they would be able to do would be to submit and go along with Wolters's decision.

Only Bill Maister was sufficiently prepared to take care of the situation. His fellow teachers could learn from him how to handle the case. Bill listened to the arguments of Wolters. He understood the position Wolters was taking, and he saw the helpless reaction of Holland and other teachers. Their outrage was going nowhere from Wolters's point of view, except for strengthening the conflict with budget facts. Bill's mind worked quickly, and in the midst of the tempest he said loudly to Wolters, "Excuse me, excuse me, Jim."

Wolters was suddenly brought to Earth by this skillful use of his first name. He was no longer a superior principal executing a higher will on a bunch of teachers—he had a name, and his name was Jim, not Principal

Wolters. He reacted as Bill expected, by saying with irony, "Yes, Bill?" Maister said, "I think I can guarantee that this year's show will make money." Wolters had no choice but to say, "I am listening." He was sure that no such solution existed, but Maister did catch his attention. Perhaps, if the proposal had any chance of making sense and succeeded in some savings, Wolters could show to the Board of Education how well he could manage the school.

Maister proposed, "What if we get some of the football players to be the dancers in the show and people come to the show to see how they fall on their asses?" He looked at Holland to meet his eyes and create understanding. Sarah opposed the idea initially by pointing out that she did not want the show to turn into a farce. But Maister knew what he was talking about: "It wouldn't be a farce, because we can get them to be better than the damn best dancers, and now that would shock the hell out of everybody." Wolters asked, "Who will teach the football players how to dance?" Maister was ready for that. He said he would do it himself. When suspicion in Wolters's voice was about to tell everybody this would not fly, Bill said, "I minored in modern dance."

By this statement, his competence was announced in official terms and Wolters no longer felt able to readily object. Holland understood Bill's idea. He confirmed, with as sure a voice as he could afford at the moment, that Bill did minor in modern dance. And Bill went on to explain that his coach in college had them do it to be more graceful. He stood up, asked Holland to help him keep one of his legs above the table, and he moved his hands above his head as a dancer would. People laughed and Bill was terrified for a moment that he had overdone the case. But Wolters only sighed and accepted the plan to produce "The Gershwin Review."

FEATURE 9. PROFESSIONAL GROWTH

Recall how Iris told Holland that he was not doing well as a father and said, "You know what? Your best is not good enough. So, go on. Write your music." Holland's reaction was very strong, as if his anger had accumulated for a long time and finally was released from deep within himself when he shouted, "Write my music? Write my music. When do I get time to write my music?" He broke the pencil in his hand and went out of the house, slamming the door behind him.

This scene illustrates one of the most important aspects of Holland's career as a teacher. Initially, Glenn Holland told Bill Maister that he decided to teach to have time to compose music, and Bill laughed at him. Fifteen years later, Holland understood that teaching was time consuming far beyond his imagination. Writing music turned out to be in conflict with his being a husband, a father, and a teacher. When Iris encouraged him to take the job, she also thought it was only a gig. But what really happened points out that throughout his whole career, Holland had a deep problem with fulfilling his ambition as a musician. He was teaching students by showing them how and why he loved music, but he could not show them that music loved him back.

Why? Was he so bad a composer? No, that would be too easy to say because fortune and fame do not always go hand in hand with true value, and true value is often suppressed for the wrong reasons. But one thing is clear: Holland is not shown even a single time making or performing music outside his school. The film also does not show any instance of his contact with professional musicians who could appreciate his music and perform it with him. Therefore, we claim, he had to suffer from the feeling of being not creative enough, not productive enough, and thus not appreciated enough by the outside world, and especially, by his beloved world of music.

Holland's lack of professional satisfaction in music became particularly transparent when he advised Rowena. She found him at a diner working on his composition, as he did from time to time in spare moments. She wanted to tell him how much she liked his class, the way he taught—he made her love music. Holland was very happy to hear that. Since she was a senior now, he asked her what she was planning to do after she graduated from high school. Rowena did not think seriously about going to college. Her mother and father had established a restaurant, her dad's dream, and her family wanted her to stay and help with running it. Holland asked what she herself wanted to do. If she had just one wish, what would she do? Rowena said, "Sing. I think I would rather sing than do anything. Sometimes I dream about going to New York and being on the stage in front of thousands of people. That's what I wish for." Rowena spoke in a deep voice from the bottom of her heart, and Holland knew she trusted him and wanted his advice. He said, "Maybe I shouldn't tell you that, Ms. Morgan, but you have a great talent. And if you have the passion, if you have the hunger, then you ought to go to New York and do what you want to do. No matter what anyone tells you." Rowena heard him well. She left and Holland went back to work. He told her what he had wanted to hear when he was young.

Finally, at the end of the film, Holland's lack of success as a composer was acknowledged by the Governor, Ms. Lang, his former clarinet student. At the farewell ceremony for Holland, when he was forced to retire, she said, "Mr. Holland had a profound influence on my life, on a lot of lives I know. And yet I get a feeling he considers a great part of his own life misspent. Rumor had it he was always working on this symphony of his. And it was going to make him famous, rich, probably both. But Mr. Holland isn't rich. And, he isn't famous, at least not outside our small town. So it might be easy for him to think himself a failure. And he would be wrong because, I think, he has achieved a success far beyond riches and fame. Look around you. There is not a life in this room that you have not touched. And each one of us is a better person because of you. We are your symphony, Mr. Holland. We are the melodies and the notes of your opus. And we are the music of your life."

SEPARATION OF ART FROM SCIENCE

It is as obvious as the difference between day and night that when push comes to shove educators and the general public believe, even if reluctantly, that science and math are more important for education than music and visual arts. That assertion requires no documentation. In this regard, *Mr. Holland's Opus* is a fictional and yet realistic description of these attitudes. Principal Wolters appeared in the film as an advocate of rigorous math and science education, giving them higher priority than music. He supported his decision by saying, "When I am forced to choose between Mozart and reading and writing and long division, I choose long division." Holland's reaction was, "Well, I guess you can cut the arts as much as you want, Jim. Sooner or later these kids won't have anything to read or write about."

The critical issue is that the separation between arts and sciences is largely artificially and arbitrarily created by schooling. There are three related points here.

The first point is that the concept of a context of productive learning is applicable to the teaching of any subject matter, and if the context is, in fact, an unproductive one, the intellectual and personal assimilation of the subject matter will be minimal at best and at worst totally counterproductive.

The second point is that our schools and even universities teach math and science in ways that turn off the interest of students forever.

The third point is that the intellectual and personal processes involved in musical and other artistic endeavors are precisely the same as many of those that are critical in the processes involved in learning math or physics or other sciences, and vice versa.

Exposure to any of these subject matters can have positive and negative consequences depending on whether the context in which they are taught is productive or unproductive. We will elaborate on these points in the next chapter, where we discuss the relationship between productive learning in the arts and sciences using three other well-known films.

At this point, you may still wonder what Einstein has to do with education and the context of productive learning that we discussed so far using only music and Mr. Holland's story. But you can go back to the beginning of this book and read again what Einstein said about the interpersonal relationship between a teacher and a student. This relationship is the driving force of our culture and science equally, and we are going to discuss the meaning and implications of this statement further in this book. The story of Mr. Holland illustrates what we have to keep in mind when we consider $E = mc^2$.

4

Transition From
Music to E = mc²

I f you take the features of the context of productive learning seriously, the first task is to determine as much as you can and as quickly as you can about the mindset with which the learner is approaching the task: feelings, thoughts, attitudes, expectations. This is no easy task even under the best conditions. At the same time, we cannot gloss over the fact that the teacher comes with a mindset shaped by, among other things, a predetermined curriculum that has to be covered in a specified period of time. So, we are always dealing with two mindsets: one of the students and the other of the teacher.

The central goal of a context of productive learning is that the two mindsets produce a degree of mutual understanding that engenders and reinforces wanting and proceeding to learn more. What is made clear in the case of Mr. Holland is that his mindset and that of his students were initially radically different and opposed. It was only when he was hit, so to speak, by the recognition that he and the students were on different planets that he began to deal with the implications. From that time on, the context of his classroom began to resemble a context of productive learning.

We make the very reasonable assumption that if you were to watch the film or only have read a presentation of it in the previous chapter, a number of questions would arise in your mind. Different viewers or readers will not be asking the same questions. Why are the power relationships between students and teacher, teachers and teachers, and teachers and administrators what they are? Why are music and other arts considered expendable, kinds of frills or luxuries? Why was Mr. Holland so unprepared for the realities of the culture of the school? Why is Mr. Wolters promoted from assistant principal to principal? Why did not Mr. Holland blame himself for the poor performance of his students on the test he gave them when he was beginning to teach? Why did he blame and derogate the students? Why was it that neither Mrs. Jacobs nor Mr. Wolters or anyone else sat in his classroom, observed what was going on, and sought to understand and help this neophyte? Why has the educational reform movement been so unsuccessful in increasing the number of classrooms that are contexts of productive learning? These are only a sample of the questions one can ask.

This is by way of saying that the film or our chapter contain no explanation of why schools—in this case, high schools—are what they are. We hope, of course, that seeing the film or reading the previous chapters helps you appreciate some of the important problems that should be studied and clarified. We use the word "appreciation" in its literal meaning: an increase in value of what you have seen or what you have read. It could be a person, a work of art, or a particular subject matter. When we say we appreciate something or somebody, we mean they have more positive value for us than they did before. Appreciation, however, is not explanation. You may now have more appreciation of matters educational, but that does not mean that you understand why and how schools are what they are. In other words, you do not have the "whole" story. Without some knowledge of that story, you are very likely to grossly underestimate why schools have been so intractable to a gamut of reform efforts.

Put it this way: The history of the development of compulsory education in America toward the end of the nineteenth century illuminates why schools today are what they are. Of course, they have changed in many ways. But in terms of the rationale for their organization, structure, governance, and ever-increasing complexity, they have changed remarkably little. For example, the New York City school system is not what it was at the end of the nineteenth century or in the first decades of the twentieth century. Today, it has about 1,100 schools and well over a million students. You need to know no more than these two facts to predict that the school system has a surfeit of problems. If New York is at the top of the scale in these respects, it is more a matter of degree than substance.

If you had to choose one factor, one of many important factors, in the history of American schools, it would be the waves of immigration in the nineteenth and early-twentieth centuries, which the society and educators were hardly prepared to confront. And yet, they were certain about only one thing: The goal of education was to tame and socialize the children of immigrants and, in effect, to make them different from their parents. The goal of these schools was to make those children Americans in attitude, behavior, and values. This in no way is intended as a criticism but rather as a partial explanation of how immigration gave rise to schools and school systems as they were and largely are today. The rationale of a context of productive learning was simply inconceivable to the majority of educators of those times. John Dewey was a monumental exception. He saw what was happening as a travesty of what America stood for. If Dewey stood for anything, it was against passive learning, drill, memorization. We need not remind the readers that in the past half century, smaller waves of immigration have had a similar impact as the earlier waves.

If we had started this book with a couple of long chapters on the development of schools in the past century, it would signify that we assumed that a context of productive learning could only be appreciated through knowledge of that history. In fact, we eschewed history because it would have no personal meaning or relevance for readers. For too many people, museums, like history, are regarded as collections of relics from the past, perhaps interesting but not applicable today.

By eschewing history we are not derogating it. We mention it here for the readers of this book who seek some kind of understanding of what they saw or read about *Mr. Holland's Opus.* If you do, it will be an instance of "the more you know or learn the more you want to know and learn." Having said that, let us now come back to the issue of learning in the arts and sciences.

The first published work of German astronomer Johannes Kepler (1571–1630), *The Sacred Mystery of the Cosmos,* appeared in 1596. It became well-known and helped him enter into a correspondence with Galileo and Tycho Brahe, who were the most famous astronomers of his time. After Tycho's death in 1601, Kepler succeeded him as Habsburg's imperial mathematician. Kepler discovered regularities in the orbital motion of planets, which are called Kepler's laws. Sixty years after the publication of Kepler's work, Newton still considered Kepler's data as having the greatest precision (better than one-tenth of a percent in the case of size of orbits of Mars and Venus in comparison to the orbit of Earth). Having formulated mathematical principles of physics, Newton was able to logically explain the regularities observed by Kepler. Kepler's work on optics is said to have been the first reading of Newton as a student at Cambridge.

It is much less known that in his works *Epitome of Copernican Astronomy* and *The Harmony of the World,* Kepler had paralleled the mathematical regularities observed in the planetary motion to the regularities known in harmonic sequences of sounds in music.[1] At the end of Chapter 4 of his *Harmony,* Kepler wrote that

> In Chapters 5 and 6, the single planets will be compared to the choral music of the ancients and its properties will be exhibited in the planetary movements. But in the following chapters, the planets

taken together and the figured modern music will be shown to do similar things. (p. 1,034)

Indeed, the title of Kepler's Chapter 5 says that "In the Ratios of the Planetary Movements Which Are Apparent as It Were to Spectators at the Sun, Have Been Expressed the Pitches of the System, or Notes of the Musical Scale, and the Modes of Song [Genera Cantus], the Major and the Minor." Chapter 6 is titled "In the Extreme Planetary Movements the Musical Modes or Tones Have Somehow Been Expressed." Chapter 8 has the subject "In the Celestial Harmonies Which Planet Sings Soprano, Which Alto, Which Tenor, and Which Bass?"

Considerable portions of Kepler's text refer to musical notes in order to describe how planets move. The mathematical equations required for description of planetary motion did not exist in Kepler's time and he could not use them. He was trying to make sense of the regularities he was observing in the motions of the planets, and he found it helpful to think about the large numbers of data in terms of sound scales that were familiar to him from music. The planets moved in ways he wanted to understand, in ways not created by humans. In order to organize his thinking about how the planets were moving, he used music that was created by humans and contained regularities that were familiar and useful to him in trying to understand the planetary regularities. He was comparing ratios of frequencies of various sounds in a musical scale with ratios of apparent velocities of the planets in their motions. Kepler's knowledge of musical scales helped him to see the regularities in planetary motion that are named Kepler's laws. Clearly, Kepler appreciated the structure and "sounds of music" and was influenced by them when he was investigating and thinking about the planetary motion, with the highest accuracy of the times.

The reason we quote Kepler's work here is that our preceding discussion of *Mr. Holland's Opus* concerned the concept of a context of productive learning in the case of a music appreciation class, and now we want to make a transition to a discussion of the same concept in the case of other disciplines, and in particular in the case of teaching science. Einstein is quoted as saying that after a certain high level of technical skill is achieved, science and art tend to coalesce and great scientists are also artists.[2]

The concept of context of productive learning does not change when we make the transition from art to science. The discipline, of course, changes. The inculcated opinion that different disciplines, like music and astronomy, are completely different regarding key characteristics of productive learning appears to be one of the results of "learning" about art and science in the practice of the classroom. Kepler's example suggests that this particular perspective may be unique to educational institutions and that it does not necessarily reflect the reality of how scientists learn about the world, what motivates them, how they discover regularities of

Nature, and how they eventually arrive at useful generalizations. Students need to understand how discoveries are made in order to think about it. And whether students want to discover the world is far more important for productive learning than whether they can memorize a formula and pass a test. For example, if a student thinks about stars in association with music and gets some idea to pursue, a teacher may very easily extinguish the birth of a flame of interest in the student or help it grow in a fruitful direction, depending on how the teacher understands the relationship between art and science and how he or she can use this understanding to help the student pursue an interesting line of thought.

We recommend that the reader sees three films that concern productive learning in three disciplines. The first film, *Stand and Deliver,* is a true story about a computer expert, Mr. Jaime Escalante, who chose to become a teacher in a poor minority school in Los Angeles. He taught mathematics to a class of 18 troubled students so well that they passed an advanced placement calculus exam and "got a ticket out of the barrio" through admission to college. He taught many more students afterwards. The second film is called *October Sky,* a true story of high school student Homer Hickam, Jr., who lived in Coalwood, West Virginia, in a traditional mining family. When Hickam saw the satellite Sputnik on October 4, 1957, with his own eyes, he decided to try to build a rocket, and he pursued that goal despite his father's disapproval. His father wanted him to be a miner like himself. Let us mention that Homer Hickam had an outstanding career as a NASA engineer, and he is now one of the leading voices among those contributing to a discussion of the future of the space program. The third film is *Billy Elliot,* based on a true story from England. It is about a boy who wanted to be a ballet dancer, not a boxer as his father wished. The boy sought admission to the Royal Academy of Dance. Needless to say, he had a great career in dance. The three films abundantly illustrate features that commonly characterize contexts of productive learning independently of the disciplines: mathematics, rocket science, and dance. The dominant aspect is a relationship between a teacher and a student.

But the films also show that learning processes in different disciplines are differently perceived by the public. We expect the readers to have difficulties with a transition from thinking that the key characteristics of productive learning processes are different in the case of art classes and science classes to thinking that the key variables and their changes are actually very similar, if not the same, independently of the subject matters taught in schools.

The source of this difficulty is how we are taught in schools. Let us compare the stories of Mr. Holland and Mr. Escalante to illustrate this point in concrete terms.

Escalante made students in a poor inner-city school want to learn mathematics. They deeply desired a better life than the one they feared would become their fate unjustly. They felt trapped in the barrio and they did not know how to change their situation because there was no hope of their passing standard tests and graduating.

Escalante set the goal of learning for them: to pass an advanced placement math exam and go to college. Mr. Escalante was convinced that his students were capable of learning math as well as students in other schools. He was a minority member himself, and he knew he had no reason to assume that the minority students were inferior to others. In order to motivate them to learn before they could appreciate what math was about, he made it clear to them that unless they learned math, they would end up washing dishes or frying chicken in the restaurants of the same poor neighborhood forever and never see a change in their lives.

He also took them to a computer company to show them a part of the different world outside their neighborhood. One can infer from the film that the visit was not an empty excursion to a point of interest, like so many other school trips. The film shows students walking freely in a large computer room, touching things, and asking questions. It is clear that they never saw such a place before. And it is perfectly clear that they could not and would not ever imagine such places before they saw one. So, they could not have any concrete image of what math could be good for. The visit showed them an impressive example of a place where people had to know math in order to do their job. And they liked the place. It was clean, sophisticated, appealing in its design, comfortable to be in, and full of secrets. And eventually, after a long ordeal of study, the students passed the exam and their appreciation of mathematics greatly increased.

Music is presented in *Mr. Holland's Opus* as a form of expression of one's self, and math is presented in *Stand and Deliver* as a way to graduate to a higher level of education and a better job. Escalante is shown drilling students in solving mathematical problems for this purpose. In contrast, *Mr. Holland's Opus* explains the human value of music that Holland helped students appreciate. This value motivated his students and it did not depend on the existence of colleges and admission criteria. Music was not included in SAT or similar tests. By this contrast, we may conclude that *Stand and Deliver* does not explain the value of math beyond the concept of social advancement.

The difference between the films may suggest that music serves expression of humanity, while math is only a drill that some desperate students practice for the reward of breaking through an otherwise impenetrable social barrier. And minority students could succeed only if they had an unusually interpersonally sensitive teacher. Several examples of Escalante's sensitivity were shown in the film to explain how he engaged students in learning math. No other teacher in the school was able to achieve that.

Escalante observed students closely and looked for ways to gain their trust. He thought about students' problems outside school and helped them solve those problems. He was similar in this respect to Holland. For example, when a student was afraid that members of his gang would see him carrying books home, Escalante gave him more books so that the student could keep one always in the classroom and one always at home. When another student had to quit because her father wanted her to work in the family restaurant, Escalante explained to the father that she had a chance to go to college and study medicine, as she wanted to. This case resembles the case of Holland's student Rowena Morgan, who had a great talent for singing and did not want to work at a family restaurant for the rest of her life.

Thanks to his understanding of what was going on in the minds of the students, Escalante, like Holland, was able to talk with them about their problems in their language, and he connected math problems with examples from their lives. In one case, he even formulated a problem about the number of girls each gigolo had in a certain neighborhood. Students did not understand the mathematics of the example right away, but they saw some relevance of the calculation in their world.

The close contact with students served Escalante as a vehicle to tell them that they were on the margins of social life. He skillfully created in them a hopeful desire to learn math and pass the exam. The importance of the teacher-student relationship for understanding how to motivate students to learn is repeatedly shown in both films. Escalante's relationship with his students was contrasted with attitudes of other teachers who stayed away from close contacts with students. The same contrast is visible between Holland and Wolters.

Nevertheless, we would like to observe that Mr. Holland did not motivate students to learn in the way Mr. Escalante did, namely, by suggesting failure in life if they did not learn music. And Holland's criteria of productive learning did not include test scores. Thus, the verification of learning by exams was an important aspect that distinguished what Holland and Escalante were doing with students. Escalante dealt with a different situation. There was a set of mathematical formulas that students ought to know how to apply in order to solve problems of a well-defined type. These formulas and problems were the subjects of the tests that the students had to pass. The meaning of the mathematical formulas that they were learning was never addressed in the film.

The essence of the difference in presentation of productive learning processes in *Mr. Holland's Opus* and *Stand and Deliver* lies in the following. Ms. Lang was shown to play the clarinet, and viewers could hear that at a certain moment she managed to play it right. In *Stand and Deliver*, no student was shown solving a math problem that viewers could understand and see that the solution was right. In other words, in the case of music the criterion of success appeared to be verifiable by viewers through direct inspection of how students performed, while in the case of math, no such inspection was available to the viewers. Thus, the key criterion for productive learning in math remained invisible. Productivity of learning was thus effectively identified in the viewers' minds with a score on an exam. This difference may easily support the opinion that music is a part of "social life" while math is an abstract invention of nerds for nerds, or even a tool to raise and sustain social barriers. And it is hard to see similarities between learning processes in music and math when one is used to thinking in terms of such different images.

Are math and music so differently perceived because music is fun and speaks to us without requiring conscious analysis while math is boring and cannot be comprehended without willful, conscious effort of the mind? Or, perhaps more likely, math is taught in schools in ways that make it incomprehensible and appalling?

Let us observe that exactly such an opinion about classical music was visible on the sullen faces of students in Holland's class before he understood that his students had a false—or no—image of classical music in their minds and that he, as their teacher, would have to do something about it. If Holland's students did not appreciate classical music in his class at the beginning of his teaching career, it was certainly not because classical music was boring or incomprehensible. The lessons were boring and incomprehensible because they had little to do with music.

Is it possible that algebra and calculus are like classical music, but students are not given opportunities to notice the similarity of mathematics to the operations they already do and like to do in the context of their lives?

It is conceivable that arithmetic of the sort of 1 apple + 1 apple = 2 apples is as natural for us as listening to the basic rhythms and sounds of the world. And further, the simple popular music may be analogous to everyday operations like $10 + $10 = $20, while classical music can be similar to algebra and calculus. If Holland's students had to be given opportunities to connect the music they already knew with classical music in order to become able to study the latter with great interest, what could one say about algebra and calculus, or physics, or chemistry?

Let us also invoke, here, a scene from *October Sky*. In a scene in which Hickam "proved" to the school principal that his rocket could not be blamed for the fire in the forest three miles away from the launch pad that Hickam and his friends had built, Hickam drew figures and wrote equations on the blackboard. The principal said he was "duly impressed." But if viewers looked closely at what Hickam actually wrote on the blackboard, and if they carefully listened to what he said to the principal, they would notice that his speech did not make any clear mathematical or physical sense. It was blurting out sequences of words that sounded relevant but did not constitute any proof. His explanation was as far from any acceptable scientific reasoning as the sounds that were initially produced by Ms. Lang on her clarinet were distant from music.

Could the film audience notice that Ms. Lang did not play well? Yes, they could. Would the same viewers notice that Hickam's speech made no clear sense? Most people would not, and this is also the reason why the scene could be a part of a popular film. Should we conclude that a good performance in music is easy to recognize but in science it is not?

Now, is this particular example telling us that science is so complicated that it is impossible to present it clearly in a film intended for the popular audience? Why should any filmmaker expect that the audience would be convinced that Hickam's speech had scientific merit as long as it contained a hodgepodge of figures drawn on a blackboard and words such as rocket, velocity, acceleration, time, square, gravity, or distance? The troubling answer is that our educational systems do not provide us with the ability to recognize harmony in science. This is why the jumble is accepted as representative of a scientific argument. We simply are not provided with means to judge on our own.

Instead, we accept that the less understandable the figures on the blackboard in a science class, the more "scientific" they are. Therefore, we may even identify our act of shutting off our minds to details of reasoning as a sign that the content we are facing is "scientific." And when watching the film, we take for granted that Hickam did make sensible statements even if his speech did not make any sense.

Unfortunately, Hickam's statements concern concepts that belong well within the scope of a usual high school curriculum. Thus, if Hickam's speech is accepted as "scientific," the film reinforces a feeling in the audience that their ignorance of science is expected, somehow "reasonable," and perhaps not a significant issue. Perhaps the level of our average appreciation of science is analogous to the level of appreciation of music by students at John F. Kennedy High when Holland was beginning to teach. But this would mean that we are not appreciating science much as a society. And since we do not have sufficiently many teachers like Mr. Holland to change the situation in teaching, in art and science, we grow up in the mode of ignorance until we finish school. And then there is no more opportunity to change that mode.

So, can science be appreciated by a typical student? If this is not the case, it is a consequence of the miserable schooling system. In order to show what we mean, let us quote here an example that demonstrates how science can be recognized through its clarity. The example concerns a brief exposition of an argument that also pertains to rocket science, this time made by a physicist.

During congressional hearings about the tragic mission of the space shuttle Challenger, long and confusing statements blurred the investigation of the cause of the explosion that killed several astronauts. As a member of the investigating team, physicist Richard Feynman spent a long time studying available data, talking to engineers, and pondering the issues involved. Eventually, he changed the style of the proceedings when he clearly showed to everyone in the hearing room that the explosion was most probably caused by the malfunction of large washer rings in the fuel tanks.

As part of his argument, he showed a piece of the washer ring in his hand to be flexible and resilient, capable of sealing adjacent parts of the fuel tanks at room temperature. Then, Feynman put the washer in a glass of iced water, which had a temperature similar to the rocket tanks on the launch pad at the time of takeoff. The washer material became stiff and thus incapable of properly sealing the joints.

This example shows that science is not a hodgepodge of words and concepts. Its quality, analogous to harmony in music, is reflected in the clarity of statements concerning experimental facts, their interpretation, and predictions that logically follow in a harmonious theory. Buying Hickam's "explanation" is possible only when we do not learn at school the meaning of science. The irony is that the principal of Hickam's school said he was "duly impressed" when the audience of the film was offered the hodgepodge. This is an example of how our lack of appreciation of science is perpetuated—we are told we are doing the right thing when we miss the point. Exactly as it happened when Holland said, "Good" about a miserable performance of his orchestra.

One might think that learning how to dance must be quite different from learning how to launch rockets. The subject matter is completely different. But both Billy Elliot and Homer Hickam were helped by teachers who were able to create an interpersonal relationship between the boys and them. These relationships were key to the boys' successes. The teachers knew what was happening with the boys, and they had the talent to act accordingly and help the boys in critical situations. Hickam's teacher inspired him, helped him go to a science fair, and supported him in his relationship with his father. Elliot's teacher encouraged him to dance, helped him in qualifying for the Royal Academy of Dance, and supported him in his relationship with his father.

In the process of learning, both boys did essentially the same thing: They were learning by trial and error how to reach the goals they were pursuing. Hickam knew he had learned how to build rockets when one of them eventually went straight up so high that he could not see it any-more. Billy made endless pirouettes in front of a mirror before he learned how to keep his balance. If something did not work, both boys had to make a change and try again. No lesson was lost because each of the lessons showed that something did not work and should be changed, or that something did work as intended and should be kept. This is exactly how scientists and artists learn. This is how they make progress in their work.

Hickam was immensely happy when his father admitted that Hickam's rocket was an impressive achievement. Similarly, Billy Elliot danced in front of his father to show what he had accomplished. The boys believed that they learned a lot, and they demonstrated what they learned to their fathers. They were hoping that their fathers would appreciate it. In both cases, the events were great lessons to their fathers. Holland's understanding of his relationship with his son Cole developed in a similar sequence of steps.

These examples hint that contexts of productive learning in all disciplines have common features. Many omnipresent variables occur and change equally in the processes of productive learning, independently of disciplines. The key factor is the understanding between a teacher and a student. But this relationship is not easy to understand.

We do not point out this difficulty lightly. If the key teacher-student relationship were easy to understand, we would not have ever-increasing problems and need for educational reform. Most students would want to learn and become whom they can be like Ms. Lang, Homer Hickam, or Billy Elliot did. But instead, their stories are so unusual that they became subjects of films.

What is so hard to understand about the context of productive learning? Is there a way to explain why reform efforts do not solve the problem despite great expense, time, and work put into them?

We shall offer a path to certain answers to these questions in the next chapters. The subject of the next chapters is Einstein's formula $E = mc^2$. The subject is chosen very carefully in order to point out several aspects of the educational challenge in a number of mutually related ways. But our main purpose in these chapters is to explain the origin, meaning, and implications of Einstein's relativity. The formula $E = mc^2$ is one of these consequences. We want to use this subject matter later, toward the end of the book, in order to demonstrate by analogy what we see as the central reason for failures of educational reform. The history of schools explains how it happened that they are as they are. But to understand the reason for continuous failure of reform is a different matter. You cannot claim it is easy to understand the problem after tens of years and billions of dollars were invested in the reform and did not fulfill their promise.

We will use our story of $E = mc^2$ to explain that the problem of educational reform is similar in certain ways to the problem that Einstein solved by formulating his theory of relativity. You know that the subject of $E = mc^2$ is difficult. It appears to be very "scientific," abstract, and hardly an opportunity to learn. And it seems much more difficult than problems with schooling. One cannot touch or see relativity as one can see a classroom, a teacher, students, or touch an object on a table. For another thing, we know that for the great majority of students, math, physics, and other sciences are subject matters to be endured, not embraced, to be avoided, not struggled with. For college-educated people, $E = mc^2$ is an educational witch's brew they have absolutely no intention of tasting. But these same educated people would be very surprised to be told that sophisticated scientists, famous or not, regard school education as a similar witch's brew. We will explain in the next chapters in what way and why the problem of educational reform, and in particular the concept of productive learning, is more complex and harder to comprehend than Einstein's relativity.

Both authors of this book have spent many hours with many scientists trying to understand why educational reform is such a monumentally difficult problem conceptually, theoretically, and in the research arena. Serious scientists require no help from us about the importance of educational reform. They need no convincing. They are socially responsible and concerned people. But as soon as they get a glimmer of the scores of variables that one cannot overlook in educational research or action, they would rather throw up their hands in frustration and thank God they have something else to do.

In telling the story of relativity, we include the historical origins that ultimately led Einstein to make the contributions he did. If, instead, one starts right off by focusing on the formula $E = mc^2$, we learned by experience that people quickly get overwhelmed by concepts and their relationships that have no resonance in their lives and thinking.

So, for example, it is one thing to say that light travels at the speed of about 186,000 miles a second—people will accept that as a fact. But at the same time, they will be asking themselves, How was that speed determined? In a context of productive learning, the learner has to feel safe enough with a teacher to ask that question. If you tell the learner that $E = mc^2$ in words means that energy is a function of the mass of an object times the speed of light squared, he or she will accept that statement as a fact written on a scientific tablet brought down by Einstein from a scientific Mount Sinai. But the learner will be mystified when you tell her or him that energy, mass, and light are not three independent variables but part of one unitary process, a conclusion that flies in the face of the way people see their earthly world. There are many examples like that. And this is why experience taught us that the developmental history of relativity is of discernible help to learners.

Unlike the case of music in *Mr. Holland's Opus*, where the readers or viewers can see teachers and learners in action in classrooms that are similar to those in which the readers or viewers themselves have also spent years of their lives, we have no movie with the title *Mr. Einstein's Opus*. We have only statements in language as a means for conveying what Einstein did. In using language, we are trying to be as sensitive as we can possibly be to where the readers are most probably coming from in respect to the story we are telling. And we very consciously made the decision that we would make no effort to tell "the whole story," but enough so as to allow the readers to conclude that they have learned and understood key aspects of the story. What we do want the readers to understand, using our story of $E = mc^2$, is the magnitude of consequences that a clear understanding of the context of productive learning may have for the future of our society.

In short, to begin with, we want readers to be able to say that they appreciate what they have learned about relativity and that it has a greater value for them than before. Other authors have attempted to do the same. If we have serious reservations about how some of them went about the task, in no way do we criticize them because we know how excruciatingly difficult it is to bend language to the purposes of new and challenging concepts. Our main reservation of these previous efforts is that they are not informed by a conception of learning that makes it necessary to be appropriately sensitive to the mindset of the learners or readers.

There are millions of college-educated people who have been robbed of the opportunity to grasp what selected high school seniors grasped about some basic aspects of the theory of relativity when we taught them. With no exception, they truly valued what they learned. *We allow ourselves to believe that this book will also be found rewarding for those college-educated individuals who are curious about Einstein's contributions.* But we have no doubt that future authors who will write on the subject of relativity and $E = mc^2$ will find this book wanting in some respects.

However, our ultimate goal will be to draw some critical lessons from our story of $E = mc^2$ and move on to the issues of educational reform and the context of productive learning. We not only aim at a better explanation of what is meant by the context of productive learning but also at an indication of what such better understanding may bring as its consequences. Einstein's relativity and the formula $E = mc^2$ as its consequence, and great practical implications of that formula to our planet, will help us in sketching the magnitude of issues and forces that are involved in matters educational and in the context of productive learning. We will take this up in the last chapter.

5

A Letter to the Reader

Dear Reader,

The chapters that follow discuss the content and meaning of the formula $E = mc^2$. The discussion described here has been preceded by several attempts to organize material that could either be applied in a classroom or a small group activity. We have studied for a couple of years how those materials worked, and none was truly satisfactory. The more we learned about the difficulties that our task encountered, the better we understood that those same difficulties were present in the discussions between the two of us as different individuals.

What you will read in these chapters is the result of a process of discovery that a psychologist and a physicist went through trying to do two things at the same time. One of the goals of our efforts was to understand and explain the content and meaning of the formula $E = mc^2$ itself. Another goal, a more important one for us, was to understand and explain the content and meaning of the concept of context of productive learning, using the example of the formula.

The most important feature of the process of discovery that we went through in the period of study that included writing these chapters is that we both became a teacher and a student at the same time. We became "friends in mind" as a result of the processes of learning and teaching that we were going through. A psychologist who never hoped to understand Einstein's ideas eventually grasped the essence of them and found them natural and comprehensible, meaningful, consequential, instructive, no longer a mystery but a source of inspiration. A physicist who never before comprehended how differently the world is seen by other people eventually understood that his own conception of learning by human beings was limited to his own experience of learning in the community of physicists. His conception of learning was expanded by many orders of magnitude by his engagement in the teacher-student relationship whose results are reported here. Only then did he begin to understand the role played by the psychological interpersonal relationship between a teacher and a student in the process of productive learning.

The authors come from very different worlds. Our disciplines differ greatly. We had to find a way to understand each other, translating our thoughts that so far were expressed only in the different languages of our different disciplines. In order to be able to proceed, we had to trust each other and become mentally able to openly disclose how confused we were by what the other was saying. We had to find new ways to help each other understand what was unclear. We had to eventually overcome our personal fears of appearing ignorant of some "obvious" stuff, fears dating back to our own education. We did not give up. We unlearned illusions that were inculcated in us in their youth and later in their our lives, and we continued our search for a meaningful ordering of the material.

The transforming effect that the process of productive learning produced for us resulted from the interpersonal teacher-student relationship that cannot be recreated in the format of a book. We could talk with each other, ask questions, display stress or confusion on our faces, argue, get excited, challenge each other's deep beliefs, see connections of what we were doing and saying with how we lived and what was happening to us; we could be honest with each other about our feelings of inferiority in the area of specialty of the other and learn, learn that our fears could be overcome by a meaningful discussion, that our ignorance about something we wanted to learn about did not have to be hidden but could be appreciated and rewarded with help in understanding. We began to trust each other when each of us observed in the action of the other that neither of us was being judged when he sought understanding of something that was bothering him, even if the ignorance level initially looked really embarrassing. Once this difficulty was faced, it was overcome to our satisfaction. It typically was turning out that confusion was justified, was related to an interesting question, required considerable discussion, and opened new views on the subject. This experience cannot be recreated for a reader in a book. We can only employ written language, and we have no way of interacting with the readers.

So, what should we do? Providing a record of our discussions would be inappropriate. We stopped taping them. More important was what we could incorporate in our discussions and what we have learned from interactions with others. But thanks to the discussions between the two of us, we could better understand the difficulties that others had, and we could identify the points concerning the content and meaning of $E = mc^2$ that required explanation in the book. Over time, we felt more and more comfortable by building a story that needs to be told to the reader in order to create the contexts in which things, concepts, words, and entire sentences that we can write may become recognizable, understandable, so that the readers can read from our sentences what we wanted to say by writing them. A new concept has to be built in the mind of a learner before the name of the concept can be used in a meaningful way.

The need for building the imagery required for understanding became more or less clear only through the analysis of very concrete cases, such as the analysis of simultaneity of definite events by two different observers. We could slowly begin to see that we were largely not understanding each other as intended and expected on the basis of our initially naive approach. It became clear that we were not understanding each other even when we were using the same words in apparently similar sentences. It turned out that the subject of $E = mc^2$ required precise thinking and careful talking far beyond the commonly accepted level of precise language. Most intriguing was the fact that we could not separate the meaning of what we were talking about from the relationship between the two of us as people. The questions we were asking concerning time, space, motion, speed, or our own learning were too deeply related to the ability to think clearly by each of us, and to our self-images, for us to react without emotion to the difficulties we were encountering.

All experiments we have done before with teaching $E = mc^2$ to high school students, university students, or adults whose "education" was already "completed" appeared in a new light. We became able to remove one illusion after another and clarify misconceptions about what one of us thought about the understanding of what the other said; what was truly clear or what was only assumed to be clear; what was only said and never comprehended; or what was repeated many times, always apparently clearly confirmed as understood, and what was eventually discovered to contain some essential misinterpretation.

Such a learning process is missing in schools. Our goal is to point that out. But since in a book we can only write and hope to be read, our combined experiences suggested that the best thing we could do is to write a story of $E = mc^2$. In that story, we could write about concepts that are difficult to grasp in such a way that they will not involve major confusion. This level of clarity was always achieved in the practice of our interaction by talking about concrete familiar contexts. We had to describe those contexts in detail. But please do not expect that the chapters that follow are in the how-to-do-it category. We are not presenting a curriculum or a detailed instructor's guide. We try, instead, to take the reader on a tour around the mountains that require exploration.

Even if the following chapters cannot be a substitute for a live context of productive learning, the chapters do present $E = mc^2$ in the context of a story that illustrates what is missing in schools. All we have found in interaction with other people, and all that eventually happened between us, led us to writing the chapters that follow and eventually culminated in the conclusions that concern basic issues of educational reform: what it means to learn and what it means to teach. The famous formula $E = mc^2$ is explained here in ways that cannot be found in classrooms or popular books about Einstein and relativity.

If our relationship with you as a reader is inevitably not an optimal interpersonal one, there are several things we feel we can tell you about the mindset a person may have in relation to Einstein, relativity, $E = mc^2$, and the like at the beginning. Here are the things we know about the majority of people.

1. One may be curious about Einstein's ideas but also feel utterly incompetent or ignorant in understanding why Einstein is, like Newton, considered a secular god who has changed our view of how the universe works. One may have resigned in one's mindset to accept the role of an ordinary mortal who will never comprehend why Einstein is accorded such a role in human history.

2. Many people have never taken a course in physics, either in college or high school. If somebody did take such a course, she or he very likely put its content in the file-and-forget category.

3. The same is true for mathematics. Some people may have passed such courses, but they were never taught those contents in relation to their daily existence or relationship to the sciences generally. They probably knew that other people found mathematics mystifying and a source of "math anxiety," which they controlled by ensuring that they chose a career in which mathematics is not necessary.

4. Some people probably have concluded that they do not have the kind of mind "wired" to understand an exact science. They may not know that for many decades, no more than 30% of all teachers of science in our schools have had some formal credentials to teach science. As someone said, "Science teachers are as rare as hen's teeth."

5. Many people probably do not distinguish between the problem that someone like Einstein is struggling with, a conceptual problem concerning the real world, and the mathematics that is necessary for making precise predictions and comparing them with results of actual measurements. We do assume that people are generally capable of grasping what the problems were that puzzled Einstein, without or with minimal knowledge of mathematics. The problem is that they are overwhelmed by the impression that the required mathematics is so important and complex that they have no chance of understanding what the leading ideas were. That is why, in the

chapters that follow, there is little mathematics but a great deal on the origin and nature of the questions Einstein was seeking to answer.

6. There is one feature of the reader that is his or her great asset: curiosity, desire to understand more. It powers the willingness to read, to think things through again, and overcome the socially acquired feeling that one misses something important because of one's own inadequacies.

The chapters that follow are intended as an *introduction* to the understanding of relativity and its consequences. For readers who may be inclined to initiate their own study of the subject beyond the main text, the Appendices discuss elements of Einstein's relativity theory and related matters, including some mathematics.

Sincerely yours,

The Authors

6

Light Carries Energy

Imagine yourself waking up early one summer morning and walking outside in a thin t-shirt and shorts. Imagine how you are getting goose bumps from the night chill that lingers in the shadows. Do you remember the sunshine passing through a gap between the trees? You may step into the light, and right away you can feel its warm touch on your face, arms, and legs. What causes this feeling? Is light warm? How does it happen that it warms up your body? You may try to look toward the Sun, but it is so bright that looking toward it is painful, and you have to shut your eyes. Even with closed eyes you see the strong, bright light through your eyelids.

The light warms you because it carries energy. Your body absorbs this energy. When a ray of light reaches a molecule of your skin, it imparts a sequence of rapid impulses that shake the molecule. The molecules of your skin vibrate more after the absorption of light than before. This increase in intensity of vibrations of atoms in your skin is what you feel as the warm touch of the Sun. Your eyes are much more sensitive to light than your skin is, and you must close your eyes when you look straight toward the Sun. Otherwise, the energy of light would destroy the retinas at the back of your eyeballs. The pain associated with looking directly into the Sun is caused by the rapid absorption of energy in such large amounts that the capacity of your eyes is greatly surpassed.

Your eyes are not designed to look toward the Sun. They are tuned to see the light reflected from the objects that surround you in your natural environment. The reflected sunlight has less intensity than the light coming straight from the Sun. It is the reflected light, reflected from the ground, plants, and animals, that is the primary source of information about the world that our brains receive through our eyes. Since our eyes must be sensitive to the relatively small amounts of energy carried by the reflected light, they are not able to withstand the direct exposure to sunlight. As a result of these conditions, millions of years of evolution produced a mechanism that automatically narrows our pupils whenever it gets too bright. This mechanism keeps in check the amount of energy that is absorbed in our retina. By the same evolutionary design, in the extreme case when we attempt to look straight toward the Sun, we feel pain and instinctively close our eyes to protect them from the energy carried by light directly from the Sun.

What element or entity in the Sun could be the source of this energy that sunlight brings down to the Earth? Before we answer this question, let us observe that all processes of life on the Earth are effectively propelled by this source. The light powers life by first being absorbed in plants: It strikes molecules of water and carbon dioxide and additional atoms and provides the energy that allows all of these atoms to be welded together in the form of substances called carbohydrates, like sugar. This complex process is called photosynthesis and has many phases. The resulting molecules of carbohydrates are like batteries freshly loaded with the energy of light. The energy is accumulated and transported in such molecular batteries in all living cells of a plant. The cells can grow and function because the energy from the little batteries is unloaded in the cells wherever it is needed.

Up the food chain, plant eaters consume the energy of light stored in plants, and meat eaters consume the same energy by devouring plant eaters. Humans are at the top of this ladder of consumption of the energy of light from the Sun. Thus, we not only see the world thanks to the energy of light, but we also live in every material way thanks to the energy that comes to the Earth from the Sun carried by light. Moreover, the photosynthesis in plants produces the oxygen in the Earth's atmosphere, which we need to breathe. Thus, not only our stomachs but also our lungs are effectively fed by the energy of light.

When you take a magnifying glass and concentrate sunlight on a sheet of paper, the paper will heat up and start burning when its temperature reaches about 450° Fahrenheit (230° Celsius). Your lens collects light only from a small area of your magnifying glass. But every bit of the landscape around you, to the horizon and beyond, collects the energy of light with similar intensity. The amount of energy carried by light that the Earth receives from the Sun must be enormous.

So the question is, Where does the Sun get this energy? The answer to this question was first found in the twentieth century: The Sun burns its mass inside its core according to the formula $E = mc^2$. We have begun our discussion of this formula with a description of the morning scene in order to point out that the formula $E = mc^2$ is relevant to practically everything that happens around us all the time! However, the meaning of the formula $E = mc^2$ is wider and deeper than the explanation of the source of subsistence of life on the Earth. The formula $E = mc^2$ stems from facts that concern realms far beyond our solar system. We intend to discuss these big aspects of the formula $E = mc^2$ with you in the following chapters.

In terms of symbols, the formula $E = mc^2$ connects the energy of a piece of matter, E, with the mass of that piece, m, and the speed of light, c. The equation states that the energy of an amount m of mass (it can be a mass of an entire body or of a part of it) is equal to m multiplied by the square of the speed of light, which means multiplied by c once and then another time. Unfortunately, the notions of energy, mass, and speed of light are not as familiar in contemporary society as they should be, given the role of energy in our life. This lack of authentic familiarity with the energy of mass is a consequence of how our educational system teaches us. It is quite possible that the notions of energy, mass, and speed of light have so far appeared to you as somewhat artificial, not as clearly understood as you might wish to have them understood.[1]

But in the context of the summer morning and its interpretation that we have just described, the notion of energy of mass can appear as less artificial than it seems to be at school. It is a curious subject of apparently far-reaching implications. In fact, the concepts of energy, mass, and speed of light were conceived as a result of studies by researchers who were driven in their studies by curiosity. They were puzzled about the mechanisms of their own existence and their perception of the world. They wanted to grasp the right image of the universe, and they could not stop asking questions and seeking answers. The history of their investigations is fascinating and itself a subject of study by historians of science. This book is written in order to respond to your own curiosity about the world.

The formula $E = mc^2$ is a perfect point of focus for our discussion about the context of productive learning because it is relevant to our existence, it has a great depth in meaning, it is directly related to our understanding of our place in the universe, and it will be very helpful to us in our later discussion of the concepts of learning, teaching, and the goals of education. We did not choose the subject of $E = mc^2$ lightly or randomly. Besides explaining the origin of the power of our Sun, the formula $E = mc^2$ allowed people to build new sources of usable energy on the Earth. When one plugs an appliance into a wall socket in the United States, one uses the power of electricity that in about 20% is drawn from burning small amounts of mass according to the formula $E = mc^2$ in nuclear reactors in U.S. power plants. In France, this percentage is in the order of 70. These are manifest examples of relevance of the formula $E = mc^2$ to our everyday life.

The less tangible aspects of $E = mc^2$ are related to how much, or rather how little, every one of us knows and understands about the formula. What does it really say? How did it come about? Is there more to learn in the apparently remote land where it comes from? Is this formula famous only as a symbol of something incomprehensible by mortals? Why are we so ignorant about the formula that seems to undergird the world as we know it? And in the context of the last question, What, why, and how are we learning in schools? Are art and science taught in schools in ways that give us enough authentic comprehension of our world, or are we taught in ways that give us as little authentic comprehension of the world as we obtain regarding the meaning and content of Einstein's discovery from a century ago? Do we learn in productive or unproductive ways? What does "productive learning" mean? What do we mean by "learning"?

In order to explain how $E = mc^2$ was discovered by Einstein, we will have to discuss the theory of time that provided the foundation for his discovery. The formula $E = mc^2$ emerged from the precise theory of time that Einstein conceived while trying to understand paradoxical results obtained by other physicists. The concept of time that resolved the observed paradoxes is more basic and of bigger significance to our image of the world than the formula $E = mc^2$ itself. Besides, the formula will remain incomprehensible without a study of the concept of time. Therefore, we shall devote considerable room in our discussion to the concept of time. But we are not going to discuss the theory of time in abstraction. We will describe contexts in which the study of time becomes as natural as stepping into the sunshine on a summer morning to see how it feels.

Einstein was motivated to review the concept of time by his puzzlement about the properties of light. Likewise, we shall start by discussing what is known about light. It is also most appropriate to begin our discussion with what has been learned about light because the formula $E = mc^2$ was derived by Einstein for the first time by analyzing how the energy of a piece of matter changes through an interaction with light, a process akin to what we experience when we step into the sunlight on a summer morning.

7

How Fast Is Light?

Our first step toward the formula $E = mc^2$ is to get acquainted with light as a phenomenon. The speed of light, c, appears in the formula and we need to understand why. The depth of the reasons for why this speed appears in the formula will surprise you. Also, light played a critical role in the history of discoveries that eventually led Einstein to the formula $E = mc^2$. We would like to show you how our understanding of what light might be has evolved and how puzzling the behavior of light was. The puzzles eventually forced physicists to review their understanding of the concepts of time and space, and this process culminated in Einstein's theory of time. It was this theory that resulted in the prediction that $E = mc^2$.

Remember how you played with a mirror in your hand, reflecting sunlight and seeing it bounce around on the ceiling or walls of your room, reaching any point you liked? Perhaps you also had fun playing with a flashlight in the dark. You could just turn your flashlight on and a beam of light would immediately shine on the objects that you wanted it to reach. The slightest move of your hand caused the beam of light to turn, and you were able to instantly decide where the light would go. There was no visible delay, no waiting. In contrast, if you played with a water hose and suddenly turned it in a new direction, you would see how the stream of water was curved, delayed, not able to turn with its far end from one direction to another as fast as the hose in your hand did. No such delay is visible when one turns the flashlight. The bright spot far away is right there as soon as you point your flashlight in the new direction. How fast is light?

This question was posed by generations of people. Galileo tried to measure the speed of light but did not succeed—it was too fast. In fact, until the seventeenth century, people had every right to believe that the speed of light was infinite. This meant that light appeared to move instantly from a source, like a lighthouse, to a receiver or detector, such as the eye of a sailor on a ship in the sea. There was no earthly phenomenon that showed any delay between sending and receiving light. So how did it happen that people found that the speed of light was finite instead of infinite? We shall now tell you a story about how it happened. The story is long enough for you to wonder what it has to do with $E = mc^2$ and the context of productive learning, but the connections will become more and more clear to you along further reading of this book.

The first estimate of the speed of light was reported by Römer in 1676. He estimated the speed of light on the basis of his observations of the motion of the moons of Jupiter over several years. The largest four moons of Jupiter were discovered by Galileo around 1610 (it is known today that Jupiter has 16 moons). Galileo's rival astronomer, Simon Marius, gave the four moons the names of mythological figures with whom Jupiter fell in love: Io, the closest to Jupiter; Europa; Ganymede; and Callisto. These moons are about the size of our Moon. They are about three to four times smaller in diameter than the Earth. Figure 7.1 shows how Jupiter and the moons appear in a telescope.[1]

Our story of how Römer estimated the speed of light will be helpful in our discussion of $E = mc^2$. Among other things, the story illustrates how science develops in its social environment, which in turn is conditioned by history. The complex social environment provides the context in which scientific discoveries are made. The context of scientific discovery will be important also in our discussion of $E = mc^2$. More generally, the issues of context matter in how people learn, what they choose to learn, and why they do so. We invite you to compare our stories with how people learned about science in your school. The role of context, when clearly noted, will help us in discussing the concept of productive learning, as distinct from unproductive, and in establishing what requirements reform efforts must meet if they are to encourage productive learning.

In order to understand what and why Römer was studying, we need to first take a brief look at the magnitudes of distances and times that were involved in his studies. He was investigating the solar system, in which distances are enormous. So, imagine yourself to be so huge that the Sun appears to you to be the size of an apple. Then the Earth would appear to you to be the size of a poppy seed, while Jupiter would be like a blueberry. These scaled-down proportions are the same as in the real solar system. In order to imagine the distance between the Earth and the Sun in proportion to the actual sizes of the Sun and Earth, think now that the poppy seed (the Earth) circles around the apple (the Sun) at a distance of about 30 feet. This corresponds to the real distance between the Earth and the Sun (about

Figure 7.1   Jupiter and, from left to right, Europa, Callisto (barely visible), Io, and Ganymede, as seen through a telescope from Warsaw, Poland, on Thursday, November 21, 2002, at 3:17 A.M. in the direction of southeast, at an angle of about 45° above the horizon. See the Sky Charts by P. Chevalley at http://www.astrosurf.com/astropc/.

150 million kilometers, or about 90 million miles) in this analogy. The blueberry (Jupiter) circles around the apple at a distance of about 150 feet, about five times farther away from the Sun than Earth. Io moves around Jupiter in an orbit that appears to be only about two inches across. All planets circle around the Sun practically in one plane and in the same direction, as if they all originated from some primordial swirl of matter around the Sun.

The Earth circles on its orbit around the Sun once in a year (one such full circle defines the year). This means that the Earth moves with the speed of about 30 kilometers per second (about 19 miles per second) along its orbit.[2] Jupiter circles on its orbit around the Sun once in about 12 years. Io needs only about 1.8 days to complete its orbit around Jupiter. When looked at from the Earth through a telescope, Io periodically disappears behind Jupiter on its one side and shows up again on its other side. We know today that the diameter of Jupiter is about 140,000 km, almost 40 times the size of Io, whose diameter is about 3,600 km. Today we also know that Io moves around Jupiter at a mean distance of about 422,000 km with the average speed of about 17.33 kilometers per second (km/s).

Christensen R. Römer was born in Denmark in 1644. He became known as a skillful astronomer when he was quite young. He went to work in the Royal Observatory in Paris in 1672. In the course of his work, he was investigating the movements of Jupiter's moons because Galileo proposed that the motion of the moons, especially Io, could be read like the hands of an ideal reference clock by all people on the Earth, no matter where an observer was located on the globe. The idea was similar to one that people were used to, a reference clock on the main tower in town. When people wanted to adjust their own clock, they would look at the tower clock and set their time accordingly. The moons of Jupiter could play the role of such a reference clock for people even if they were separated by large distances, much larger than the size of a town. The issue of knowing time concerned all serious travelers who crossed oceans and explored new continents.

The main motivation to conduct research on Io stemmed from the desire to have a reference clock that could be used for keeping accurate time over large distances for establishing geographical longitude, which means the position on the surface of the Earth in the direction of east or west. We will explain below why knowledge of time was needed for finding the longitude. Precise knowledge of longitude was also necessary for drawing precise maps of the Earth. Good maps were essential for safe sailing. None of these needs could be satisfied without having a precise reference clock to set time at remote places.

In contrast to longitude, the geographical latitude, which means the position in the direction of north or south on the globe, was relatively easy to find. Sailors traveling over large distances could establish how far north or south they were by measuring the angle at which they saw Polaris, or the North Star, at night. The North Star lies on the firmament in the direction of the Earth's axis, around which the Earth turns once a day. So, if a sailor were at the North Pole, the North Star would be straight up above his head. If he were on the equator, the North Star would be seen by him on the horizon. At intermediate geographical latitude, the North Star would be visible at a corresponding angle in the sky. Measuring this angle, a sailor could find his geographical latitude. Quite accurate instruments were built to make such measurements. A similar procedure could be used on the southern hemisphere using stars visible in the south.[3] Thus, sailors could always establish how far they went toward north or south by looking at the sky. But there was no such direct method for precise determination of how far one had traveled toward the east or west.

One could not tell the longitude by looking at the sky because the Earth was turning around its axis once a day, and the sky appeared to be in constant motion. There was no reference object that could pinpoint the longitude. This problem could be solved for a sailor if he had an accurate clock that would tell him the time that was displayed by the reference clock in London. Knowing the time, and knowing how stars were positioned in the sky above London at any given time, the sailor could observe the positions of the stars above his head and infer his longitude by measuring the angle by which the stars he was seeing were apparently turned away from the positions they had in the sky visible over London at the same time. The angle of the turn he would see would be equal to the difference between the longitude of the sailor's observation point and the longitude of London. Of course, the French sailors would prefer to have Paris as a reference point, rather than London.

The critical problem was that a minute of error in time meant an error of about 30 kilometers, or 20 miles, in position on the sea or land. This magnitude of error comes from the fact that the Earth rotates by its entire circumference (about 40,000 km at the equator) every 24 hours. Thus, the Earth's surface shifts at the equator by about 1,700 km in an hour. This rate is the same as about 30 km per minute. But the accuracy to a minute was not easy to achieve for a typical clock on a voyage over long distances. The ships were sailing for weeks and months over the oceans, on rough waters. There was no clock that could work in such conditions with the required accuracy.

The lack of an accurate, universal method to determine time prevented people from finding their longitude and from drawing accurate maps. This was a great impediment in sailing. For example, a ship could sail westward along a given latitude in order to find an island that was known to have fresh water. But when the ship neared the island, a storm could push the ship some distance to the south and some unknown distance farther west. After the storm, the sailors could return to the correct latitude and continue west. However, that could be a grave mistake if the storm had pushed them so far west that they were already past the longitude of the island. They would eventually notice that they had missed the island. But it might be too late for their survival if they ran out of fresh water and the wind continued to blow west. Even more dangerous, however, were reefs, rocks, shallow waters, quicksand, and areas in the possession of enemies. Great losses were suffered by entire fleets because of running aground or falling prey to foreign powers or pirates. This could happen just because the position of ships and land could not be determined precisely.

Kings of England, France, and Spain had ambitions (each of them in competition with the others) to conquer new lands, govern over them and the seas, and draw freely on their natural riches. It was devastating to their plans for supremacy overseas that their captains could not figure out the longitude. And their commerce was losing large investments in men, ships, and merchandise due to the longitude problem. At its core, the problem could be reduced to otherwise innocent-looking small errors in determination of time. Thus, the problem of determination of common time at distant locations became a major obstacle to the European trend for expansion. The king of France established the Academy of Longitude to solve this problem.

When Galileo built his telescope and discovered the moons of Jupiter, he also found that the motion of Io was so regular that it could perhaps serve as a universal reference clock that could be read through a telescope from all places on the Earth. If astronomical research could establish how to read time from the periodic motion of Io, the longitude problem could be solved. It is probable that Römer was working at the Royal Observatory in Paris on precise tables that would translate the positions of Io into time. We do not know for sure what Römer was working on because his work belonged to the Academy of Longitude and it was kept secret. The secrecy was dictated by the goal to achieve dominance of France over the seas and distant lands in competition with England and Spain. Also, the library that kept Römer's own notes burned, and there is no detailed record of what he was doing. But there is no doubt that Römer was studying the motion of Io very precisely.[4]

Römer's initial assumption was that Io was circling around Jupiter with a constant period, which we know today to be 42 hours 27 minutes and 33.5 seconds. But when he observed Io with great precision over the entire year, he found that for half a year the period appeared to keep slightly increasing, and then, for another half a year, slightly decreasing, eventually returning to the initial value. Römer tried to explain this effect, and after four years of detailed studies of minute changes of Io's apparent period, he made enough observations to conclude that the most natural explanation of the small changes was that the speed of light was not infinite and had a concrete finite value. The distance between the Earth and Jupiter was changing during the year and, at different seasons of the year, the light from Io would need different amounts of time to travel to the Earth.

Römer assumed that Io's motion around Jupiter had a constant period (we remind the reader that this period is about two days). Suppose that Römer measured the time when Io emerged from behind Jupiter on some day in August, 1676 when he knew the Earth was nearest to Jupiter (the Earth was between the Sun and Jupiter). About 100 days later, after Io would make, say, 50 complete circles around Jupiter, the moon should emerge from behind Jupiter at a definite time, equal to 50 periods of its motion around Jupiter, counting from the observation made in August, 1676. Knowing precisely the initial time when Io was emerging from behind Jupiter in August, Römer could predict when Io should come out from behind Jupiter on November 9, namely, after the 50 periods.

This conclusion would hold if the speed of light was infinite and there was no delay due to the travel of light from Io to the Earth. But Io appeared later than Römer could predict this way, by about 10 minutes. This delay could be explained by saying that indeed, the 50 periods passed as they should, *but in the meantime the Earth changed its position and moved away from Jupiter.* Therefore, the light that was bringing to the Earth the image of Io emerging from behind Jupiter would travel over a longer distance in November than it did in August. The November distance should be longer than the August distance by about one-quarter of the Earth's orbit, or about the radius of the Earth's orbit. The image of Io needed the additional 10 minutes to reach the Earth on November 9. Thus, Römer claimed that light had a speed of about one radius of the Earth's orbit in 10 minutes. This was an enormous speed, but finite. Römer could divide about 150 million kilometers by about 10 minutes, or 600 seconds, and he obtained an estimate for c, the speed of light, of about 250,000 km/s.

If it were so fast, it would take light only about a second to travel between our Moon and the Earth. Also, light would be capable of flying around the Earth, still a giant distance from human perspective, in about one-seventh of a second. No wonder that it seems to move instantly from place to place according to our daily experience.

Let us point out some features of the above story that are relevant to the concept of productive learning. According to that story, Römer was investigating the movements of Io with a clear, practical goal in mind. He was painstakingly collecting data to achieve that goal. He discovered a tiny departure from the simple theory of Io's movement, which said that the period should be constant. He had to find a reasonable explanation for the departure. He did not accept any explanation that did not sound entirely clear to him. The irregularity was interesting to Römer because it surprised him and he did not know why it existed. We may assume that he also wanted to explain the origin of the delay he observed in order to incorporate this understanding in his tables for Io's movement as a clock, and we know that 10 minutes meant about 300 km of the longitudinal distance. Apparently, the only explanation for the variation in visible Io's movement Römer found convincing was that light had a finite speed. Römer could estimate the magnitude of the speed of light that explained the data he had collected. It is almost certain that Römer 's discovery of the finiteness of the speed of light was not an intended goal of the longitude research program that the Academy worked on.[5]

We do not learn at school about the context in which Römer was carrying out his observations. His discovery, if it is discussed in detail at all, is presented as a product of a genius who, for no earthly reason, gazed at stars and came up with a brilliant conclusion. Römer's studies are not described in schools as a search for an explanation of a small, actually very tiny and entirely unexpected, but verifiable phenomenon that was observed by a curious mind trying to carry out a project designed for different reasons.

Einstein's discovery of the formula $E = mc^2$ is usually spoken about in a similarly misleading fashion, taken out of context, incomprehensible, and unproductive in its ultimate effect of de facto telling teachers and students that such a process of discovery is not something they can experience themselves no matter what they do. We shall try to break away from this devastating habit in our chapters on $E = mc^2$.

Before we continue, let us note that the magnitude of the speed of light is enormous, about 300,000 km/s. The formula $E = mc^2$ contains the speed of light squared. When such enormous speed is squared, the energy one obtains is great even when the amount of mass, m, is small. The magnitude of c also tells us that even though we can feel the warm rays of the Sun due to increase of energy carried by molecules in our skin, the corresponding increase in the mass of our body is too small for us to notice. On the other hand, to shine as it does, in each and every second the Sun is burning an amount of its own mass equal to about a thousand times the combined mass of all people living on the Earth. Most of the energy of the burned mass goes out into space in all directions. Since the Earth is far away from the Sun and quite small, only a very small part of the Sun's radiation falls on the Earth. In total, only about one 120-millionth part of the energy radiated out by the Sun falls on all planets in the solar system. All the rest travels with the speed of light out of the solar system.

In order to understand how $E = mc^2$ was conceived, we have to learn much more about light than the magnitude of its speed, c. Precise measurements of c, especially toward the end of the nineteenth century, revealed unexpected properties of light, puzzles that forced physicists to question their understanding of basic concepts. In particular, Einstein noticed that in order to explain properties of light, one had to revise the concept of time. We have to grasp the historical and scientific contexts in which Einstein revised the concept of time. The very structure of the formula $E = mc^2$ is a consequence of a clear definition of time that Einstein was first to formulate.

In preparation for the intellectual adventure of learning what Einstein did, we have to tell you some more stories about how people thought about what light was, how fast it moved, how much energy it carried, and what was happening to the energy of a material object that emitted or absorbed light with a definite amount of energy. The formula $E = mc^2$ will finally emerge in a story about how the energy of a piece of matter increases when this piece absorbs light. However, in order to imagine the energy of light in some concrete way, and to understand how Einstein deduced the formula $E = mc^2$ in his reasoning that involved a revised concept of time, we first need to learn more about the intriguing properties of light.

8

What Is Light?
What Is Ether?

A prism splits sunlight into many rays with different colors in a beautiful pattern. The pattern shows that sunlight is a mixture of light with different colors. A rainbow displays the same spectrum of colors because drops of rain that fall in the air reflect light of different colors at different angles in a pattern similar to a prism. All objects reflect and absorb light of different colors with varying efficiency. We see the objects as having the color of light that is most effectively reflected by them. The light of other colors is absorbed by the objects or reflected in directions other than the direction from an object to our eyes.

So, what is different about two beams of light that have different colors? The difference lies in how fast the light "vibrates." Color is a quality that can be associated with some kind of frequency that light exhibits in the process of absorption in our retina. The faster the light "vibrates in our eye," the more violet it appears to us. The slower it "vibrates in our eye," the more red we see in it. And there is a whole spectrum of colors between the red and violet. Different colors correspond to different frequencies of the "vibrations," ranging from the smallest at the red end and highest at the violet end of the visible spectrum. The concept of frequency of light will play a central role in our discussion of Einstein's discovery of the formula $E = mc^2$.

Our eyes are sensitive only to a very narrow band of frequencies of vibrations that sunlight carries.[1] Sunlight also contains components with smaller frequencies than the red light has. These components are called infrared. It also contains light with frequencies larger than that of the violet light. These are called ultraviolet. The entire known spectrum of frequencies is unimaginably larger than the range of frequencies visible to the human eye.

But how can one imagine the frequency of light? A classical picture of light that was commonly accepted toward the end of the nineteenth century, the one that Einstein was learning about at school and university, represented light as a wave of electric and magnetic fields. We will say more about these fields below. In the wave picture of fields, the frequency of light that shines on a molecule is analogous to the frequency with which waves of water rock a boat. We need to understand more about the nature of light.

The main investigator of the electric and magnetic fields was Michael Faraday (1791–1867) in England. Faraday studied forces acting between charged objects and forces acting between magnets. An electrically charged piece of metal or other substance will attract or repel another electrically charged object as if one of them is creating in the space around it something that influences the other. The observable effect is the force that one such charged object exerts on the other. But one can imagine that a charged body modifies the space around itself, and other charged bodies feel the modification. Faraday also investigated forces that acted on wires carrying electric currents when he placed them near magnets. When you put a wire next to a magnet and make an electric current flow through the wire, the wire will move as if the wire with a current is pushed by something that the magnet produced in the space around itself. Also, when you move a magnet near a wire, there will be an electric current induced in the wire as if the magnet was creating something in the space around it that was able to cause the current in the wire.

These forces and their effects could be described by introducing the concept of electric and magnetic *fields,* those altered conditions of the medium which we perceive as empty space. The electric field could be imagined to have some strength and direction in every point in space around a charged object. Moreover, one could think that if one places an electrically charged object in such an electric field, the object is pulled in the direction of the field with a force proportional to the strength of the field. It did not matter any more how the field was produced. The existence of the field in space was sufficient to explain how charged objects would behave in the space with the field. The magnetic field served the description of magnetic forces in the same fashion. Magnetic fields also had some strength and direction in every point in space, varying from place to place.

The person who developed the theory of the electric and magnetic fields was Scottish physicist James Clerk Maxwell (1831–1879). His theory is considered on par with the contributions of Newton and Einstein, and

Maxwell is seen as an intermediary between the two. Maxwell wrote equations that described in mathematical terms the behavior of the electric and magnetic fields in the presence of electric charges, magnets, and wires with currents. He also discovered, and this was his greatest achievement, that the same equations implied that the fields did not actually need any currents, magnets, or charges to exist in space.

The fields could vibrate in space, with the changes in the strength of the electric field being related to the changes in the strength of the magnetic field. A repetitive sequence of changes would have some *frequency*. The fields could keep changing and move from one place to another, forming what was called a wave of the electromagnetic field. A snapshot of such a wave can be imagined as a train of crests and troughs, the high points and the low points of the fields spread in space, almost like a sequence of crests and troughs of waves on water. Maxwell's theory predicted that the speed of these waves should be equal to the speed of light.

German physicist Heinrich Hertz (1857–1894) discovered those invisible waves of electromagnetic field in the laboratory and studied their properties between 1885 and 1889, working as a physics professor at the Karlsruhe Polytechnic. Einstein was a small boy at that time. Hertz produced electromagnetic waves and measured their velocity and length, the latter defined as the distance between the successive crests, or between the troughs. His measurements showed that the waves of electromagnetic fields exhibited properties of reflection and refraction (the change in direction of a wave passing from one medium to another, like from water to air or glass) that were the same as those of light. *All kinds of light and their behavior in optical phenomena could be explained using the picture of waves of electric and magnetic fields.* This was the great triumph of Maxwell's theory.

The frequencies of vibration of the waves of electromagnetic fields may lie anywhere on the frequency scale, inside or outside the range that our eyes are sensitive to. An entire spectrum of electromagnetic waves is used today in radio, television, satellite, and cellular telephone communication. The frequency is measured in units of hertz, named after Heinrich Hertz and abbreviated Hz. One Hz means the arrival of one crest or trough per second, 2 Hz means two crests per second, and so on.

It was Hertz's discovery that opened the new era in communication: One could arrange a device made of wires with currents and use it to send invisible waves of electric and magnetic fields through open space with the speed of light and receive and decode them at a distant place. This is how radio works. Vibrations of radio waves have frequencies in the range between hundreds of kHz (kilo Hz; kilo stands for one thousand) and hundreds of MHz (mega Hz; mega stands for one million). You can see the frequencies marked on the tuning scale of every radio, including car radios.

The frequency of radio waves is too small to trigger a reaction in our retina, and we do not see the radio waves or other infrared waves. The light that has frequencies greater than the violet light spears through the cells in our retina. The oscillations are too fast to be properly detected in the eye. But the ultraviolet electromagnetic waves are so energetic in their vibrations that they can damage molecules in our body. Sunglasses are used to prevent that. The electromagnetic radiation with very high frequencies includes X-rays, which we also cannot see with our eyes. These are produced in the Röntgen apparatus for medical purposes. The X-ray waves penetrate matter enough to allow us to inspect bones or lungs using shadows that are visible on X-ray films after processing. Still higher frequencies characterize so-called gamma-rays of light that emerge from nuclear reactions. The fact is, however, that all these kinds of radiation are just one phenomenon, light, except that the frequency has different values. Microwave ovens work by sending light with a frequency of about two and a half thousand MHz toward the food to be cooked. The energy of this light heats up the food. One cannot see the microwave light, but one can see how fast the light pumps energy into the food and cooks it. The Sun shines light that is a mixture of rays with all frequencies, but the Earth's atmosphere protects us from the X-rays and gamma-rays. The ultraviolet rays are largely absorbed in the air. On the other hand, the visible light and warm infrared light penetrate the air. The infrared part of the sunlight spectrum causes the warm effect in our skin when we are in the sunshine.

Thus, *light of different colors can be understood as waves of electromagnetic field with different frequencies. All waves of light move with the same speed, c, but the distances between crests (or troughs) can be of different magnitudes, and the corresponding frequencies can take different values.* But when it was understood that the behavior of light could be explained using the wave picture, physicists were confronted with a new question. *What was the medium (see below) whose motion was detectable as the waves of the electromagnetic fields, including the visible light?* Einstein was learning physics at the time when these developments were fresh and the questions concerning the nature of electromagnetic fields and light were pressing.

All kinds of waves that physicists knew were due to some kind of vibration in a medium in which the waves were propagating, in a similar sense that the waves of water propagated in the sea, or as the oscillations of pressure and density propagated from place to place in the air in the form of sound. The oscillations of pressure can travel in the air and they cause vibrations of a little drum in our ears. This is how we hear sound, provided that it has a frequency in the right range for the human ear. We do not hear very low frequency sounds, such as some sounds made by whales, and we do not hear very high frequency sounds, such as the sounds used by bats for orientation in the dark.

Physicists know how to think about waves that spread from one place to another, like sound. Namely, the waves spread in the process of motion of some medium: The motion of one part of a medium in one area is transferred from that area to another part of the medium, in another area, through the vibrations of the medium in between. That light is a wave of the electromagnetic field with some frequency was a very successful idea, but physicists were challenged by the question of what was the supportive medium which oscillated in the form of these waves that were interpreted as vibrations of the electric and magnetic fields. *It had to be a curious medium, because one could not see or feel it, and we still do not see or feel it today. This medium was called ether. The magic was that this medium appeared as an empty space, vacuum. And still light moved through as a vibration of this medium with some frequency. What was this medium that undergirded everything we see?*

WHAT CAME OUT FROM THE SEARCH FOR ETHER?

Having to deal with light that zipped through the lab so fast that it could not be easily followed and inspected, physicists hoped to learn about the mysterious ether medium by studying all measurable properties of light with increasing accuracy. One of the critical issues was precisely how fast light traveled through the ether. Physicists struggled to measure the speed of light with accuracy of about 1 part in 100,000. Why would scientists consider such high precision important? Why would physicists care about the possibility of the existence of effects so tiny that one could not see these effects if the precision in measuring velocity would be worse than 1 part in 100,000?

The reason was as usual: The researchers had a theory of what should come out from their measurements, and they wanted to see whether their theory could fit the data. The key point in this particular case was that if light was a wave in some medium, and if different observers of light could move with respect to this medium with different velocities, then the light should be seen by the different observers as moving with different speeds, in a one-to-one correspondence to the motion of an observer. This idea can be understood by analogy. For example, when we stand on a pier and look at waves of water coming toward the shore, we see them to have some velocity. We may denote the velocity of waves measured from our point of view when we stand on the pier by v. But when we run on the pier toward the shore with the same velocity v as the waves roll in, they remain at a fixed distance from us. We could say that their velocity with respect to us in this case is zero, that is, when we run toward the shore with the same velocity v with which the waves roll in, they appear to us as not moving away from us. And when we run in the opposite direction, that is, when we run on the pier toward the open sea, we will see the waves coming toward us faster than we were seeing them coming when we were standing on the pier. The reasoning went, then, like this.

If the light is a wave in the ether like waves of water in the sea, we should see the same type of variation in the perceptible speed of light when we move with respect to the ether. Since the Earth moves around the

Sun with the velocity of about 30 kilometers per second, we should see a different speed for the light that moves forward along the Earth's orbit and for the light that moves in the opposite direction. The fact that the Earth moves in its orbit makes us travel through the ether as if we were running very fast on some kind of a pier jutting into the cosmic space in which the ether is like some kind of a sea full of "water" that supports the waves of light. But the velocity of 30 km/s, equivalent to about 70,000 miles per hour, is still about 10,000 times smaller than the speed of light c. Thus, there should be only a tiny variation in the visible speed of light due to the orbital motion of the Earth. *In order to see any effect with clarity, one should measure the speed of light in different directions, like along the orbital motion of the Earth or against it, with greater accuracy than 1 part in 10,000. Physicists hoped that 1 part in 100,000 was appropriate to see the expected effect clearly.*

Measuring the speed of light with accuracy of 1 part in 100,000 was an incredible challenge. On the other hand, the stakes were high enough to invest time and effort in the measurements. Researchers saw a chance to measure the speed of light in different directions and determine in what direction and how fast the Earth moved in the ether. They thought that this information should be helpful in understanding more about the universe. Any clearly measurable variation in the speed of light, depending on direction, was expected to provide evidence for the existence of ether, a substance of presumably fundamental significance to the structure, origin, and function of the universe.

But there were also many other reasons to learn more about light. It was clear that the nature of electromagnetic waves, whether studied in theory or experiment, was central to how well one could use them in practice. Eventually, Hertz's discovery created realistic hopes that wireless communication would be possible, and this possibility was certainly on the minds of people leading the industrial development at the end of the nineteenth century. And as always happens in our civilization so far, there was also military interest in wireless communication. The studies of light and ether could become only more important with time. The accuracy of measurement of the speed of light reached the level of precision required to see the effect of motion of the Earth through the ether in the experiments of Michelson and Morley in the 1880s.[2]

But instead of providing insight into the nature of light according to the developed theory, the precise measurements of the speed of light in different directions brought a surprise—a surprise of a much bigger consequence than anybody could expect.

We have already encountered an example of a scientific surprise in the story of Römer. But the surprise we are beginning to discuss now shook the worldview of researchers much more. In the Römer story, we saw how precise measurements of tiny effects led to the unexpected opportunity to estimate the speed of light—and it ceased to be "infinite."

Thus, a tiny effect offered a lot to learn from it in the case of Römer's study. In other cases, the amount and significance of information contained in apparently small effects can vary. Sometimes the amount can surpass all imagination. Before we move on to further discussion of light and what was found about it by precise measurements of its speed, and how those findings challenged the worldview of physicists, let us tell you a story about another example of a tiny effect that changed our worldview. This example will give you some idea of what to expect about the magnitude of change that eventually came out from the study of the speed of light and why a solution to the puzzles that light revealed earned Einstein a permanent place in the pantheon of science.

The example we have in mind is from the sixteenth century. As a result of a lifelong effort, Copernicus published in 1543 a book that explained his new astronomical system, in which the Earth moved around the Sun rather than vice versa as all authorities maintained in his times.[3] Our story of Copernicus is following.

Copernicus was interested in the nature of movements of heavenly bodies in the sky. He was also interested in the reform of the calendar.[4] Calendars were always needed for orientation in time, for agriculture, for recording events in history, and for foreseeing what may happen in the future and when. Calendars were arranged on the basis of visible motion of the Moon, the Sun, planets, and stars. Two basic types of calendars existed: one primarily based on the motion of the Moon and another one primarily based on the motion of the Sun. First were the Moon calendars because the Moon goes through clearly visible phases. The motion of the Moon provided us with the concept of a month, corresponding to the cycle of phases that our Moon goes through in about 28 days. The calendars based on the motion of the Sun were designed later. One such calendar, called the Julian calendar, was established by Julius Caesar in the first century B.C.E. It served people in Europe unchanged for about 1,600 years.

But the records of events based on coincidence with the counted phases of the Moon and the records of the same events based on their coincidence with the visible motion of the Sun could not be exactly connected by a perfectly firm formula because the phases of the Moon and the visible movements of the Sun could never be measured exactly. The Moon's phases recur on the same days of the solar year every 19 years, or after 235 lunations (lunation is the period of time elapsing between two successive new moons). But astronomers could not say with perfect accuracy how many lunations should be in a year as defined by the movements of the Sun. The rate at which the Moon moved around the Earth and the rate at which the Sun moved were in some ratio. The ratio was known only with some approximation. Astronomical tables could always be improved as the time was passing. Still, after many years, every scheme for dividing years into days and months would show some tendency to drift away from the intended calendar order. In particular, after the one and a half millennium that passed from the times of Julius Caesar to the times of Copernicus, the apparent difference between the real full moons and when they should occur according to the Julian calendar reached about 10 days. A discrepancy of 10 days over 1,500 years is tiny. But such discrepancy was enough to become a major issue. Basic questions concerning the calendar required answers.

For example, the calendar uncertainties posed a problem for the Pope as the head of the Church in Rome. In order to speak in concrete terms, let us consider the question, When should the anniversary of the resurrection of Jesus Christ be celebrated? The Bible gave the date in terms of the motion of the Moon, used in the ancient Moon calendars, while the Julian calendar used by the Church was arranged according to the motion of the Sun. Since the Sun and the Moon move differently in the sky, and just a little bit differently out of step than it was assumed in the design of the Julian calendar, the differences accumulated to such extent that after 1,500 years one could ask questions of the sort "Which Sunday after which full moon was the right Sunday for celebration of the resurrection of Jesus Christ?"

Just to imagine what might be involved in attempts to solve this kind of problem,[5] suppose that the Bible said that people should celebrate the resurrection "on the first Sunday of April after the full moon." The actual Bible reference to the right time is not that simple. Possible interpretations involve the concept of one day during the spring (vernal equinox) when the night has the same length as the day. Encyclopædia Britannica explains that[6]

> Western Christians celebrate Easter on the first Sunday after the full moon (the paschal moon) that occurs upon or next after the vernal equinox (taken as March 21). If the paschal moon, which is calculated from a system of golden numbers and epacts[7] and does not necessarily coincide with the astronomical full moon, occurs on a Sunday, Easter day is the succeeding Sunday. Easter, therefore, can fall between March 22 and April 25. This rule was fixed after much controversy and uncertainty, which lasted in various parts of the church until the 8th century. In the Eastern Orthodox church, however, a slightly different calculation is followed, with the result that the Orthodox Easter, although sometimes coinciding with that of the West, can fall one, four, or five weeks later.

Since the actual astronomical and theological issues are very complex, let us simplify our discussion tremendously and suppose that over many hundreds of years the night of the full moon that was supposed to occur on the same day of the calendar was actually wandering slowly but steadily toward earlier days and eventually happened about a week or two early, already in March. Finally, the full moon would happen so early in March that "the first Sunday of April after a full moon" could mean not the Sunday at the beginning of April after the full moon in March, but instead the Sunday at the end of April after the full moon that occurred already in April. If such a simple course of events were true, one would have to explain if, why, and when the jump should occur.

The question of how one should interpret the Bible regarding time of events as important as the resurrection of Jesus Christ could not be left unanswered by the Pope. He could not freely alter the Bible to conform with the shifts in the calendar, and he needed the help of theologians and astronomers to find the right way to handle the details of the calendar and interpret the meaning of scriptures. One could also not change the fact that days and years were accumulating over centuries to produce a discrepancy between the accepted interpretation of the Bible and the course of events in the real world. But the division of the year into months was arbitrary and could be arranged according to some rule in order to solve the problem. The rule would have to be very precise in order to resolve the issue for a long time. In addition, the rule should not shed doubts on the foundation of the Church.

The number of days in a year was not exactly 365, or 365 and a quarter, as the Julian calendar assumed. The rule for counting months and days in a year required an accurate number. The real number corresponded to the real structure of the solar system. But at that time, the solar system was still perceived as having the Earth in its center. This assumption was in perfect agreement with the scriptures. When, after about 1,500 years, the solar calendar accumulated the shift of about 10 days, arcane details of astronomy had to be considered and turned out to be important in an unusually bold way. The ambiguities in existing knowledge accumulated to an effect that became very visible to all concerned. Since the divine power of the Pope, presumably coming from God, would appear questionable if the Pope did not know which day was the right one for the celebration of Christ's resurrection, Copernicus was not the only astronomer who worked on the details of the calendar.

But instead of just solving the Pope's problem, Copernicus's studies of the "details" produced results that reached far beyond the fate of the Catholic hierarchy at those times. Copernicus discovered that many tiny problems with the astronomical calendar could be explained in a far more parsimonious way if one changed the image of the solar system from the one where the Earth was in the center to the one where the Sun was in the center. Things started to fall into place. We can say that the new image of the universe came out of "tiny effects." But the conclusions were shocking.

One of the main shocks came with the realization that the Earth was not at absolute rest in the center of everything. The conflict with scriptures was obvious because the Bible declared that God created the Earth to be in the center of it all. The scripture as a founding element of Christian religion was in jeopardy. In science, the concept of absolute rest, associated with no motion with respect to the ground, began to crumble. The traditional principle that said that all matter was attracted down to the center of the universe, meant to be the Earth, had to be abandoned if the Copernican system were to be adopted.

Our story about the calendar and Copernicus's discovery serves the purpose of stating that an analogously profound change also occurred in our concept of the universe as a result of precise measurements of tiny effects regarding the speed of light. These tiny effects led to a new understanding of time. Tiny details in the speed of light became explicable if time was not considered as absolute as everybody was used to thinking in the context of their daily lives. This dramatic change in the comprehension of time was also the main ingredient in Einstein's derivation of the formula $E = mc^2$. This is why we will need to discuss the concept of time in our story of $E = mc^2$.

We want to stress here that physicists who had been trying to measure the speed of light had no idea about what was coming. They wanted to see how the speed of light on the Earth varied with the direction of observation. They wanted to deduce from this variation how the Earth moved with respect to the ether. The detection and properties of this substance were at stake.

Surprisingly, careful measurements were showing that the speed of light was not changing with direction as expected on the Earth, and no variation was found with considerably better accuracy than 30 km/s. Thus, propagation of light could not be used to detect motion of an observer with respect to the ether because the expected effect of the motion of the Earth through the hypothetical ether on the observed speed of light was absent. This result posed a problem: *The medium that physicists were looking for had to have two conflicting properties. It vibrated in the form of waves of the electromagnetic fields, but the speed of propagation of these vibrations was the same for all observers no matter how they moved with respect to the vibrating medium.* There was a clear contradiction to resolve, incomprehensible within the commonly adopted worldview.

As is usual in such circumstances, a whole range of new guesses were coming to mind and many were allowed to be considered by authoritative scientists. Always when we learn something new, see a problem, and cannot see a solution, we go through a period of confusion and try to come up with new ideas. Physicists do the same. For example, one explanation might be that the ether could have been dragged by the Earth, and by the apparatus that was used to measure the speed of light. But that would imply also a drag of the ether in many more circumstances, and the hypothesis of dragging the ether by the Earth could not be sustained. For example, the light from stars was coming to the Earth on straight paths while the drag would have to lead to bent paths. There was also a concept that all material objects were shortening in the direction of motion in the ether. If the rulers used to measure distances in the procedure of measuring the speed of light were shortened in a universal way due to the motion of the Earth, the shortening of the rulers could compensate for the effect of motion and the speed c could be the same in all directions on the Earth. But the hypothesis of such shortening seemed to have no deeper explanation than just the wish to explain the observed lack of variation in c. It appeared like a cure for a symptom of a serious illness without explanation of the cause of the illness, and nothing was understood about the ether.

History showed that nothing much was to be understood about the ether in the years to come either, because the great puzzle of the constancy of the speed of light found an unexpected resolution that was independent of the concept of ether. Thus, the activity that aimed for learning more about the ether led instead to the conclusion that light behaved in ways inexplicable within the worldview that was the basis of the plan to investigate the ether. As a result, the search for ether was overshadowed by the discovery of the new puzzle: How could it happen that the speed of light c does not change from one observer to another as expected? Einstein was struggling with this problem, and $E = mc^2$ followed from his solution.

The above story confirms again that productive learning does not occur according to a prescribed schedule. Instead, a student follows his or her path of interest and discovers what to do next. The art of teaching is to help students get on the path of discovery and enable them to learn as much as they can as soon as they can through discovering the features of the world they shall live in. They should feel encouraged and free to ask questions that occupy their minds and the discussions with their teachers should be helping them to understand how to proceed. It is unproductive to teach students that learning occurs through reading and reciting a Bible in a classroom without understanding why.

Our story about the confusion concerning light and ether at the end of the nineteenth century suggests that the notions of "vibration," "frequency," "wave," "medium," or "speed," *all pertaining to light*, were not as obvious as everybody thought they were. The understanding of these concepts that Einstein brought to the scene was of a new kind and required that the absolute concept of time be abandoned. The new concept that Einstein introduced allowed him to write an expression for the energy of light. He then used this expression to predict the change of energy of an object that had emitted or absorbed light. Using the predicted change, Einstein deduced that $E = mc^2$. Our goal is to understand elements of Einstein's reasoning, their content, and implications.

9

How Can We Describe the Energy of Light?

Our story brought us so far to the point where we may think that light is some kind of an oscillating wave of electric and magnetic fields. The wave has an inexplicable property of moving with the same speed according to all observers. We are puzzled by this property because to us, the velocity of every material object depends on whether we follow the object or move in the opposite direction. If we are on a station platform and begin to run after the train, we experience the fact that the train does not ride away from us as fast as when we stand on the platform. And when we run in the opposite direction, we see the train moving away from us very fast. If the speed of light is the same for all observers no matter how they move, how do we reconcile it with the observed variation of velocities of all material objects that do depend on the motion of observers? Do we really know what to make of light if its speed is the same for all observers? We already know that light carries energy. But if the speed of light surprises us with its properties, what image of a beam of light should we have in our mind in order to describe its energy? We will discuss these questions and then proceed to a description of the process of absorption of light by material objects. Once we resolve the puzzle of the constancy of the speed of light for all observers, the process of absorption will help us deduce that $E = mc^2$.

The question of what light is has fascinated people from the beginning of history. But to find any realistic image of light was extremely hard. One reason we already know: The speed of light is enormous. It is impossible to follow the light and look at it at rest. We have also learned that the speed of light is strangely constant. Not only is light too fast to follow and inspect at rest, but even if we try to follow it, light turns out to escape us always with the same speed no matter how fast we move.

The more that was found about light, the more questions came up. This was the situation when Einstein was learning about light. We can only imagine how confused he was by the information he read in scientific journals concerning the speed of light as a wave in the ether. Not only was the speed of light behaving in an inexplicable way, but also the concept of light as a wave in a medium was in doubt. The puzzle intrigued Einstein immensely. He was also aware of additional facts that we have not mentioned yet and that we need to discuss now because these facts did not agree with the idea that light was spreading in space like a wave. These additional facts helped Einstein understand how one can describe the energy of light.

Since the energy of light is central to the reasoning that led Einstein to the conclusion that $E = mc^2$, we need to discuss here the concepts that will help us in visualizing the energy of light. This is done in terms of the frequency of light. The frequency and energy of light are the key to understanding our whole story of $E = mc^2$.

In order to explain how light carries energy, Einstein proposed a new heuristic picture of light. He pictured light as made of particle-like lumps of the electromagnetic field. The word "heuristic" that he used to describe his picture means "exploratory," helpful in the process of learning about something by trial-and-error, supporting our intuition when we attempt to understand something that puzzles us. In Einstein's picture, a beam of light was no longer a wave but a large number of "particles of light" made of concentrated electromagnetic fields. This new picture will help us in building an image of the energy of a beam of light as a sum of the energies of all the particles that form the beam. But we are not going to overwhelm the reader with mathematical details and a complete history of the research. Instead, we shall focus on the key physical ideas and those aspects of our story that are directly relevant to the concept of productive learning.

What we want to accomplish in the discussion that follows is analogous to what Mr. Holland wanted to do when he understood that he ought to explain to his students why he himself was drawn to music—it was fun. Physics is also fun, the fun of firsthand learning about natural phenomena. Having said that, let us note that Holland's students did not have to start from understanding note-by-note how Bach or Beethoven wrote music. They also did not have to write music themselves. Instead, Holland introduced them to the value of music in terms of concepts that they already knew. Holland helped his students observe resemblances between a rock-and-roll hit they knew well and a Bach minuet they did not know. After observing the connection, a student could see the goal of studying music more clearly and could begin to listen to music with new interest. In the same spirit, but in the area of physical sciences instead of music, we intend to discuss connections between basic facts and ideas and how they form together a harmonious whole in the minds of physicists. Pursuing this harmony is "the fun" for physicists, in an analogous way to the way the pursuit of harmony in music is "the fun" for musicians. Our goal in this book is to show you the harmony in physics from a distance and give you a chance to become interested in knowing more.

Einstein was bothered by the fact that the continuous nature of waves of the electromagnetic field, which was used to represent light, was in sharp contrast with the discrete nature of matter. This was odd to him, not harmonious. He thought that either both light and matter should be continuous or both should be discrete. By all means, matter was discrete. It was made of atoms. In addition, and more strikingly, Max Planck, an older physicist contemporary to Einstein, suggested that all vibrations of atoms are also discrete.

Planck thought that the vibrations of atoms are discrete in the sense that the magnitude of swing in the atomic oscillations appeared to vary only in discrete units. It was as if the energy of vibrations could not be marked anywhere on a continuous scale but only on equally separated discrete points. This is not the most felicitous or technically appropriate way of putting it, but consider when you order a glass of beer and the bartender puts the glass under the spigot, pulls the lever and out comes a continuous, homogenous fluid that can be collected in the glass in any amount one wishes. Beer can also be portioned in bottles so that one may only buy one bottle, two bottles, or more bottles, but never a fraction of a bottle. The second option appeared to be the case for the energy of atomic vibrations—it could only be a multiple of some well defined discrete units or portions.

Planck published his theoretical article on the discrete character of atomic vibrations in 1900. Planck's work concerned colors of light emitted by a hot body, such as a hot piece of iron that a blacksmith works on with a hammer. The color of light was related to its frequency and the frequency of light emitted by vibrating atoms was related, in Planck's theory, to the frequency of the vibrations of the atoms. Planck discovered that it was possible to explain the spectrum of colors of light emitted by a hot body if the energies of oscillations of atoms in the hot body could not be arbitrary in magnitude but occurred only in multiples of discrete units. The observed spectrum of colors could not be explained otherwise.

Planck conceived his idea still using a wave picture of light. In that picture, oscillating molecules emitted electromagnetic waves. The mechanism resembled the one in which a vibrating stick generates waves in water. The frequency of a wave of light emitted by an oscillating molecule is the same as the frequency of the mechanical oscillation that characterizes the emitting molecule. Since the frequency of light was in one-to-one correspondence to its color, Planck was able to connect the colors of light emitted by a hot body with the frequencies of vibrations of molecules in that body. For example, the larger the number of the molecules oscillating with a given frequency, the greater the wave of electromagnetic field with the same frequency and the brighter the light of that frequency. Thinking in such terms, Planck related the intensity of light of a given color, or frequency, with the number of molecules oscillating with the same frequency.

In order to explain the observed mixtures and intensities of colors of light emitted by a given body at a given temperature, Planck had to develop a theory of matter that could predict the right numbers of molecules that oscillated with various frequencies. Planck obtained the right predictions when he assumed that there exists some basic unit of energy for every atomic oscillation with a given frequency f (we will use the symbol f to denote frequency throughout our whole story of $E = mc^2$). Let us denote this unit of energy by E_f. This basic unit meant, according to Planck's picture, that the energy of all possible oscillations of hot-iron atoms oscillating with frequency f could only be a multiple of a certain unit.

Moreover, Planck discovered that if he assumed that the unit E_f itself is proportional to the frequency f, he obtained agreement with the observed intensities of different colors of light emitted by a hot body. This latter result meant that the larger the frequency of an atomic vibration, f, the larger the corresponding unit of energy, E_f, for vibrations with that frequency. We stress that in Planck's theory not only do all atomic vibrations of frequency f have discrete energies, namely, E_f, $2E_f$, $3E_f$, and so on, but also that the very unit E_f is proportional to the frequency f itself.

Most strikingly, however, the proportionality constant between the unit of energy, E_f, and the frequency f itself had to be the same for all frequencies of all kinds of oscillations for all kinds of atoms or molecules in all kinds of bodies. The universal proportionality constant is denoted by h. It is called Planck's constant and belongs to a few most fundamental constants of Nature that we know. Planck showed that the relationship $E_f = hf$ for atomic vibrations was the right relationship that explained very accurately the relative intensities of all colors of light emitted by matter at all available temperatures.

Planck's formula worked very accurately for an impressive number of measured cases. It exposed a new and still mysterious harmony in a large body of data. The agreement with data strongly supported the idea of discrete energies of oscillations of atoms. Nothing spoke against this idea except the lack of an answer to the question, Why should the oscillations be discrete at all? The problem was that the classical picture for all oscillatory motions, like a pendulum or a swing, implies that such motions can have continuously varying amplitude, that is, the magnitude of the swing can be arbitrary. Thus, the energy of vibrations should also vary continuously. Namely, the larger the amplitude, the larger should be the energy of the swing. But the real atomic vibrations apparently did not obey this rule.

Their energies do not vary continuously and, instead, appear to exist only as multiples of well-defined fixed portions. The puzzle was insoluble by the classical models of oscillating objects.

But no matter how puzzling it was, the data on the spectra of light emitted by hot matter was irrefutable. Planck's idea that vibrations of atoms could only have energy equal to a multiple of a fixed unit for a given frequency was realistic. The amount of energy $E_f = hf$ was named a quantum. The word "quantum" originates from Latin, where it has more than one meaning. All of these meanings are related to the English term "how much" of something one considers, or what "amount," or "portion," or "quantity," of something one deals with.

Knowing Planck's work, Einstein was confronted with the picture of matter as built from discrete atoms that could vibrate with only discrete energies, while light was a wave of electromagnetic field that is continuous, not granular like particles and their oscillations. Einstein believed in ultimately unified basic laws of Nature. If matter was granular, the electromagnetic field should also be granular, and the continuous picture of waves of light was not appealing to Einstein.

But light was described by physicists as a wave of continuous electromagnetic field for a good reason. Namely, all optical experiments were explained this way. The principles of how a magnifying glass, a microscope, a telescope, a prism, and all other optical devices work were provided using the wave picture of light.

On the other hand, Einstein knew that some new experiments performed in the beginning of the twentieth century demonstrated that light could behave in ways that cannot be explained using the concept of a wave of a field. The particular example that Einstein considered in his studies was the photoelectric effect, investigated by Philipp Lenard: A beam of light can knock electrons out of a metal plate. Einstein proposed that the beam of light was knocking out the electrons one by one as if the beam was a shower of particles of light, each particle of light striking electrons individually. This picture is quite different from the wave picture in which light is like a surf of electromagnetic field that pushes electrons like a big wave and displaces them like a sea wave can wash many tiny boats onto the shore.

A brief description of the Lenard experiment of 1902 will help us appreciate the meaning of the formula for the energy of light that Einstein proposed in his explanation of the photoelectric effect.[1] We should remember that at the time of carrying out his experiments, Lenard did not have the concept of light that was described by Einstein three years later, that is, in the beginning of 1905. A schematic view of Lenard's experiment is shown in Figure 9.1.

An electric arc is created between two carbon electrodes and produces light that contains all visible colors. The light comes to a filter, which lets only one color pass through. We already know that this means that the

Figure 9.1   A schematic view of Lenard's experiment

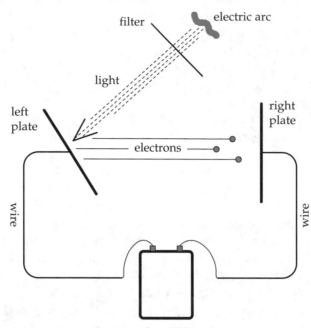

battery of variable voltage

a. The electric arc produces light.
b. The light reaches a filter, which lets only one color through, or one frequency.
c. The light that passes the filter has only one frequency, f.
d. The light hits a metal plate on the left.
e. The light acts on the electrons in the plate.
f. The electrons absorb the light and gain its energy.
g. The energy of light is turned into the energy of motion of the electrons.
h. The electrons fly from the left plate toward the right plate.
i. The stream of electrons sinks in the right plate.
j. The stream flows through the wire, like water in a pipe, back to the left plate.
k. The same electrons are knocked out by light again.
l. When the arc light is on, the circulation of electrons goes on.
m. There is a measurable current in the wire.
n. The battery can work against the flow of the current.
o. When the voltage of the battery is high enough, even the fastest electrons are stopped.
p. The larger the energy that electrons gain from light, the faster they move.
q. The faster they move, the larger the voltage required to stop the current.
r. Lenard measures the voltage V required on the battery to stop the current.
s. Lenard observes that the stopping voltage V does not depend on the brightness of light.
t. If light is a wave, the brighter light means a bigger wave.
u. A bigger wave should eject faster electrons—this is not what Lenard finds.
v. By changing the filter, Lenard finds that V depends only on the color of light.
w. This means that V depends only on the frequency of light, f.
x. This in turn means that the velocity of the fastest ejected electrons depends only on f.
y. This in turn means that the energy imparted by light onto electrons depends only on f.
z. Three years later, Einstein suggests that light of frequency f is made of "particles of light," each of which has energy E_f given by the formula $E_f = hf$. They are absorbed by electrons one-on-one, and this explains Lenard's results; light is discrete.

light that passes the filter has only one frequency, f. Then the light shines on a metal plate (the left plate on Figure 9.1) and acts on the electrons in the plate. The electrons absorb the light and gain energy from the light. The energy of light is turned into the energy of motion of the electrons, and those that have sufficiently large velocities are able to emerge from the metal and they fly away. Many of these emerging electrons fly toward the plate marked "right" on Figure 9.1. Then the stream of electrons sinks in the right plate and flows down the wire back to the left plate, like water in a pipe. Wires are for a stream of electrons like pipes for a stream of water.

The same electrons are knocked out by light again when they arrive back at the left plate through the wire. The circulation of electrons goes on when the arc light is on. There is a current of electricity in the wire. This current can be measured precisely, and one can study how the magnitude of the current depends on various variables in the experiment.

The key study of Lenard was based on the possibility of installing a battery with variable voltage in the circuit, as shown in Figure 9.1. The battery can work against the flow of the current. One can tune the voltage of the battery so high that even the fastest electrons ejected by light from the electrode are stopped. This stopping voltage tells us about how much energy the light can impart onto the electrons at most. The larger the energy that electrons gain from light, the faster they move between the plates. The faster they move, the larger the voltage required to stop them. The current of electrons is stopped completely when even the fastest electrons are stopped. But the fastest electrons are those that carry most of the energy that they could gain from light. Thus, the complete stopping of the current occurs in the situation when the voltage that influences the electrons becomes able to counterbalance the energy of light that knocks the electrons out of the left electrode.

Lenard could measure the voltage V required on the battery to stop the current. He observed that this voltage V did not depend on the brightness of light produced by the arc. This is not explicable by the wave picture of light because if light is a wave, the brighter light means a bigger wave, and a bigger wave should eject faster electrons. This was clearly not what happened—the greatest velocity the ejected electrons could have for a given frequency of light f did not increase with the brightness of the arc. It also did not diminish when the arc was moved farther away from the plate. But if a wave is coming from a source at a larger distance, spreading in space, the magnitude of the wave at the plate should decrease. Then the ejected electrons should be slower and the stopping voltage should be smaller for arcs placed further away from the plate. This was also not the case.

Most interesting, by changing the filter, Lenard found that the stopping voltage V depends on the color of the light. This was the only variable in the experiment that influenced the stopping voltage. This meant that V depended only on the frequency of light, f. This finding was most striking because it meant that the velocity of the fastest ejected electrons depends only on the frequency f of light, which in turn meant that the energy of light absorbed by the electrons depends only on f. The classical wave-picture of light had no simple way to explain how that result could come about.

Three years after Lenard's experiment, in his work from March of 1905, Einstein suggested that the result found by Lenard could be explained if light of frequency f was made of a huge number of "particles of light" and each of them had the energy E_f proportional to the frequency f. If these particles of light were absorbed by electrons one-on-one, the maximal energy of a knocked-out electron would depend only on the energy of the "particle of light" that knocked that electron out, E_f. But E_f depends only on the frequency f and no other variable. This conclusion was in perfect agreement with data in Lenard's experiment. The brightness of light would depend on the number of particles of light, while each of the particles would have energy that was independent of the brightness and would always be E_f. Therefore, the stopping voltage can depend on the frequency and not depend on the brightness of the arc. The voltage would also not depend on the position of the arc because it would not matter from what distance a particle of light would come carrying the definite energy E_f that contributed to the one-on-one knockout process. Moreover, if the energy E_f is proportional to the frequency f, the stopping voltage should also be proportional to the frequency f, and this prediction by Einstein could be verified experimentally. *Most insightfully, Einstein predicted that the coefficient of proportionality should be the same constant h that Planck proposed to describe the energies of vibrations of atoms.*[2]

Einstein would not be able to make his heuristic predictions unless (1) he had been struggling with the concept that light is a continuous wave of electromagnetic field; (2) he had the insight to see that Planck's constant is clearly applicable to the concept of light as discrete, comprised of articles of a new kind; and (3) he was fascinated by the subject and wanted to understand it.

Einstein found many arguments to support the idea of particles of light and that their energy E_f should be equal to the Planck constant, h, times the frequency f. Einstein called a particle of light a quantum of light, and the energy carried by a quantum of light a quantum of energy. In about 10 years, the name "quantum of light" was replaced in the language of physicists by the name "photon."[3] The new name was welcome because it reflected the fascination of physicists with the nature of the "particles of light," which was leading to more questions the more it was investigated.[4]

In view of the two different images of light, the wave picture and the photon picture, it is interesting to note that the story of how physicists were learning about the nature of light is dramatically different from the ready-to-swallow lessons that are typically offered in the education of teachers in colleges and subsequently transferred to students in schools. Nothing in the true story of learning about light happened according to a rigidly scheduled curriculum. Instead, it all happened as a result of inquiry guided by curiosity and critical thinking. The scientists moved back and forth regarding the ideas they had about light and atoms and their interactions, and the ultimate verification of their ideas came not from any authority but from experiments.

But the process of experimental verification does not mean 100% agreement between theory and data. A need for new corrections to the theoretical picture one has already built is uncovered when careful measurements show that some tiny corrections remain to be explained. No matter how small the corrections are, they may have big implications. This way, whatever is learned leads to the need and desire to learn more. The maxim of science and of all productive learning is that the more you know the more questions come up and the more you want to know. The scientific image of the world is far from the ultimately "certain" and "unique" image that is conveyed in typical classrooms where there is no room for open-ended questions and discussions. Such questions and discussions are essential in the life of scientists who attempt to learn as much as they can about Nature. The questions and discussions by no means imply that Nature is ambiguous or that one never knows what to think. Quite the opposite, the more one learns the more accurate the representation of reality we are able to build in our minds. But the more accurate image of reality allows us to see new unknowns. The unknowns become visible in departures of reality from the precise predictions based on the image we have already built.

It is known from Einstein's own writings that he was unsure about what to think about the nature of light. Einstein was awarded the Nobel Prize in 1921[5] "for his services to theoretical physics, and especially for his discovery of the law of the photoelectric effect," that is, especially for the paper about the discrete nature of light[6] that he published in March, 1905. In that March paper, among other supporting arguments for the discrete nature of light, Einstein explained the results of Lenard's experiment using his hypothesis that light is made of particle-like objects. But three months later, at the end of June, 1905, Einstein submitted to the same journal another paper,[7] in which he developed his theory of space and time in the context of a classical theory of light, represented as a wave of the electromagnetic field. This means that light was treated in the June paper without mentioning the discrete, particle-like picture proposed in the March paper. In the next article, submitted to the same journal at the end of September, 1905,[8] Einstein described his formula $E = mc^2$ for the first time, using again the wave picture of light. But all he actually used in his reasoning was how the energy of light changes with observers. This change is precisely the same as for frequency of photons that light is made of. In our story of $E = mc^2$, we avoid dealing with the complex mathematical theory of electromagnetic field. Instead, we use a simple model for photons and directly connect the energy of light to the frequency of photons, $E_f = hf$, taking advantage of Einstein's earlier paper from March, 1905. The model of photons that we describe explains how one can think about the frequency and energy of light in agreement with experimental findings but without the complex mathematics of the theory of fields. Using this shortcut, we provide the reader with the imagery of light as made of photons, which explains the formula for the energy of light that Einstein used in his September paper about the equation $E = mc^2$. It would be very interesting for the readers and the authors to discuss possible explanations of a relationship between the sequence of Einstein's papers from 1905, the development of the quantum theory during the century that followed, and the content of lessons about light, $E = mc^2$, and related subjects that are taught at schools of all kinds.

In 1951, after a most accurate, experimentally motivated quantum theory of light and charged particles had already been formulated by other physicists, Einstein confessed in a letter to his friend Michele Besso, whom he knew from his youth in Switzerland, that all these years of pondering had brought him no nearer to answering the question, What are light quanta? Einstein complained that most people who think they know what photons are have little idea of what they are talking about. In his private letters, Einstein wrote also that he had thought a hundred times as much about the quantum problems as he had about his theory of time.[9]

The above story illustrates that what happens in the real world is represented only in a limited way by concrete models that people build in their minds. One model uses waves of a field, the other is based on photons. The fact that scientists can work on explaining the same phenomena in different ways is almost never conveyed in classrooms, where knowledge is usually handed down as certain and as if there was never any question or doubt encountered on the way it was gained by scientists. The reality is, however, that we may never know for certain in all detail whether our imagined "construction" is "right." This fact is especially important to realize in all cases where the "true picture" cannot be inspected with our eyes, ears, nose, and labor of our own hands. The inner structure of photons belongs to that category and still escapes the means of scrutiny available to physicists—photons continue to be known more for what they "do," and how they "do" it, rather than for what they "are."

Since photons move with the speed of light, it is hard to talk about their "inside." One cannot move as fast as a photon and "take a look." And so far, the only way to "look" at anything is to detect the light that comes from it. But that means that we "see" as a result of absorption and hence disappearance of the photons in our eyes, where they are absorbed by the molecules in our retina. Thus, we cannot see photons like we can look at a bus that passes by. All we can do is to "absorb the bus as a whole." But then the bus no longer exists, because it is already absorbed. The act of absorption informs us that a photon did exist before absorption. We are told about the existence of a photon in the past by the effect in our eye that the process of its absorption has caused. But there is nothing for us to look at any more after we have learned that a photon had existed. The issue is that we see only as a consequence of absorption of light and in this process light disappears, so that even in principle we cannot "look at light."

Note that in the morning scene with which we started our story, we become aware of the energy of light when we feel it. Then we say "the light caused my feeling of warmth." But we cannot "see light," "feel light," or be witness to its existence before the light is already absorbed and its existence is over. So, there is some danger of circular reasoning about light and our vision of it. Since our eyes are our primary tools for inspecting the structure of matter, and they work by absorption of photons, it is confusing that to inspect photons themselves is not possible with our eyes. Most questions that concern the mental images that people build in order to imagine photons can be answered only partially and only indirectly. We cannot truly see what is inside photons because we see by "swallowing" photons in our eyes.

But even if we cannot unambiguously imagine what is "inside" photons, we can still construct a model of photons that helps us describe the energy of photons. It suffices to visualize the frequency of photons, f. As soon as we come to some understanding of the concept of the frequency of a photon, we will be on the road to studying and comprehending the energy of photons by multiplying the frequency f by the Planck constant h. As soon as we obtain some understanding of the energy of photons, we will use this understanding for the derivation of the formula $E = mc^2$.

One possible way to imagine a single photon for the purpose of describing its energy is to imagine that it is composed of a sequence of signals. These signals move one after another like cars in a train, if only a train could move with the incredible speed c. Every two successive signals in the train are separated by a fixed distance. In the case of visible light, this distance is between about four- to seven-tenths of one thousandth part of a millimeter. That means more than a thousand signals in a millimeter.

When your eye absorbs a *single photon*, you can think about it as a succession of events that constitute reception of an entire *train of signals*. In every one of these events, your retina receives just one signal from the entire sequence that constitutes the photon. You need to visualize a train of these signals in your mind in order to understand the concept of frequency f for a photon. The concept of frequency for photons is central to the entire reasoning that follows, and eventually leads to $E = mc^2$.

We can interpret the frequency of a photon in terms of how often the signals constituting that photon arrive in our eye, or some other detector. The more often the signals arrive in our retina, the larger the frequency of the photon from our point of view, and the larger its energy. The less frequently the signals arrive, the smaller the photon frequency and its energy from our point of view. If we were to tell the frequency, we would wait and count the arriving signals during some period of time. Suppose that the signals arrive one after another at equal intervals. Let us denote the duration of one such time interval by T. Suppose that we wait till some number N of signals arrive. We know how long we have to wait for N signals: N times T. The frequency f of the arrivals of the signals will be given by the number of registered signals, N, divided by the total time of waiting, which is NT. When we divide N by NT, we obtain $\frac{1}{T}$.

$$f = \frac{\text{Number of signals}}{\text{Time of waiting}}.$$ [9.1]

Thus,

$$f = \frac{N}{NT} = \frac{1}{T}.$$ [9.2]

For example, if there were just 3,600 signals coming at equal intervals during one hour, successive signals would be separated in time by 1 second, and the frequency would be 3,600 signals divided by 3,600 seconds, or

$$\frac{1}{1 \text{ second}}.$$

The relation between frequency f and the time interval T, that is $f = \frac{1}{T}$, is called inverse. Thus, one can say that the frequency f is an inverse of the period T.

A high-energy photon comes to us as a train of signals that are very closely following one after another, as if the train were built from very short "cars." The shorter the distance between the signals in the train—in other words, the shorter the length of a single "car"—the shorter are the time intervals between arrivals of the successive signals. Remember that photons move always with the same speed c. The shorter the "cars" in a photon, the more frequently one "sees" the "cars" coming. The frequency is in one-to-one correspondence with the distance between signals, called a wave length, because the speed of photons is always the same c and the time intervals between arrivals of successive signals are all equal to the wave length divided by c. Therefore, a photon with a short wave length comes as a very rapid sequence of signals, its frequency is high, and its energy is high. A photon with a longer wave length comes as a less frequent sequence of signals, which means that its frequency is lower and its energy is lower.

Let us note a very important property of the frequency f of a photon: It is defined in the process of absorption of the photon in the eye of an observer. In other words, it depends on an observer and may be different for different observers of the same photons. We will adopt this image of frequency of photons for our further discussion.

The advantage of imagining the frequency of photons lies in the fact that the energy of photons, E_f, is given by the Einstein formula $E_f = hf$.[10] The size of the Planck constant is so extremely small that the energy $E_f = hf$ of one photon is very small even for quite large frequencies f. But we may have a very large number of photons with any given frequency f, each having a small energy E_f equal to hf. Zillions of photons may have together quite large energy even though h is so small. When a regular bulb shines, zillions of photons fly out from the filament. In the case of the Sun, the numbers are still zillions of zillions times larger.

10

The Principle of Conservation of Energy

T he mental image of a photon that we introduced for thinking about light in terms of a collection of a great number of photons is compatible with what is known about how photons interact with matter. All interactions of photons with matter conserve energy. *The term "conservation of energy" means that the sum of energies of all objects involved in an experiment is the same before and after the experiment. No energy can disappear to nothing or get produced from nothing. The total amount of energy in an isolated system, one that does not exchange energy with any other system, remains constant forever. Energy may be transferred from one part of the system to another, like from one particle to another when they collide, or from one form to another, like when atoms collide and emit light so that the initial energy of the motion of the atoms is eventually carried in part by the emitted light. But the system of atoms and light as a whole has constant energy.*

The principle of conservation of energy is established so well by so many experiments that if any reasonable experiment is ever conceived as perhaps leading to some nonconservation of energy, even with a very tiny chance to see such nonconservation, the possibility will intrigue many people and they will try to check what happens in such an experiment. So far, it always turns out that the energy is conserved. Any finding that energy would indeed not be conserved in some process, even only one, and even only by a tiny amount, would mean a great, bottom-up alteration of our worldview. One can say that our worldview is built on the principle that energy is conserved.

We have no reason to believe that the law of conservation of energy is violated anywhere in the universe. We can think about billions of other systems, like our solar system, visible through telescopes. There can be life in those systems. We can think about the processes that proceed in the stars of those systems, how mass burns in them according to the formula $E = mc^2$ and produces light, and how this light may fuel strange forms of life in these systems. In all the processes that we can think about on the basis of all of our experience, the energy is conserved.

Thinking in this spirit, we can observe that the formula $E = mc^2$ and the concept of conservation of energy provide us with a context of learning that has an incredibly large scope. It ranges from the secrets of how atoms and their parts interact with light at the microscopic scale to the secrets of formation of planets and stars and galaxies. Within this range, we encounter the secrets of life at its molecular level inside cells of our bodies and the inexplicable ability of the human mind to learn. At the scale of a society, we find many new phenomena and among them an educational system that puzzles us, too. The context of $E = mc^2$ appears to open an interesting path for learning about the world. This chapter in this book is but one step on the path that can be followed by every person as far as he or she wants.

The formula $E = mc^2$ was conceived by Einstein using the law of conservation of energy. We will need this law in our discussion. We will have to consider three forms of energy: *the energy of mass, the energy of light, and the energy of motion.* Let us begin with the discussion of the energy of motion. The energy of motion of a given body that moves with a given velocity depends on its mass. Therefore, we first discuss the concept of mass.

WHAT IS MASS?

When we throw a stone, we see that the smaller the stone, the easier it is for us to throw it. A very small stone is easy to throw. When we throw a small stone we mainly feel how our own hand moves. When the stone flies out of our hand we do not feel much of a change in the movement of our hand. But when we attempt to throw a large stone, the size of a fist or a football, we feel that we have to give a lot of push to the stone to make it fly. We feel the resistance of the stone to be moved fast. One of the sports in the Olympic games is shot put. The sportsmen are very big and strong and still they need to whirl around and push the iron ball a lot before it gains the speed they want it to obtain. We also have to put effort into accelerating (increasing the velocity of) the stone by constantly pushing it with our hand. We accelerate it gradually until it has some considerable speed. Eventually, we let it go forward from our hand with a feeling of relief. We can conclude that the big stone is harder to make fly than the small one. The quality that quantitatively describes this feature is called mass. Big stones have large masses and small stones have small masses.

But the concept of mass cannot be understood as related to the size. A pillow filled with feathers can be much larger than a stone, and we have no trouble throwing a pillow. A stone of the same size as a pillow would be much harder to make move equally fast as we can make a pillow move. So, a large pillow must have much smaller mass than the stone. Let us look at some other examples.

It is much easier to make a small airplane move fast than it is to make a big airplane move equally fast. When an airplane begins to get going on the runway, its velocity is small. When the engines work at full throttle, the plane gains speed quickly enough to take off before the runway ends. But a big plane needs a much more powerful engine than a small plane. A small plane can gain the required speed using an engine comparable to the engine of a truck, while a big airplane requires an engine with great power to reach the same speed. The big plane has a big mass in comparison to the mass of a small plane. However, a big plane may be empty or full of people and cargo. When a plane is fully loaded, its size does not change but its mass does, and the engines have to work very hard to take off. If we overload the plane, the engines will not be able to accelerate the plane enough to take off before the runway ends.

The general statement that characterizes these examples is that bodies have inertia; they have to be worked on in order to change their motion. We say that the harder we have to work the greater is the inertia. The measure of inertia is called mass, and the bigger the mass of a body, the harder it is to make the body move as we want. In other words, the mass of a body is a measure of resistance of the body to the change of its state of motion to a new one. This is why the mass of a body is also called the inertial mass of that body. When the mass of a body is large, it is hard to accelerate the body. When the mass is small, it is easy to accelerate the body.[1] Spacecrafts are easy to accelerate when they have a small mass and hard to accelerate when they have a big mass. Cars with a big mass are hard to accelerate. This is why large trucks need powerful engines and a motorcycle can have a little motor and still accelerates much faster.

The same concept of mass applies in the case of slowing down, or braking, which is also a change in motion. The bigger the mass of a car, the harder it is to slow down its motion. In general, the bigger the mass of a body, the harder it is to change its motion. The mass of the body measures its inertia, the resistance to attempts to make a change in its motion. The inertial mass of a body is denoted by the letter m, and it is this inertial mass that appears[2] in the equation $E = mc^2$.

THE ENERGY OF MOTION
FOR DIFFERENT OBSERVERS

When a body moves, it has an energy of motion. When we work on a stone with our hand, we transfer chemical energy from our muscles to the energy of motion of the stone. The energy of motion of the stone increases at the expense of the energy that our muscles lose through our effort. Consequently, when the stone goes out of our hand, it has energy larger than the energy it had before it started moving. The difference is equal to the energy of its motion, which in turn is equal to the energy that we have spent in order to make the stone move.[3] The energy is conserved but changes form. Initially, it was contained in the molecules in our muscles, and finally, it exists also in the form of the energy of motion of the stone.

This brings us to the critical issue of how energy depends on an observer. Namely, when we say that the energy of a moving stone is larger than the energy of a stone at rest, we have to admit that while the stone moves fast from our point of view, it also moves with a smaller velocity from the point of view of somebody who rides on a bicycle in the same direction in which we have thrown the stone. This means that the rider on the bike must see the energy of motion of the stone as different than we do. Does this mean that energy depends on the observer? And what about conservation of energy if different observers see energy as different?

The state of motion, and therefore the energy associated with motion, both depend on the observer. By that we mean that the same object—a truck, a planet, a plane—can move with respect to one observer and remain at rest or move differently with respect to another observer. This means that the state of motion is not absolute. Whether an object is at rest or in motion depends on who is looking: *The state of motion depends on the observer of an object, and it is not a quality or property of the object itself, but of its relation to an observer.* And since the energy of an object includes the energy of motion, we have to discuss the dependence of the energy of objects on the observers who see them. Only then we will be able to follow Einstein in his reasoning regarding $E = mc^2$. He discovered the energy of mass by considering the energy of motion of a body of mass m from the point of view of two different observers.

Let us begin our analysis of how the observed energy depends on motion by considering an example that requires that you imagine something practically impossible. If we sit on a plane, we clearly see that other passengers do not move with respect to us. But we know that both we and they move with a great speed when looked upon by somebody on the ground. When another plane flies parallel to us, it appears to us as motionless. When the other plane comes toward us and we fly toward that plane with the same speed with respect to the ground, we see the other plane approaching us with a great speed, twice the speed that our planes have with respect to the ground. When this happens above foggy, structureless clouds that provide no point of reference, we have no way to tell which plane is flying how fast. All we see is another plane coming at us with a great speed. And we have literally no way to tell by looking outside through a window how fast our plane moves. All we can see is how our and the other plane move with respect to each other.

Now comes the impossible. When a plane flies 600 mph with respect to the ground, it has a speed comparable to a bullet shot from a gun. When you see a plane flying toward your plane, its speed with respect to you can be twice as large, 1,200 mph. This is more than the speed of a shotgun bullet. Suppose that a metal ballpoint pen held by a passenger in his hand on the other plane could miraculously enter the cabin of your plane. It would be like a bullet, able to pierce through your body, the seat, and another passenger because it has so much energy of motion from your point of view. This energy is real and the ballpoint pen would act like a real shotgun bullet. The same pen, however, is steadily held by the passenger on the other plane in his hand. He sees the pen as not moving much with respect to him, no more than the passenger intends his pen to move. And the pen does not have the energy of motion from the point of view of its owner that it has from your point of view.

CONSERVATION OF ENERGY FOR DIFFERENT OBSERVERS

The fact that the energy is conserved does not mean that all observers measure the same amount of energy for the same objects. Instead, it means that whatever process people observe and measure, they always come to the conclusion that *the total energy that they measure at the beginning of a process equals the total energy that they measure at the end of the process.* Two different people who move with respect to each other with a constant speed may see different amounts of energy, but both will conclude that the amount they see is preserved in time.

The energy of light is also different for observers who move with respect to each other, despite the fact that the speed of the light is the same for them. Consider that you run away from a light that follows you. This can last only a moment because light moves so fast that it is impossible to outrun it. Let us simplify our consideration and talk about moving with respect to a source of light, instead of the light itself. The energy of the light appears smaller to you when you move away from the source than when you do not move with respect to the source. And when you move toward the source, the light has larger energy from your point of view than when you are at rest with respect to the source. These effects can be understood qualitatively by observing that *when you move toward the source you will be meeting the signals that constitute every photon more often, or with larger frequency f, than in the case when you do not move with respect to the source. And when you move away from the source, the signals constituting every photon will come to you with smaller frequency f than in the case when you do not move with respect to the source.* The energy of the photons is, for all observers, equal to the Planck constant h times the frequency f, and it differs between observers according to how the frequencies f they see differ. Physicists have measured the energy of light with suitable devices in countless circumstances, and it is confirmed with great precision that frequencies change with the motion of observers but the energies are always proportional to the frequencies with the universal Planck constant h.

However, the fact that you see a different frequency, and thus different energy of light when you move differently, does not change the fact that energy remains conserved in all processes involving photons. The principle of conservation of energy is universal for all observers and all kinds of energy, including the energy of light. Einstein used this fundamental assumption in his reasoning that led him to conclude that $E = mc^2$.

Conservation of energy implies that the energy that is gained by a body of mass m through absorption of photons must be equal to the energy of the absorbed photons. Knowing the energy of the photons, one can deduce the change in the energy of the absorbing body. The same rule of conservation of energy is valid for all observers of the absorption process. For one observer the body may appear at rest. This observer sees energies of the photons to be of some magnitude. Another observer may be moving with respect to the body with some velocity v. This observer sees the body as moving and photons as having somewhat different frequencies, correspondingly to the velocity v. The photons have a different magnitude of energy for this observer because their frequencies are different from the point of view of this observer.

ENERGY OF MOTION OF A BODY OF MASS m AND VELOCITY v

In order to understand the principal steps in the reasoning that Einstein used in his derivation of the formula $E = mc^2$, we need to discuss the dependence of energy of motion of a body on its mass m and velocity v. Let us consider again the case of throwing a stone of mass m with our hands, this time straight up. Our first observation concerns the height that the stone can reach when we throw it with some initial velocity v. We know that the stone will fly higher when we throw it faster. It will fly up to certain height and then it will fall back to the ground. The maximal height it reaches is a measure of the energy of motion that the stone has at the beginning, that is, at the moment when it leaves our hand with the velocity v.

When the stone moves up, it is slowed down by the pull of the gravity of the Earth. It goes up to the height at which it loses its speed entirely due to the gravitational force. This happens at the moment when its motion upward turns into the motion downward. At *this moment,* the energy of motion of the stone is absent from our point of view because the stone does not have any velocity. But, instead, it is at the maximal height above our hand. Let us denote this height by H. Since the gravity continues to pull the stone downward, as it always does, the stone starts to move down and continues its accelerated motion downward under the influence of the same gravity force that slowed it to zero velocity in its motion upward. When the stone reaches the level of departure, which we assume to be the level of our hand, it has again the same velocity v, except that the velocity points downward instead of upward.

The more energy of motion the stone has at the beginning, the longer it takes for the gravity to stop it because the gravity force near the Earth's surface is always the same along the stone's path, and the same gravity force must work over a longer distance to stop the more energetic motion. Therefore, the faster we throw the stone up, the higher it goes. In essence, the gravity can be imagined as acting like some kind of a rubber band that tries to keep the stone close to the Earth. The analogy is not precise because a real rubber band exerts a different force, not a constant force like the gravity exerts on stones near the surface of the Earth. But the essence of the effect we describe is similar. When we throw the stone up, the distance between the Earth and the stone is growing, and the gravitation pulls back like a rubber band that is being stretched. This "stretching" accumulates energy in the gravitational "rubber band." The energy for "stretching the gravitational rubber band" is drawn from the energy of motion of the stone, until the latter is consumed entirely. The initial energy of motion of the stone is turned completely into the energy of the "stretched" gravity when the stone reaches the maximal height H. Hence, the height H at the top of the path of the stone is a measure of the initial energy of motion of the stone when it leaves our hand with the velocity v.

Now, we can throw the same stone with different velocities v and measure how high the stone will reach. The experimental finding is that H is proportional to the square of the velocity v with which we throw the stone. The proportionality to v^2 means that if we throw a stone twice faster, it will fly four times higher, and 2 squared is 4. And if we throw the stone three times faster, it will fly nine times higher, and 3 squared is 9. The same proportionality to v^2 means also that when we throw the stone with twice smaller velocity, it will reach four times lower height, and $\frac{1}{2}$ squared is $\frac{1}{4}$, and when we throw it with three times smaller velocity, it will reach nine times smaller height, and $\frac{1}{3}$ squared is $\frac{1}{9}$, and so on.

As a side remark, let us stress that the rule of H being proportional to v^2 works only as long as we are close to the surface of the Earth and v is small enough so that the body does not fly very high, or even out into the space away from the Earth. But the value of our reasoning is independent of the limitation to very low heights. We use the Earth's gravity only to find out how the energy of motion depends on v for small velocities. The same expression can be obtained in many other ways, too. We use the example of throwing stones to be concrete.

We are now introducing a new bit of information: The gravitational energy of a stone above the surface of the Earth is proportional to its height H. It is hard to justify this statement. But, for example, the higher we climb on a mountain, the more effort it requires. More energy must be spent to get to a higher level. Physicists, beginning, in particular, with Newton, have worked out details of the gravitational energy and checked their ideas very precisely. The conclusion is that near the surface of the Earth the gravitational energy of a stone, and every other body, grows proportionally to the height. The more gravity is "stretched" by increasing H, the more energy this "stretch" contains. So, let us adopt this measure of energy intuitively.

Now, we have already accepted that the more energy of motion we impart to a stone when we throw it straight up, the higher it will fly. The energy of motion that the stone has at the beginning is turned completely into the gravitational energy at the maximal height H, where the stone stops moving upward. Then, from the experimental result that the height H is proportional to v^2, combined with the finding that the gravitational energy of the body at the top is proportional to H, and using the law of conservation of energy, we can conclude that the initial energy of motion of the stone that has velocity v is proportional to v^2.

What is the proportionality factor? Our daily experience suggests one ingredient in this factor: the mass m. The bigger the mass of a body, the more energy it has due to motion with a given velocity v. Suppose we drop a baseball from a building and look what happens to the sidewalk where the ball hits it. We do not see any change in the pavement. Suppose that we drop an iron ball from the building. The gravity of the Earth accelerates the iron ball to the same velocity as it accelerates the baseball. But the iron ball breaks the pavement like a cannon ball. Its energy of motion is so large that it is able to do the work required to break through the pavement. One can follow this intuition, carry out many experiments (do not do them by dropping balls on sidewalks from buildings, any ball from any building), and the analysis leads to the conclusion that the energy of motion of a body of mass m that moves with the velocity v is proportional to m times the square of v. To complete a formula for the energy of motion, one has to provide a factor one-half in front, so that the final result for the energy of motion is $\frac{1}{2}mv^2$. That the factor in front of mv^2 in the energy of motion should be just $\frac{1}{2}$ can be explained in many ways, and one of them is given in Appendix A.

Knowing that the energy of motion of a body that has mass m and moves with velocity v is proportional to the mass and the square of the velocity, we see that an observer for whom the body is at rest will assign to it zero energy of motion because v for this observer is zero. An observer A, who sees the body as moving with some velocity v_A, will say that the body has the energy of motion corresponding to v_A. And another observer B, moving with respect to A, may see the same body as moving with some other velocity v_B, and he will then observe that the energy of motion of the same body is the one that corresponds to the velocity v_B. *The energy of motion of a given body depends on the observer. It is not an absolute quantity.*

11

Max and Ming

Light in the Matchbox

W e now proceed to the analysis of how the energy of a material body increases when the body absorbs light. Imagine a box of matches lying on the table in front of you. Let the matchbox have a little hole in it and let a beam of light enter the box through the hole. We know that if the beam of light is like the one that we can obtain by focusing sunlight with a lens, the beam will bring in enough energy to ignite a match inside. The ignition makes it evident that the light brings in energy. However, we are not interested here in the possibility of ignition. *What interests us is the fact that when the light enters the box, the energy of the box is increased by the energy of the absorbed light.*

In order to understand how to describe this increase of energy in detail and how this increase is related to the increase of mass, there are several things we need to understand. Einstein knew those things when he considered the interaction of light with matter and discovered that $E = mc^2$. We need to learn what Einstein knew before we will be ready to discuss the critical reasoning concerning the process of absorption of light by a body. This knowledge cannot be gained by reading just a page or two, and we have to move step by step, introducing new elements in the development.

To give you an idea how much Einstein knew and understood when he conceived the idea to consider the interaction of light with matter, let us list the main points.

1. Einstein knew that different observers would measure the same speed of light no matter how fast the observers were moving with respect to each other. This result is not comprehensible in the pre-Einstein way of thinking about motion, time, distance, and speed.

2. Einstein found how to explain the constancy of the speed of light. His explanation was based on a precise understanding of the concept of time, which showed that time depends on the observer. It is hard to exaggerate how difficult Einstein's conception of measurement of time was for many physicists and other scientists to understand. It was as revolutionary as the works of Copernicus and Newton. The reader inevitably will have some difficulty understanding and appreciating Einstein's conception of time. "Difficulty" may not be the appropriate word. After all, when you are presented with a new conception of time that challenges the usual, millennia-old conception that has worked well for us in our daily chores, and when you are then told that the way we tell time does not apply in explanation of the entire universe including the Earth where we live, you should expect you are being asked to unlearn and then learn a great deal.

3. Einstein intuited that his new understanding of time would have consequences for how all processes of Nature are traced in time by us as observers, and he was checking the consequences of his new way of thinking about time. In brief, if time is not absolute because it depends on an observer, many of the explanations of physics would have to be rethought and could change. The question was, how? Put in another way, Einstein was very happy to have found a profound explanation of the constancy of the speed of light and was on the path of thinking about what his new finding implied when he analyzed the question of energy changing form in the flow of time and how the form of energy changes when light interacts with matter.

4. Einstein knew how to describe the process of interaction of light with matter from the point of view of two differently moving observers in the pre-Einstein theory, which did not account for the constancy of the speed of light.

5. Einstein knew that his new theory, which did account for the constancy of the speed of light by introducing a precise concept of time, was different from the previous theory, and he was curious what would follow regarding the energy of light and matter in interaction, if he used his new understanding of time.

6. Einstein knew that energy was conserved in all processes, and he assumed it should also be conserved in his new theory.

7. In his new theory, Einstein knew precisely how to relate time coordinates of events according to two observers in motion, and he could tell how the energy of light according to one of the observers would be related to the energy of light according to the other observer.

8. Einstein analyzed the interaction of light with matter using his understanding of the energy of light and discovered that there must be a relationship between the energy of matter and its mass, in order to conform to his theory of time.

The above points are the basis for our starting with the matchbox example. We need to clarify these points step by step, and we will use the matchbox example for that purpose. This is why the example provides the point of departure for our tour of reasoning that will lead us to the conclusion that the increase in energy of a body implies also an increase in its mass. The amount of change in the mass is related to the amount of energy that the light brings in. We will find how the amounts of mass and energy are related by studying implications of the law of conservation of energy *according to two different observers.*

One observer moves with some small and steady velocity v with respect to the matchbox. We will, from now on, call this observer **Ming,** an abbreviation of the word "moving." Another observer sits at the table with the matchbox. We will systematically refer to that observer as **Max,** an abbreviation of the word "matchbox." Max remains at rest with respect to the matchbox and he will consider the matchbox to be at rest because the matchbox does not move with respect to him. Since Ming moves with a small velocity v with respect to the matchbox, he also moves with respect to Max, and Max will see Ming as moving with the small and steady velocity v. We will derive the formula $E = mc^2$ from comparison of the results of measurements of energy that the two observers will make in the process of absorption of light in the matchbox. Max will look at this absorption process at rest while Ming will look at it in motion. The relationship between energy and mass will emerge from the results of Ming once we compare his results with those obtained by Max.

Max considers the matchbox to have some unspecified energy before the absorption of light. We will denote this **initial** unspecified energy of the matchbox by E_{before}. The energy of the matchbox **after** absorption will be denoted by E_{after}. The energy E_{after} will be greater than the energy E_{before} by the amount that the light brings in. We will assume that the light brings in an amount of energy that will be well-known to Max. Let us denote this energy by the symbol Δ_{Max}. In physics and mathematics, the Greek letter delta, Δ, is often associated with the amount of change, and here the energy of the matchbox is changing due to the absorption of light. We add the word "Max" as a subscript to Δ because the change of energy we are now talking about is seen by Max. Assuming that from Max's point of view energy is conserved, the energy E_{after} will be equal to the sum of the energy E_{before} plus Δ_{Max}.

Ming, who moves with respect to the matchbox, will see the matchbox as moving with respect to him. It may sound strange to the reader to say that when the observer moves the matchbox is moving relative to that observer because the reader *knows* that the matchbox is at rest on the table.

But the table also appears to Ming, as observer, as moving. The concept of motion depends on the observer, and the energy of motion also depends on the observer. *That the matchbox is at rest relative to the table does not mean that it is at rest relative to the observer who moves with respect to the table.* This was also discussed in Chapter 10, page 115, using the example of two airplanes. When two planes are flying parallel to each other at the same velocity with respect to the ground, each appears to the other as not moving. *But to somebody on the ground, both are in rapid motion.* When the planes fly toward each other, each of them appears to the other as moving at great speed even though the passengers of each of the planes see themselves as at rest. We will say more about the perception of motion by different observers later. What counts here is that Ming will see the matchbox not only to have the energy E_{before} but also the energy of motion. That is to say, if Ming approaches the matchbox with velocity v, he perceives the matchbox as approaching him with the same velocity v. In order to imagine this situation, erase the ground from your mind, as if all this is happening in empty space and neither Max nor Ming can see or refer to the ground. We know from the previous section that the energy of motion of the matchbox is given in terms of its mass and velocity by the formula $\frac{1}{2}mv^2$. Let us denote this energy by E_{motion}.

What we have said in the above paragraph means that Ming will see the initial energy of the matchbox as equal to the sum of E_{before} plus E_{motion}.

Ming will also see the light that is absorbed by the matchbox, and he will be able to measure the energy of the light from his point of view. Let us denote the amount that he sees by Δ_{Ming}. We need to understand how Δ_{Ming} is related to Δ_{Max} because our goal is to describe how the moving observer sees the process of absorption of light. The formula $E = mc^2$ will emerge in our analysis of the energy conservation from the point of view of Ming, who sees the absorbed light carrying the energy Δ_{Ming}.

The question is, How large is the energy Δ_{Ming} of the absorbed light that Ming sees in the case in which Max at the table sees the absorbed light to have energy Δ_{Max}? If Δ_{Ming} differs from Δ_{Max}, then by how much? What conclusions will follow from the assumption that the law of conservation of energy is equally valid from the point of view of both observers even if they see the energies as different? Einstein found a theory that allowed him to tell the amount of energy of light, Δ_{Ming}, that the moving observer sees if the observer at rest with respect to the absorbing body sees Δ_{Max}. Our intention is to discuss the meaning and implications of Einstein's theory in a sequence of steps of increasing detail. This sequence of steps will eventually lead us to the conclusion that $E = mc^2$.

Assuming that energy is conserved, the final energy of the matchbox after absorption of light will be seen by Ming as equal to the sum of three contributions: E_{before} plus E_{motion} plus Δ_{Ming}. The nature and value of E_{before} is not specified, and we will not need to know more about E_{before} for the time being. E_{motion} is already known to us to be $\frac{1}{2}mv^2$. The magnitude of Δ_{Ming}, that is, the energy of the absorbed light according to the observer who moves with respect to the matchbox, is the subject of our further study. We need to find out how Δ_{Ming} and Δ_{Max} are related depending on the velocity v of Ming with respect to the matchbox. This dependence is the origin of the formula $E = mc^2$.

Our discussion of the absorption process must account for the fact that the line of reasoning concerning energy, which we want to describe, involves a new understanding of the concept of time. Time gets involved because the energy of light is proportional to its frequency, and frequency is measured through measurements of time. Measurement of time is also involved in the measurement of the speed of light and velocities of all material objects. Einstein introduced his new understanding of time in order to explain why the speed of light c is the same for two observers even when they move with respect to each other with some non-zero velocity v and even though the velocities of all material objects change from observer to observer if they move with respect to each other.

Before Einstein solved the puzzle of the constancy of the speed of light, a physicist would expect that if the observer at the table sees the light to have speed c, the observer who moves with velocity v with respect to the table will see the same light to have the speed equal c plus v, or c minus v, depending on the direction of motion of the observer. This expectation is based on experience with all familiar objects. For example, when we ride in a car on a highway, the cars that travel in the opposite direction appear to us to move very fast. From our point of view, *our velocity with respect to the ground* adds to *their velocity with respect to the ground,* and as a result we see the cars that move head on toward us as very fast, as in the case of our example with the airplanes. From our point of view, their velocities are sums of our velocity and theirs. On the other hand, the cars that travel in the same direction that we ride in appear to us to move slowly with respect to us. From our point of view, our velocity with respect to the ground sub-tracts from their velocity with respect to the ground, and we see them moving with respect to us only with the velocity that is equal to the dif-ference. Thinking in the same way about light, we expect the speed of light to be modified by addition or subtraction of the velocity v of an observer who moves in the opposite or the same direction that the light moves in.

The pre-Einstein way of thinking about the moving observers and speed of light is so deeply rooted in everybody's mind that there is no other way to continue but to discuss first how the absorption process can be described in the pre-Einstein manner.

MING, MAX, AND THE MATCHBOX

We begin our discussion of the process of absorption of light by our match-box on the table within the pre-Einstein way of thinking.

For Max at the table, the matchbox is at rest and the initial energy of the matchbox is equal only to E_{before}. Ming sees the initial energy of the matchbox as equal to the sum E_{before} plus E_{motion}.

We also need to describe the energy of the absorbed light from the point of view of Max and Ming. We have already discussed how to describe the energy of light in terms of the energy of photons (see Chapter 9, page 109). Light is made of photons, and every photon carries energy equal to the Planck constant h times the photon frequency f. But the beam of light that enters our matchbox is made of zillions of photons, each of which carries only a small part of the energy of the whole beam. In order to simplify our discussion, we shall not consider the entire beam of light but only a couple of photons. This will allow us to reason without worrying about all the complicated processes that may occur in the case of a real matchbox on the table when it does absorb zillions of photons.

We will make additional simplifications in order to avoid some other difficulties as well. The key value of these simplifications will be to remove all clutter and expose the bare bones of the ideas that will eventually lead to the conclusion that $E = mc^2$. Thanks to the simplifications, our matchbox example will cease to have features that are specific to boxes of matches. As a result, our discussion of light in the matchbox on a table will bring us to conclusions that are expected to be valid for all known bodies in the universe. Our reasoning will grasp some of the essence of the laws of Nature that equally apply to matchboxes, atoms, and stars.

Let us now observe that when we consider absorption of just one photon coming into the box through a hole on one side, the photon not only brings in the energy to the box but also pushes the box in the direction of the motion of the photon. Thus, if we were considering conservation of energy in the process of absorption of just one photon, we would have to figure out how much energy of motion is imparted to the box. This complication can be avoided when we assume that the matchbox absorbs precisely two identical photons and one of them comes from your left side while the other one comes from your right side. When we consider absorption of two identical photons coming from exactly opposite sides at the same moment, the same push is provided from opposite sides and there is no motion imparted to the matchbox. The desired consequence of setting up the absorption process this way is that the matchbox never moves on the table. All that happens is that the two photons enter the matchbox at the same moment and the energy of the matchbox is increased by the energy of the two photons while the matchbox lies always still on the table.

Let us also observe that a real matchbox may contain many matches, and they can move inside. If ignited, they can burn using oxygen in the air and produce smoke and heat. All these processes involve energy in one form or another. We would have great trouble if we had to analyze how energy changes place and form in all these processes. To avoid this type of complication, we assume that the two photons have very small energy, insufficient to ignite matches. We imagine that there is no air around, no wind or resistance to any motion of any kind. Even more radically, we assume that our matchbox constitutes one indivisible whole so that we will not have to consider any matches inside the box as separate parts, analyze their motion individually, and so on. We also assume that our matchbox has mass m that is so well measured that we can think that there is no ambiguity in the value of m in our reasoning.

On the basis of our simplifying assumptions, we can now say that the energy of light that is absorbed by our matchbox from the Max point of view, denoted by Δ_{Max}, is equal to twice the energy of one photon, or $2E_f$, where 2 comes from two photons and $E_f = hf$ is the energy of one photon (we remind the reader that f stands for the photon frequency and h is the universal Planck constant). Therefore, in agreement with the principle of conservation of energy, the energy of the matchbox after absorption is equal, from the Max point of view, to the sum of the energy of the matchbox before the absorption *plus* the energy of the two photons. The energy that the matchbox has before the absorption of two photons, E_{before}, whose nature we did not specify, is increased by Δ_{Max} to the new value of energy after absorption, which is denoted by E_{after}. This can be written as E_{before} plus Δ_{Max} equals E_{after}, and we know that Δ_{Max} equals $2hf$.

There is a virtue in writing these statements in terms of mathematical equations. When we use language, there is an ambiguity allowed by the fact that everyday language is not very precise. For example, when we say "He is six feet tall," we do not truly care whether the man is 6 feet and $\frac{1}{100}$ of an inch tall or 5 feet and 11.99 inches. As another example, we say that "It is 2 P.M." without really paying attention to whether it is 2 P.M. and 0.01 seconds or 1 P.M. 59 minutes and 59.99 seconds. The practice of our daily life does not require that we distinguish such tiny differences because by the time we say the words "It is 2 P.M." the time has already changed by a couple of seconds and the accuracy to one hundredth of a second is irrelevant. The accuracy to one hundredth of a second in our language does not come to the fore except in special situations, such as clocking runners or swimmers at Olympic games. Otherwise we do not need such great precision in our daily chores, and our language does not need to be precise.

So, when we just say that the energy X plus energy Y gives energy Z, we do not say how precisely the *equation* $X + Y = Z$ is satisfied. Our language does not indicate the degree of precision of our statement. Does it hold with accuracy to 1%, 0.1%, or 0.01%? Or is it an exact statement, with no room for any ambiguity in it? A mathematical equation implies no ambiguity. Therefore, when one writes an equation that is supposed to describe some aspect of the real world, one means an exact statement about the world. If one then observes some deviation in the real world from the exact statement, the existence of the deviation implies that one's understanding of the world was incomplete. How much of a mistake was made is not as important as the fact that the world turns out to be different than expected. Such turning points come about as a result of measurements that are carried out so precisely that a deviation from some mathematically stated equality becomes appreciable. Although the magnitude of deviation is important, what counts in the first place, regarding ideas and imagination, is not so much the magnitude of deviation but that the exact statement one had previously derived turns out to be not satisfied in reality. Recall that in Copernicus's studies of the calendar[1] and in Römer's studies[2] of the movements of Io it was the very tiny departures from precisely stated expectations that led to important revisions and conclusions about the world. The formula $E = mc^2$ also emerged from consideration of effects that in normal circumstances are very small.

In order to see a tiny effect, we first need to precisely describe what we expect. The equations $E_{before} + \Delta_{Max} = E_{after}$ and $\Delta_{Max} = 2hf$ serve this purpose. They are considered an idealized, exact description of how Max should see the absorption process and conservation of energy. These equations will enable us to identify tiny effects in Ming's observations when he passes by with some small velocity v with respect to the matchbox on the table and watches the absorption process.

Regarding mathematical equations, we should stress that although they are used for formulating exact statements that can be compared with experiment and reveal new realms through small corrections, the equations originate from a deeper source. They come as a result of imagining what one wants to describe.[3] *The equations provide a useful language in which precise statements can be made concerning what one thinks about. The situation is similar to music and notes. Notes on the page are not music. Music is only described by notes. When a musician writes or reads notes, the music plays in his mind.*

Since the energies of the individual photons are different for Ming and Max, a complete pre-Einstein description of the absorption process requires that one answers the question, What is the energy of photons absorbed by the matchbox, according to Ming? We denoted this energy by Δ_{Ming}. We can find the amount of this energy because we know that the energy of photons is simply related to their frequencies, and we are able to determine how the frequency changes from one observer to another. The pre-Einstein reasoning that predicts the energy of photons according to Ming from the knowledge of their energy according to Max can proceed as follows. *The reader should remember that the pre-Einstein reasoning contains a flaw because we still miss the explanation of the paradox of the constancy of the speed of light for all observers.*

One first imagines closely how Max sees the situation and then one extrapolates the picture to Ming's point of view according to the pre-Einstein theory. Max sees two photons that approach the matchbox. They are coming from opposite sides and simultaneously sink into the matchbox. More concretely, one photon is coming from the left and one from the right. To be precise, it is assumed that both come exactly on the same straight path of flight, which one can think about as if it were a single line in space. In other words, when one thinks about the photons as trains of signals, they are coming on the same track from opposite directions. And they are to ride into the matchbox simultaneously.

The photon coming from the left will be called the left photon, and the photon coming from the right will be called the right photon. The matchbox can be thought about as standing on the track that the photons ride on. And Max sits at the table where the matchbox is.

One should also imagine that the photons are coming from two sources that are located on the same track far away from the matchbox, the source of the left photon far to the left and the source of the right photon far to the right, so that the situation near the matchbox looks more or less as depicted in Figure 11.1. Ming should be thought about as if he traveled along the same line of flight or rode on the same track. He moves from left to right with velocity v. His velocity v is much smaller than the speed of light c. Shortly before the photons sink into the matchbox Ming is nearing the matchbox, and it is helpful to imagine that he arrives at the matchbox simultaneously with the photons.

Figure 11.1   Schematic view of the matchbox; moving observer (Ming); and the two photons, right and left, shortly before the absorption takes place

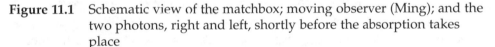

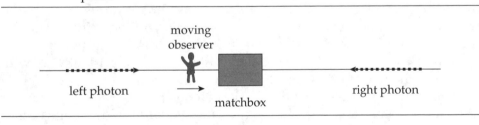

Since we assume that Ming comes toward the matchbox from the left, the photon that comes from the right source moves head on toward Ming. The photon that comes from the left source approaches Ming from behind. Ming cannot see the photons because to "see" them means to absorb them, and they are to be absorbed in the matchbox, not Ming's eye. But we can imagine how Ming would see the photons if instead of sinking into the matchbox they sunk into his eyes. Our goal is to describe the energies of these two photons as they would be seen by Ming if they sunk into his eyes. To see the right photon, Ming would look forward, and to see the left photon, Ming would look behind.

So, we have to consider what energy would the right photon have for Ming, the one that comes to meet him head on, and what energy the left photon would have for Ming, the one that trails him from the back. Since the matchbox is to absorb both photons, we need to add their energies up, and the resulting sum will tell us the total energy Δ_{Ming} that the absorbed photons bring into the matchbox according to Ming.

Thus, we are going to determine what energy the right photon has from Ming's point of view, what energy the left photon has from Ming's point of view, and what is the sum of these two energies, which will give us Δ_{Ming}. Our assumption is that Max sees Δ_{Max}, which is comprised of two equal parts, h times f for the right photon and the same for the left photon. Thus, Δ_{Max} is equal to 2 times hf.

Let us start with the energy of the right photon that moves head on toward Ming. Its energy will be seen by Ming as equal to the Planck constant h times the frequency that Ming sees. We need to find this frequency under the assumption that Max, sitting at the table, sees the frequency of the right photon to be f. What frequency will Ming see? How much different will this frequency be from the frequency f that Max sees?

In order to answer these questions one needs to proceed step by step. The reader may find it helpful to analyze the details that we have described in Appendix B. The key point of the pre-Einstein reasoning is that the speed of the right photon is expected to be seen by Ming as equal to c **plus** v. The photon "train" and Ming's eye move head on toward each other. This means that the signals of the right photon appear to Ming as approaching him faster than with the speed of light c by the additional velocity v with which Ming moves toward the signals. This, in turn, means that Ming's eye meets the signals of the right photon more often than it would if Ming did not move toward the signals with velocity v. And the frequency of meeting the signals is greater for Ming than it is for Max because Max is not moving toward the signals: The velocity of Max with respect to the matchbox is zero.

Because the frequency of the right photon is greater for Ming than for Max and the energy of the photon is always equal to its frequency times the Planck constant, we conclude that the energy of the right photon is greater for Ming than for Max. A quantitative analysis of the difference is described in Appendix B.

The left photon, it appears to Ming, according to the pre-Einstein thinking, as coming from behind with the speed c **minus** v. By the same reasoning as for the right photon, we conclude that the left photon appears to Ming as having a smaller frequency than for Max (v is subtracted from c). And so the energy of the left photon is smaller to Ming than it is to Max.

So far we have said that the right-photon energy appears to Ming as greater by a certain amount than the right-photon energy hf that Max sees. The left-photon energy appears to Ming as smaller by the same amount than the energy hf that Max sees for the left photon. The amounts of the difference are equal in size but opposite in sign because the speeds of the photons are seen by Ming as changed in opposite ways: from c to c plus v

for the right photon and from c to c minus v for the left photon. But if the energy of the right photon appears to Ming as increased by the same amount by which the energy of the left photon appears to him as decreased, the sum of the photon energies remains unchanged. *Therefore, the pre-Einstein theory predicts that the combined energy of photons seen by Ming, which we denoted by Δ_{Ming}, is the same as the combined energy of photons seen by Max, which was denoted by Δ_{Max}. The pre-Einstein way of thinking implies that Δ_{Ming} is precisely equal to Δ_{Max}.*

One can now look at the energy conservation law. According to Max, the energy of the matchbox before absorption is E_{before} and the energy of the photons is Δ_{Max}. In the absorption process, the energy of the photons adds to the energy of the matchbox. After absorption, the photons are absent and the energy of the matchbox is E_{after}. Conservation of energy tells us that E_{after} is equal to the sum E_{after} plus Δ_{Max}.

According to Ming, before the absorption, the energy of the matchbox is equal to the sum E_{before} plus E_{motion}. The energy of the photons is Δ_{Ming}, and Δ_{Ming} is equal to Δ_{Max}. Thus, on the basis of the principle of conservation of energy, Ming should see the energy of the matchbox after absorption as equal to the sum E_{before} plus E_{motion} plus Δ_{Max}. Note that we use here Δ_{Max} although we talk about Ming. It is correct because Δ_{Ming} is equal to Δ_{Max} in this pre-Einstein reasoning. But we know from Max that E_{before} plus Δ_{Max} is equal to E_{after}. Thus, we see that all that happens from Ming's point of view is that E_{before} turns into E_{after} due to the absorption of the energy Δ_{Max} and *the energy of motion of the matchbox remains unchanged.*

The pre-Einstein reasoning leads this way to the conclusion that energy is conserved from the point of view of both Max and Ming no matter how they move with respect to each other. In the pre-Einstein reasoning, the concepts of mass and energy remain different and unrelated. Although the energy E_{before} is increased to E_{after} by the combined energy of the absorbed photons, equal to Δ_{Max}, the latter is not related to the mass of the matchbox in any conceivable way. The energy of motion is accounted for in terms of the mass m and velocity v quite independently of how the initial energy E_{before} is changed to E_{after} by the absorption of photons that bring Δ_{Max}. These conclusions illustrate the pre-Einstein way of thinking about energy and mass.

It is known, however, and Einstein knew, too, that the speed of light is the same for all observers. Both the addition of v to c for the right photon and the subtraction of v from c for the left photon, in order to find speeds of the photons from Ming's point of view, are inconsistent with the experimental findings. Therefore, the pre-Einstein thinking is disconnected from the experimental facts in principle. It does not contain a single element that would suggest that the speed of light is the same for both Max and Ming.

Nevertheless, the pre-Einstein reasoning described above leads to some important conclusions. One is that if the speed of light is constant instead of varying with the observer, one needs to understand more about how this constancy may come about. This is a fundamental question, and *the answer may influence the pre-Einstein worldview in which the speed of light seems to have to depend on the observer.*

The other conclusion is that whatever explanation of the constancy of the speed of light one finds, the result will enter the consideration of the energies of the matchbox and photons in the absorption process. We can no longer trust the assumption that Ming sees the photons to have speeds $c \pm v$. The assumption contradicts the results of measurements that say that the speed of light is always c, both for Max and Ming. So, how should the right reasoning proceed?

Whatever it should be, the explanation of the paradox of constancy of the speed of light, when systematically applied, may change our understanding of the relationship between the energy of our matchbox and the energy of absorbed photons. And since the energy of motion of the matchbox depends on its mass, there is a possibility that the mass of the matchbox and the energy of light may somehow get connected in a proper theory that explains the constancy of the speed of light. *Such connection might imply that mass and energy are **not** independent concepts, as the pre-Einstein worldview suggests.*

The third conclusion is that the corrections one needs to think about are very small when the velocity v we consider is very small in comparison to the speed of light c. And since velocities of all material bodies and observers in everyday life are very small in comparison to c, we have to be very precise in our considerations and watch for apparently tiny details that need to be taken into account.

The above observations force us, as authors of this book, to invite you, as a reader, to a discussion of the relationships between measurements of frequency, and hence time, by different observers. Such discussion requires great precision of thought.

A valid theory of how the results of measurement of time performed by one observer of some event are related to the results of measurement of time performed by another observer for the same event was first found by Einstein. He wanted to understand the behavior of light. We need to discuss his theory of time in order to improve our analysis of the process of absorption of photons by our matchbox. We cannot be satisfied with the pre-Einstein reasoning because it contains the inexplicable contradiction with experiments that all say that the speed of light does not change with the observer. In the pre-Einstein reasoning we described so far, the speed of light varies with the observer, energy is conserved, and mass and energy are separate concepts with no indication that they may be connected. What will the valid approach imply?

Let us stress that Einstein found his new theory of time when he worked on the properties of light and explanation of the constancy of its speed, rather than on the energy conservation in the absorption process, as we do. But after he figured out how to explain the paradox of the constancy of the speed of light, he also saw many consequences of the explanation he found. The formula $E = mc^2$ is one of the consequences that he pointed out.

PRE-EINSTEIN THEORY OF RELATIVITY

Our examples with planes or cars illustrate the fact that the velocities of material objects are different for differently moving observers. And all our experience leads us to expect that the faster we run after light, the slower it should appear to fly away from us. We also expect that the faster we run head on toward the light, the greater the speed it should appear to have from our point of view. This is what we "know." The amazing fact is, however, that this "knowledge" is not confirmed by measurements of the speed of light in the real world. Instead of depending on how we move, the speed of light is always the same. How is it possible? What is wrong with our "knowledge?" What do we need to unlearn? Are we missing something important about how the world works? We need to answer these questions in order to re-analyze the process of absorption of light by our matchbox and see the corrections that Einstein predicted should exist.

Einstein discovered that in order to explain the paradox of the constancy of the speed of light, we have to review the concept of time. The concept of time that we apply in our thinking about material objects of everyday life is not precise enough, not thought through enough, and not verified enough for us to claim that light must obey the rules that we "know." We need to study the meaning of Einstein's theory in order to understand the incomprehensible constancy of the speed of light. And after we do that, we will be able to return to our description of the process of absorption of light by the matchbox on the table and reconsider the law of conservation of energy.

It will take an effort to grasp the idea of time that Einstein conceived, and our story will lead to some unexpected places. But the tour is worth taking, not only because later we will be able to understand how Einstein conceived the formula $E = mc^2$, but also because we will better understand what is meant by "time." The new insight is like knowing that the Earth is not flat but round. This knowledge does not change much about the flatness of pavement on the street, but we become able to think that the Earth is a ball and that it circles around the Sun. We become capable of conceiving satellites and travel to other planets.

Learning about the world outside the area of our experience is not easy because we need experience to comprehend new information. Whether our learning concerns the speed of light and $E = mc^2$ or other important features of the world, true learning always forces us to face up to our own questions that are not easy to answer and require exercise to gain experience. Using the example of light and $E = mc^2$, we may learn how it happens that our learning becomes possible and how the learning proceeds. The opportunity derives from the fact that the subject of $E = mc^2$ is an example of authentic conceptual difficulty. We know how we feel when we are acutely aware that something is unclear while we believe that it could be clear and when we would like it to be clear. We will also see how much our outlook on the world will change as a result of going through the effort to learn. We need to learn in order not to be left behind in the dark regarding basic ideas. Advanced ideas are used in the development of our civilization, and one cannot keep up with the pace without advanced skills of learning. The formula $E = mc^2$ is an example of a difficult subject to learn. But the history, content, and meaning of the formula turn out to bear heavily on many areas of our lives, including not only the issues of energy, power, peace, and war, but also and primarily on how we communicate with other people. The importance of the formula as a probe of our own learning skills lies also in our reflection on how we teach others, independently of the subject, and this is a fundamental issue in education. We cannot teach beyond the obvious without learning beyond the obvious, which requires effort of mind. $E = mc^2$ provides an example to see what this means. Our lessons from $E = mc^2$ about learning will apply far beyond the concepts of mass, energy, and speed of light. But we should not jump ahead. Let us come back to physics.

The constancy of the speed of light is only one aspect of Einstein's theory of time. The fact that the speed of light is constant contradicts our intuition because we are not used to a precise description of the relationship between results of measurements of distances and times by different observers. If we cannot make sense of the constancy of the speed of light, can we trust ourselves that we know precisely how to relate results of other observations made by different observers? For example, if one observer says that something happens 5 meters to the right, 10 meters in front, and 3 meters up, at 3 P.M., can any other observer know where and when the event truly happens? *No, the observers do not know how to translate their observations from one's point of view to the other's unless they clearly specify where is right, where is front, which way is up, what is meant by a meter, and how to determine time.* And when the observers discover that the speed of light is the same for all of them no matter how they move, the result that defies their perception of the world, they face the question of whether they really know what they are doing. They need to ask themselves whether their measurement procedures are sound, and whether they correctly relate their results to each other.

The problem is thus not limited to the speed of light. It extends to an entire theory of what and how we know about events that happen in time and space and *how we relate to each other information about what we see.* The word "relate" plays a special role here. It means that observers of the world need to know how to describe the world to each other so that each can understand precisely what the other talks about. And, technically speaking, we always see things happening only from our own point of view. In order to inform somebody else who moves with respect to us about what we see happening, we not only have to tell the person what we see but also what relationship connects our frame of reference to the frame of reference of that person. When we try to be precise, this relationship becomes an entire theory. We have to discuss the meaning of this theory. All science, from ancient times to the nineteenth century, was based on a theory of the relationship between observers that implied that the speed of light should depend on the velocity of its observer. But when the speed of light was precisely measured using the definition

$$speed = \frac{distance}{time},$$

and when the speed turned out to be constant instead of varying with the observer, it also meant that the most basic measurements of distance and time were not certain. Something basic might be wrong in what we had in our heads regarding distance and time, and the question was, what?

Another question that will follow when we expand our reasoning beyond physics is, What lessons can we draw from analysis of simple physics problems, such as the problem of the relationship between frames of reference of observers of basic physical phenomena in space and time? In particular, what can we infer for the purpose of addressing complex problems that plague our understanding of human learning? Learning occurs not merely in space and time, but also in the incredibly rich variety of dimensions in our mental "frames of reference." The concept of "frames of reference" is central to an understanding of the differences between the contexts of productive and unproductive learning. But before we can address those bigger issues, let us stick, for the time being, to the problems in physics that Einstein addressed.

Einstein wanted to find out whether it was possible that there exists a relationship between results of measurements of time and distance by different observers that agrees with the constancy of the speed of light and still matches the intuitive picture for small velocities that we know is valid in our daily life. The new theory not only had to explain the paradoxical constancy of the speed of light, but also had to consistently explain the relationships among results of measurements of time and distance performed by all moving observers. These relationships could depend on how fast the observers move with respect to each other. Einstein would not accept any explanation of the constancy of the speed of light if it did not follow from a comprehensive theory. He would also not consider any theory as a legitimate candidate for interpreting results of real measurements unless that theory clearly explained the constancy of the speed of light. Thus, Einstein accepted the constancy of the speed of light as a fact and wanted to know what that fact meant.

The leading principle in Einstein's reasoning was that how things truly happen should not depend on who observes them. This principle does not exclude that the speed of light can be the same for all observers irrespective of how fast they move relative to each other. To the contrary, the result that the speed of light is the same for all observers sounded like the simplest possible way of satisfying the condition that the nature of the world does not depend on the observer. But how could a speed not depend on how the observer moves? And what can the right answer to this question tell us about the nature of light, its frequency, and energy?

An observer states that some object moves if he or she sees that a distance between this object and some other object changes in time. This is how we perceive motion. For example, when the distance between a train and a train station grows with time, we say that the train moves. But this means that we perceive motion in terms of a reference object (like the train station) from which we can measure the distance that changes in time (like the distance between the train and the station). Thus, motion is not a concept that concerns only one object, but at least two. Motion means a change of position of one body relative to another. *There is no concept of motion of a body if we consider only one body.* The words "a body moves" refer to a change in position that is perceptible only when we see another body and the distance between the two changes. By the same token, there is no way for us to tell whether we move and how fast we move unless there is some material body to refer to. When we observe the distance between us and that body, and when the distance changes in time, we can say that we move with respect to the body.

In particular, we are psychologically preconditioned by our everyday experience to refer to the ground as the reference body. This preconditioning is so strong that we are often not aware that our concept of motion is related to the ground we live on. This is why the words "motion" or "rest" seem to us to refer to single objects, like a person or a car. In fact, we always use the ground as a reference body when we say that something "moves" or is "at rest." We consider the ground to be static, at absolute rest, because the ground is our reference body, and as such, it does not move with respect to itself. An intense mental effort is required to unlearn the concept of absolute rest and the concept of motion that says that bodies either stand or move.

It is true that bodies stand or move with respect to the ground. But whether the ground moves or not depends on the observer. This is illustrated by the example of Manhattan. New Yorkers think that Manhattan Island, the central part of New York called New York City, is a fixed place in the world. They treat New York City as a reference body. The observers in space do not treat New York City as a reference body. They may regard their spaceship as a reference body. For them, New York City is a speck on a ball that moves in a large orbit around the Sun once a year and, in addition, rotates like a top around its own north-south axis once a day.

We are also very much used to thinking about motion in the frame of reference defined by our own body. If we sit, we do not move. That makes clear sense to us. If we sit on the ground and see an object moving, which means changing its position relative to the ground and us, we think that we are at rest and the object is in motion. Our thinking proceeds as if the states of rest and motion were each somehow absolute. In fact, they are only determined relative to us as observers, and we are biased by our feeling that we sit on the ground.

If we sit on a plane, we also look at objects as moving with respect to us. We instinctively set up our frame of reference as attached to our seat and the floor of the plane. Somebody moves from our point of view when they walk down the aisle. Those who sit next to us don't move. But for an observer on the ground, our plane and all its passengers move fast. To the observer on the ground, the concept of motion relative to our seat appears clearly biased. It is valid only in *our* frame of reference.

It is much harder to unlearn the concept that the ground is at absolute rest than that our seat on the plane is at absolute rest. We can look out the window of our plane and see that we fly over roads, mountains, lakes, and towns. We see that the plane is in motion with respect to the ground, and we accept that easily. On the other hand, there is no way in our daily lives by which we can see that the Earth is moving. The planet we live on is too big for us to see clearly that we refer to the ground because of practice and convenience and not for any absolute reason. The ground is distinguished by its size and the role it plays in supporting all objects that matter in our lives on the surface of the Earth. It appears absolute because it is the biggest object there is, and everything else is observed by us in relation to the ground.

Before people could imagine that the Earth was round and that it moved around the Sun, the ground provided a distinctive frame of reference. Mountains and trees or pyramids and all other buildings did not move. Everything that did not move with respect to the ground could be considered as being at rest. Everything that moved with respect to the ground could be considered as being in motion. The reference to the ground created the impression that an absolute state of rest existed. But when the ground was recognized as moving also, the concept of the ground as a distinctive reference frame had to be abandoned, and the concept of absolute rest ceased to have meaning. There always existed a possibility to refer to the stars as providing a frame of reference. But stars are also moving, and their motion poses more questions than we can answer.

Since the frequency and energy of light and velocities of objects and energies of their motion all depend on observers, one can speak about the frequencies, velocities, and energies only in relation to an observer. On the other hand, the principle of conservation of energy that we discussed in the earlier sections holds equally for all observers. This principle is valid equally for all observers even though the frequency, motion, velocity, and energy of motion have only relative meaning and depend on observers. Physicists, and Einstein in particular, were interested in identifying those *laws of Nature that apply to observable phenomena according to all observers equally.* These laws are of special interest because they describe what happens in a more reliable way than any specific description that depends on who observes a given phenomenon and how the observer interprets what she or he sees.

Somebody who looks at cars on a one-way street only at night, and only from the back, will assure us that the cars have red lights. Somebody who looks only from the front will assure us that the cars have only white lights. What is the truth? Whose observation is more reliable if they contradict each other? We know the answer. Their points of view are different and there is no contradiction. The cars have red lights in the back and white lights in the front. But in order to suggest that this is the right answer, we have to understand the relationship between the two observers. We know the meaning of their reports taken together because we understand how the frames of reference of the observers differ and how they are related. Namely, the axes of their sight are pointed in opposite directions when they look at the same objects. When we understand the relationship between the axes of their frames of reference, we begin to see the possibility that both can be right even though they see different images. The one reality that cars have lights of two colors is true independently of the existence of the observers and their impressions. And, indeed, an observer who stands on the sidewalk and watches cars passing by will say that they have two kinds of lights.

If the reader wonders why we pay so much attention to discussion of examples that seem to be rooted in our daily lives much more than in the processes typically discussed in physics, let us point out that in the area of reform of education there seem to exist as many frames of reference as people who work on the problem. The required theory that would allow them to communicate with required precision, and which, as a result, would allow them to imagine the magnitude of the universe of valid alternatives to their point of view, is missing. This lack is one of the reasons for the disastrous incoherence of reform efforts that die out like counterbalancing fluctuations, even if they all are about to do the right thing locally in their own frame of reference. Also, the existing educational system is so large that everything is referred to it as an absolute reference frame. But the reality is that the existing educational system is not absolute in any way and can be changed. In contrast, the context of productive learning is a valid concept independently of the specific educational system. It is this concept that represents the truth and reality of learning independently of the reference frame provided by any educational system. Another special reference frame in education is the subject matter. This reference frame is treated usually as delineating some path to objective truth about learning. But it is also a frame-dependent picture, far from the essence of an entire spectrum of processes that are poorly identified and barely understood but definitely known to go on in the process of learning by a living being, practically independent of the subject matter. We add comments in the text that follows in order to point out where in our discussion of $E = mc^2$ the analogy between physics and education is being developed.

The laws of Nature that are equally valid for all observers are not biased by who observes an act of Nature. All observers can verify such laws equally, each and every one of them learning the same truth in his or her own way. Similarly, the concept of learning plays a universal role in education. We mention this point here to give the reader a preview of relevance of the discussion we go through regarding $E = mc^2$ to the issues of broad significance in schools and society at large that will be discussed in the final chapter of this book. We have designed our discussion of $E = mc^2$ so that it prepares the reader to absorb the content of that last chapter, in which we attempt to synthesize information from previous chapters about learning in art and science and draw conclusions about educational reform. We mean here conclusions that refer to and stem from the generally valid distinction between the contexts of productive and unproductive learning.

We have already said that observers verify the general laws of Nature thousands of times independently of each other, everyone from his or her own point of view. When we think beyond the problems of our daily lives and ask how it is possible that we can go to the Moon or send robots to Mars and control their movements when they collect rocks to be brought back to the Earth, or how it is possible that we have satellite TV or navigational devices in our cars, we have to realize that none of these would be possible without understanding the rules of Nature that do not depend on observers. Ironically, only looking from space do we begin to realize where we live and how little we know about the fragile balance of life on our planet. And none of these achievements would be possible without knowing the relationships between frames of reference of different observers. Without a theory of these relationships, we would not know how to isolate the information about what happens around us in ways that are independent of the observer. We would not be able to tell other observers about what we experience and what we think about what we experience if there was no good theory in existence that allowed other observers to unambiguously interpret our message and compare its content with what they experience and what they think about it.

The interest in the laws that are independent of observers led physicists to consider *the theory of relativity*. The word "relativity" means that the appearance of a real process to a specific observer is described by that observer in terms of results of measurements made relative to the frame of reference of this observer. In other words, the observer sees how things happen relative to him, or the frame that he builds, in order to locate the events in space and trace them in time.

The fact is, however, that a different observer will describe the same process using a different frame of reference, and the process will appear differently in terms of quantities measured relative to that different frame of reference. But we want to know whether the observers agree about what happens and what is it that actually happens, even if it is seen differently by different observers, as it usually is. Therefore, we need a theory of the relationship between the findings for positions and times of events that different observers measure and want to discuss. This is what the theory of relativity provides.

An agreement about common reality can be established by different observers if, and only if, they find agreement between their observations using a single, well-defined theory of relativity that provides a connection between their frames of reference. We have to admit that unless the observers know how to relate their observations to each other, they cannot firmly agree on any common understanding of what is actually going on. Especially when they want to investigate small corrections to the laws that they have already agreed upon.

Tiny corrections require precision of concepts, language, and procedures. But we already know that tiny does not necessarily mean small, in the sense of importance. We have discussed several examples of apparently tiny effects that contained a large amount of information about the universe. We have already discussed the example of Copernicus, who was studying the visible motion of the stars, Sun, Moon, and planets and how the motion changed with time measured with accuracy of about 10 days in two millennia. In details of such precise analysis, he saw tiny effects that suggested to him that the Earth was better described as circulating around the Sun, rather than otherwise, which almost everybody believed in his time. We have also discussed the example of Römer, who was studying the visible motion of Io and saw a tiny delay in Io's appearance from behind Jupiter of about 10 minutes in a quarter of a year. The small correction to the expected perfectly regular motion of Io allowed Römer to conclude that the speed of light was finite, forever invalidating the belief that it was infinite, and he could estimate its magnitude. Again, since he knew precisely how to describe the major part of Io's motion, he could study the small variation in its period. And we have described the fact that when, later, others were measuring c with accuracy better than 1 part in 10,000 in order to see the effect of motion of the Earth with respect to the hypothetical ether, according to a precise theory they had, they had found no such effect and faced a major conflict between their precise theory of the world and the result of their precise observations. The resolution of this conflict came in Einstein's theory of relativity.

All the important examples we have mentioned above involved detailed studies of the motion of several objects. Such detailed studies required an understanding of how the results of precise observations made by one observer can be compared with the results of precise observations made by another observer. For example, Römer was looking at Io from a different frame of reference every successive day because the Earth moves. He worked in Paris. But Paris moves with the Earth, and the orientation of Römer's observatory with respect to the Sun, planets, and stars was changing every minute every day. After half a year, the Earth has moved to a new place in the solar system over half of its orbit around the Sun and was then moving in the opposite direction. The same issues concern contemporary astronomers who look at the same sky from different observatories. Their observatories are differently oriented in space because they are at different places on the globe. Moreover, astronomers in the continental United States cannot see parts of the sky that astronomers in Europe, Japan, or Hawaii see at the same moment. Different astronomers need to know how to interpret time readings they use to describe what they see. Observers must know with a great degree of confidence how to communicate to others what each of them sees in his own frame of reference.

Precise comparisons between observers are possible only if *every* observer has a well-defined procedure for building his own frame of reference. This condition concerns all observers of all phenomena, not only astronomers. Only after each of the observers agrees to a set of common procedures that each of them uses in his or her own work do they begin to have a chance to start translating what one obtains to another. They begin to build a precise common picture of reality starting from a precise theory of how their observations are or should be related. A tiny correction to a law of Nature can be identified only after this effort is advanced very far. Only after the main regularities are well described, the tiny corrections may become visible and no matter how tiny they are they can open our eyes to new realms of reality. Without precise statements of what we do, what we see, and how we relate the results of our measurements to each other, our baggage of experience would be too clumsy, only qualitative, not quantitative, and the tiny windows of opportunity to see far beyond our daily existence would escape our eyes forever.

The same happened in the case of $E = mc^2$. It was discovered as a consequence of precise relations that were predicted by Einstein to hold between results of measurements of positions and times performed by different observers, each performing them in the same way from his own point of view and respecting the same set of well-defined rules of study. These precise relations between results of measurements of positions and times of the same events by different observers are the basis of the theory of relativity. Our intention is to explain the essence of these relations. We need to explain these relations in order to tell the story of how they led to the discovery of $E = mc^2$, using our example of the matchbox on the table.

12

Max and Ming Build Their Frames of Reference

Let us now describe an example of a relationship between positions and times that different observers assign to the same events. Let us consider a train that rolls through a station. Let us assume that the observer named Max stands on the station platform, and the observer named Ming rides on the train. Previously, we gave the name Max to the observer who sits at the table on which our matchbox lies, and we gave the name Ming to the observer who is moving with a steady velocity v with respect to the table and Max. Nevertheless, it will be convenient to think about Max at the table as if he was like an observer on the station platform and about Ming as if he was like an observer on the train. This way of thinking will allow us to describe how Max may build his reference frame using the station platform and how Ming may build his frame of reference using the train. *We shall begin from description of how Max and Ming build their frames of reference according to the pre-Einstein theory of relativity.*

Our conclusions from the example with Max at the station and Ming on the train, regarding the relationship between their frames of reference, will directly apply in our analysis of the process of absorption of light by the matchbox. We can think that the table with the matchbox stands on the station platform. This concrete context will help us analyze events that would appear abstract in the context of experiments with a matchbox and photons on a laboratory table. Let us begin our discussion of the frames of reference with Max.

Max attached his frame of reference to the platform. This means that Max has spent a long time walking with a ruler along the platform, and he carefully marked all points along the edge of the platform with numbers that indicate a distance from a reference point on the platform in units of the length of Max's ruler. Let this unit be called one meter. Let us assume that Max chose his reference point on the platform to be where a pole with the station clock stands. Every point on the edge of the platform has a number assigned to it equal to the distance in meters between that point and the reference point on the platform edge where the pole stands.

Thus, if you give a number x to Max, he can show you a point on the platform that is x meters away from the reference point. If the number x is positive, Max will show you a point lying on one side of the pole, say, in the direction in which Ming's train is moving, and if the number x is negative, he will show you a point on the other side of the pole. And if you select a point on the curb of the platform, Max will be able to give you the number x that corresponds to the point you chose in his frame of reference. This number is called the space coordinate of this point in the Max frame of reference. Each and every point along the platform has some coordinate x in the frame of reference built by Max. In order to indicate that a given coordinate refers to the reference frame of Max, we will write x_{Max}, instead of only x.

Ming attached his frame of reference to the train. This means that Ming has spent a long time walking with a ruler down the corridor in the train and marked points on the train floor with numbers that indicate distance from a reference point on the train in units of the length of his ruler. His unit is also called one meter because we assume that Ming and Max use identically made rulers.

Let us assume that Ming chose his reference point on the train to be at the door of one car in the middle of the train. Every point on the train is assigned a number equal to the distance between that point and the reference point at the door of the middle car. Thus, if you give a number x to Ming, he can show you a point on the train that is x meters away from the reference point. If the number x is positive, Ming will show you a point lying ahead of the reference point, counting along the train toward the locomotive. And if the number x is negative, he will show you a point lying at a distance x toward the end of the train counting from the reference point. When you show Ming a point on the train, he will be able to give you the number x that corresponds to the point you chose. This number is called the space coordinate of this point in Ming's frame of reference. Each and every point along the train has some coordinate x in the frame of reference built by Ming. In order to indicate that a given coordinate refers to the reference frame of Ming, we will write x_{Ming}, instead of just x.

Both Max and Ming can assign space coordinates to all events that happen on the platform or on the train. But to inform each other which event they are talking about using their readings of position of the events, they need to know how to relate their coordinates x_{Max} and x_{Ming} for any given point in space.

In order to understand what this means in practice, let us imagine that a lady named Mary rides on the train. Suppose she stands at a window in the first car of the train and that the distance between her and the door of the middle car where Ming's reference point is located is always 100 meters. Thus, Ming says that Mary has a fixed coordinate x_{Ming} equal to 100 meters, which does not change in time. What space coordinate x_{Max} will Mary have according to the measurements of her position made by Max on the platform?

First of all, we notice that if Mary stands on the train and the train rolls with a steady velocity v with respect to the platform, Max will see Mary as moving along the platform with the velocity v. Her position in the Max frame of reference will be changing in time. This means that x_{Max} for Mary changes in time, and we need to find out how.

As far as time itself is concerned, Max and Ming have no doubts how to assign it to events. All events are considered to have a time coordinate that says when they happen according to a reading on a suitable clock. Both Max and Ming look at the same station clock and read the time from its face, which provides them with the time coordinate of any event they consider. Thus, we can say that the time coordinate that Max assigns to a momentary position of Mary is the same as the time coordinate that Ming assigns to the same moment. But for the sake of brevity of discussion that will follow, we denote the time coordinate assigned by Max to events by t_{Max}. This notation indicates that we are talking about a time reading that Max obtains for the event in which Mary arrives at the point on the platform to which Max assigned his space coordinate x_{Max}. We also denote the time coordinate that Ming assigns to the same event by t_{Ming}. The notation indicates that it was Ming who read the time from the clock.

Our notation for space and time coordinates of events is designed to remind us about who performed the measurement of the coordinate, and thus in whose reference frame the coordinate is meant to be used. Since both time coordinates t_{Max} and t_{Ming} are equal to the time displayed on the station clock, we always have t_{Max} equal to t_{Ming}, and both are equal to the reading of time, t, on the station clock.

In order to find the coordinate x_{Max} of Mary, knowing the coordinate x_{Ming} she has according to Ming on the train, we have to establish at what time t we want to know x_{Max}, because the position of Mary with respect to the platform changes in time. Suppose that at 12 noon, which we will refer to as time $t = 0$, the door of the middle car, where Ming's reference point is located, passes by the pole on the platform, where the reference point of Max is located. Thus, the event in which the reference point of Ming passes by the reference point of Max has, according to Max, space coordinate

$x_{Max} = 0$ and time coordinate $t_{Max} = 0$. According to Ming, the same event has space coordinate $x_{Ming} = 0$ and time coordinate $t_{Ming} = 0$.

Now, at the moment $t = 0$, the reference points of Max and Ming coincide. Therefore, at that moment, the Max space coordinate of Mary will be equal to the Ming space coordinate of Mary. We can write it as an equation $x_{Max} = x_{Ming}$ at $t = 0$. This solves the problem of the precise relationship between x_{Max} and x_{Ming} for Mary at one moment, $t_{Max} = t_{Ming} = 0$. But when time goes on, the formula must change because Ming's reference point moves away from Max's reference point with velocity v.

The next step is to describe what happens at other times when the train moves on. Mary stands on the train and the train moves with velocity v. Her position on the train does not change, *but her position with respect to the platform changes in time.* Max observes that after time t, Mary has moved with the train. In fact, every point on the train has moved by the same distance, which is given by the train velocity times time, or vt. *This means that the more time passes, the greater distance Max has to add to x_{Ming} in order to obtain the space coordinate x_{Max} for Mary.* This is illustrated in Figure 12.1. We can think about the situation in terms of frames of reference as follows. At time $t = 0$, the reference point of Ming on the train is passing by the reference point of Max on the platform. But the reference point of Ming is moving with the train, and its distance from the reference point of Max changes with time and equals vt at time t. Therefore, in order to obtain x_{Max} for Mary, Max must take the distance vt by which Ming's reference point is separated from Max's reference point and add to it the Ming space coordinate x_{Ming}, which says how far Mary stands from the Ming reference point on the train.

Figure 12.1   Mary on the train has x_{Max} equal to vt plus x_{Ming}

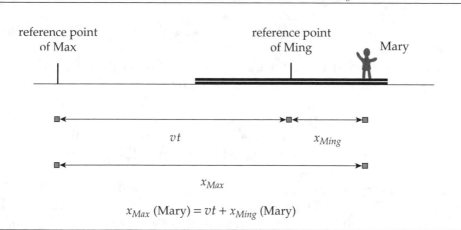

$$x_{Max} \text{ (Mary)} = vt + x_{Ming} \text{ (Mary)}$$

The result reads: $x_{Max} = vt + x_{Ming}$. Note that we can write t_{Ming} in place of the common time coordinate t. In the pre-Einstein theory, this is just a convention because t_{Ming} is equal to the common reading of time, t, and t_{Max} and t_{Ming} are the same and indistinguishable from the common t.

This reasoning shows also that the same relationship between coordinates of Max and Ming, $x_{Max} = vt_{Ming} + x_{Ming}$, is valid for all events, not only for the event in which Mary arrives at a given place on the platform. *Note that the space coordinate of Mary measured by Max at any given moment is related to both the space coordinate of Mary measured by Ming at that moment and the time coordinate of that moment.* The same holds for all coordinates of all events.

We have thus arrived at an example of a relationship between time and space coordinates assigned to the same events by two different observers who move with respect to each other with a steady velocity v. What we have just described is represented exactly by the following two equations.

One equation concerns time coordinates,

$$t_{Max} = t_{Ming}. \qquad [12.1]$$

Both times are equal to the common time t that is read from the face of the station clock. The time t plays the role of absolute time. The word "absolute" means "independent of an observer."

Another equation concerns space coordinates,

$$x_{Max} = vt_{Ming} + x_{Ming}. \qquad [12.2]$$

This relationship is written in terms of an exact mathematical equation and does not allow for any ambiguity. Thus, if we know the time t_{Ming} and position x_{Ming} of some event, we can calculate the position x_{Max} of this event. Namely, we first multiply t_{Ming} by the velocity v of Ming with respect to Max, and then we add x_{Ming} to the result.[1]

The two equations, 12.1 and 12.2, summarize the content of the pre-Einstein theory of relativity.

The pre-Einstein theory leads to the conclusion that if Mary **walks** down the corridor of the car toward the locomotive, so that she is seen by Ming to have velocity v_{Ming} relative to the train, she will be seen by Max as having velocity v_{Max} with respect to the platform and v_{Max} will be a sum of the velocity of the train with respect to the platform, v, *plus* the velocity of Mary with respect to the train, v_{Ming}. This rule of adding velocities is written in the form of an exact equation as $v_{Max} = v + v_{Ming}$. The velocities v_{Max} and v_{Ming} refer to how fast Mary moves from the point of view of Max and Ming, respectively, and the velocity v says how fast the frame of reference of Ming moves with respect to the frame of reference of Max. The conclusion that velocities add like that is a consequence of the pre-Einstein theory of the relationship between the coordinates used by Max and Ming.

We explain below how the addition of velocities logically follows from the pre-Einstein theory of relativity. Let us do it step by step.

Step 1

The Max space coordinate for Mary is given by equation 12.2 as follows:

$$x_{Max\ for\ Mary} = vt + x_{Ming\ for\ Mary}.$$

Step 2

We know that the Ming space coordinate for Mary is

$$x_{Ming\ for\ Mary} = v_{Ming\ for\ Mary}t.$$

Step 3

We now can substitute $x_{Ming\ for\ Mary}$ with $v_{Ming\ for\ Mary}t$ in the equation of Step 1. Therefore, the new equation becomes

$$x_{Max\ for\ Mary} = vt + v_{Ming\ for\ Mary}t.$$

Step 4

In order to obtain the velocity of Mary according to Max, we have to divide $x_{Max\ for\ Mary}$ by the time t. But t is common in both terms on the right-hand side of the last equation, and dividing by time t we obtain

$$v_{Max\ for\ Mary} = v + v_{Ming\ for\ Mary}.$$

It is important to realize that this law of adding velocities is an exact logical implication of the pre-Einstein theory. *The fact that the relationship between frames of reference precisely implies a relation between velocities of the same object observed in those frames will help us to appreciate that if the actual measurements contradict the rule of addition of velocities, they also contradict the theory of relationship between the frames of reference.* So, if experiment would in any way contradict the rule of addition for velocities, it would also contradict the theory of relationship between different frames of reference.

The pre-Einstein theory of relativity for frames of reference of moving observers, summarized in Equations 12.1 and 12.2, implies that *the velocity of any object according to one observer is given by the velocity of this object as seen by another observer plus the velocity of one observer with respect to the other.* This rule of adding velocities was considered in the pre-Einstein reasoning to be basically correct for all objects in the universe.

But instead of Mary walking down the train, one could consider a beam of light moving forward along the train. Ming may send a pulse of light on the train and measure its speed. He obtains c. The pre-Einstein theory implies that Max should measure the speed of the same beam of light to be $v + c$. However, experiments do not agree with this expectation:[2] Max obtains the same speed c for a pulse made by Ming no matter how fast Ming moves with respect to Max, and despite the fact that Ming always obtains the same speed c for pulses he makes. This means that the fact that the source—say, the flashlight of Ming—moves with velocity v from the point of view of Max does not change the speed that Max obtains for the pulse made by Ming. Einstein adopted the rule that the speed of light does not depend on the velocity of the source. This was one of the principles of his thinking about light. Light could be certainly thought about as a wave, according to the theory developed by Maxwell (see Chapter 8). But a wave moves with a speed that is independent of the speed of its source, precisely as in the case of waves of water that move away from a point of creation with the same speed, no matter how fast the boat that creates them moves. Einstein also adopted the rule that no observer is privileged. These two rules combined mean that Max and Ming see the same pulse of light as having the same speed c no matter how the pulse is made.[3] The speed of light does not depend on the observer. But Einstein had to ask how all these pieces of information can make sense together because they are not in agreement with common intuition concerning motion and speed.

The result that the speed of a pulse of light does not depend on how fast and in what direction the observer moves contradicts the rule of addition for velocities, which says that if Ming sees c then Max should see c + v. This conclusion poses a major problem because our reasoning that leads to the rule of addition of velocities depends only on the relationship between the time and space coordinates t_{Max}, x_{Max}, and t_{Ming}, x_{Ming} for all events. If the velocity of light does not obey the rule of adding v, then the theory of relativity that we have discussed and summarized in Equations 12.1 and 12.2 is not true. But since this theory reflects our everyday experience, it is very hard to see what may be wrong with it.

Nevertheless, the correct theory of relativity that is required to understand the constancy of the speed of light must be different from the one we are accustomed to. What is wrong? The right theory was first proposed by Einstein in 1905. We need to discuss his theory in order to improve our analysis of the absorption of light by the matchbox on the table and to derive the formula $E = mc^2$.

13

What Time Is It on a Distant Clock?

W hen Max and Ming read time from the station clock, they unreflectively assume that they see the time that the clock shows instantaneously. But if the speed of light is finite, and if they want to be very precise, they have to account for a little delay in their recording of time because light needs some time to travel from the clock to their eyes. This suggests that there may be some small correction involved in the determination of the time of events that happen on the platform or on the train far away from the station clock. The problem with precise determination of time also occurs when Max and Ming try to measure the frequency of photons absorbed in the matchbox.

The issue of delay in reading time becomes more transparent when Ming's train rides so far away from the station that Ming will no longer be able to read the station clock from his reference point on the train. And if Max follows the train along the platform, he also ends up no longer knowing how to read time from his station clock immediately. Even if Max and Ming could see the clock through telescopes, they would have to make some sizeable corrections for the time of travel of light between the clock at the station and their location. It is clear that they need some precise procedure to handle the problem of determination of time from a distance. The problem has a much longer history than the history of Einstein's work. The longitude problem that we extensively discussed in Chapter 7 in the story of Römer is just one example. The reader may find it fascinating to read the book by Galison, who reviews the history of the measurements of time.[1]

When events occur at two distant places, there is no a priori way to tell the time difference between them. The situation is like in the case of determination of time in the longitude problem (see Chapter 7). We can put one clock at one place and another clock at another place, but this is not enough because we have to know, in addition, how to decide whether the clocks display the same readings at "the same time." The intuitive notion of "the same time" is not sufficient, as it was not sufficient in the longitude problem. We cannot carry a clock from one place to another without influencing its rate of ticking. But when we understand that the required precision must be on the order of one part per million, it becomes slowly clear that we have to define what exactly is meant by the words "the same time" for events that occur separated by a large distance. Einstein was interested in how to define and check precisely whether distant clocks display the same readings "simultaneously."

Imagine Einstein, who walks on a hill above Bern after a busy week in his patent office.[2] Perhaps he is thinking about a problem related to granting or refusing a patent on some procedure for synchronization of electric clocks at a distance. He can see the clock on the town tower in Bern, and he checks the time displayed on his own watch. His intention is to check whether his watch and the clock on the tower display the same "time." The clock on the tower provides time to everybody in town.

But he has thought about physics, clocks, time, and practical issues that required understanding regarding how clocks work, and how they can be synchronized, for a long time before he came to the top of the hill. So, at this moment, his mind is at the center of focus on the problems that he was busy thinking about almost every day. And finally, after years of pondering, he sees clearly how to understand what actually happens when he checks the time on his watch with a clock at a distance. *He has the insight that when he sees that his own watch and the tower clock are both reading exactly 12 noon, it is not right to say that they show the same time simultaneously because the image of the tower clock needs some small amount of time to reach his eyes.* And Einstein comes to his ultimate understanding of what needs to be done about it. In order to say that the clocks show the same time simultaneously, Einstein should see the image of a bit earlier reading on the tower clock when his watch shows exactly 12 noon. But how could one determine the time delay precisely? This is what Einstein figured out.

One could try to measure the distance between the hilltop and the reference clock on the tower, divide this distance by the speed of light, and obtain the duration of flight of light that brings the image of the distant clock face to his eyes. That would require a lot of hard work in order to achieve high precision. But Einstein sees, now, a much simpler solution.

There can be a mirror placed on the face of the reference clock. Einstein may produce a pulse of light at some moment. Let us arbitrarily choose this moment to occur when Einstein's watch displays the time that we shall denote by $t_{producing}$. This pulse flies to the tower in some time T. Then it is reflected by the mirror and travels back to Einstein in the same time T. Einstein can look at his watch when the pulse reflected from the mirror comes back to him. Let this happen when his watch is displaying the time that we shall denote by $t_{receiving}$. At this point, Einstein can already find the time T that the pulse needs to travel to or from the tower because the difference between $t_{receiving}$ and $t_{producing}$ is equal to $2T$. Note that Einstein reads both times, $t_{receiving}$ and $t_{producing}$, on his own watch. He does not have to do any measurements regarding distance to the tower in order to find T. All he does is to send a pulse of light and wait for the reflected pulse to come back. The only condition required for this procedure for finding T to apply is that Einstein's watch does not change its position with respect to the tower in the meantime. In other words, *Einstein's watch and the tower clock must be at rest with respect to each other.* If Einstein's watch has moved with respect to the tower in the meantime, the length of path of the pulse of light on the way from Einstein's watch to the tower could be different from the length of path from the tower to Einstein's watch after it moved, and the times of flight of the pulse to and from the tower would also differ. Therefore, the procedure for finding T would not apply if the tower clock and Einstein's watch were not at rest with respect to each other. This, however, does not mean that Einstein's watch and the tower clock are at absolute rest. In fact, they travel with the Earth, and an observer from space would consider both as moving. What counts is that the distance between the clocks is not changing.

The next step is the precise statement of what is done for synchronization of the two clocks. When the mirror reflects the pulse of light, it does it in such a way that the reflected pulse carries information about the position of the hands of the reference clock on the tower at the moment of reflection. In fact, this is precisely what happens when we shine light with a flashlight on a clock in a dark room. We send a pulse of light toward the clock. The light is reflected from the face of the clock and comes back to our eyes. Our eyes register the image of the face of the clock that is carried by the reflected light. This is how we read the time from the clock that is at some distance away from us.

The speed of light is so great that we have an impression that it all happens instantaneously, but it takes some very short time. And in this tiny, tiny effect of delay, which requires razor-sharp imagery, the secret of the real development of events involved in measuring time is hidden, including the consequence that $E = mc^2$. Since the delay is tiny, we need mathematical precision in our thinking to keep track of the details. If the distances between clocks were of cosmic proportions, the delay would run into minutes (light needs about eight minutes to come from the Sun to Earth) or even hours, and we would see it as well as Römer could in the case of Io (see Chapter 7). But light needs only a fraction of a second to go around the Earth, and for all distances visible to us in everyday circumstances the delay in time of sending and receiving a pulse of light is incredibly short.

When Einstein receives the reflected pulse, he already knows all the information required for synchronization of his watch with the tower clock. He knows the times $t_{producing}$ and $t_{receiving}$ from readings on his own watch. He also knows the time that the reference clock on the tower, far away from him, was showing at the moment of reflecting the pulse. Let us denote this reading of time by $t_{reflecting}$. *Remember, $t_{reflecting}$ is read on the display of the tower clock, not on Einstein's watch, but the pulse of light carries the information to Einstein.*

Suppose Einstein's watch is correctly synchronized with the tower clock, which means that they both display the same time simultaneously. Then, the time reading $t_{reflecting}$ on the tower clock should be equal to the *middle* between the readings $t_{producing}$ and $t_{receiving}$ on Einstein's watch. Since Einstein knows the readings $t_{producing}$ and $t_{receiving}$ from his watch, he can precisely calculate the middle value, *which is just the average of these two readings.* Then he checks whether this midpoint in time on his watch matches the image of the reading $t_{reflecting}$ that the pulse of light brings to him from the clock on the tower. If his watch is synchronized with the tower clock and both show the same readings of time *simultaneously,* Einstein shall obtain the result that the average $\frac{1}{2}(t_{producing} + t_{receiving})$ is equal to $t_{reflecting}$ on the tower. If it turns out that the middle time $\frac{1}{2}(t_{producing} + t_{receiving})$ on Einstein's watch is different from $t_{reflecting}$ on the tower, Einstein will be able to shift his watch accordingly, by the difference he obtains, and then his watch will be synchronized with the reference clock on the tower. Every observer can go through the same steps and set his own watch in the same way in precisely defined agreement with the clock on the tower.

The procedure we just described is an example of a "gedanken experiment," called "gedanken" even in English because Einstein used the German word "gedanken," which means thought about, thought through, imagined, and in principle possible to carry out. Einstein used gedanken experiments in order to imagine and understand what may happen in the real world. Thinking this way, he discovered to his great delight that his gedanken procedure for synchronization of clocks could be universally applied to all clocks at rest with respect to the designated reference clock. This was a remarkable observation for him because he became able to define in this way what he, as observer, meant by measuring the time of all events around Bern. The time of any event, called its time coordinate, would be unambiguously found by reading it from a clock that belongs to a network of clocks that are all at rest with respect to the reference clock and are all synchronized with the reference clock using the same procedure. The clock in the network of clocks from which one reads the time coordinate of any given event is the clock that is located in the same place where the given event occurs. The concept of building such a network of clocks, all at rest with respect to the reference clock and all synchronized using light, is a major contribution of Einstein to physics. It defined in experimental terms what is meant by simultaneity. Such a precise operational definition of simultaneity was not known before Einstein. The reader will see later that this concept of simultaneity leads to the formula $E = mc^2$ as one of its consequences.

It did not matter any more how far the place of an event was separated from the reference clock because one had an entire network of clocks that could extend as far as one wanted, and every clock was synchronized with every other clock in the network as soon as they were synchronized with just one of them. Thus, the concept of time and its flow could be imagined as a running network of synchronized clocks. In an ideal model, one could have a clock at every point in space. Such clocks would be as small as single points in space, and this is impossible in practice. On the other hand, when we discuss events of some macroscopic size, we may imagine clocks of atomic size that are so tiny that we can consider them point-like for all our purposes. Having a network of such clocks, every event in the history of the world could be assigned the time when it happened because that time could be read by somebody on the clock that was located at the place of the event when the event occurred. The key value of this definition of measurement of time of an event was that there was no ambiguity left about what one was supposed to do in order to measure the time. Once this definition of the measurement of time was established, by all means applicable in practical terms, Einstein could ask how the measurement of the speed of light could be made. And now he was prepared to analyze what results would be obtained by two observers who move with respect to each other.

It is important to realize that the issue of comparison between the results of the two moving observers is different from the issue of how one observer synchronizes his clocks and defines time in his frame of reference. Namely, each of the observers has his own procedure of synchronization of his network of clocks. These networks of clocks are different because each moves together with the observer who builds his network. But we are now aware of the fact that these networks have to be compared with each other. The comparison is crucial and becomes possible because we know precisely how each of the two networks is built. We will describe concretely what needs to be done in the next chapter.

14

Max and Ming Review the Concept of Time

L et us continue our discussion of observers and their measurements using the example of Max on the station platform and Ming riding on the train. Let us consider that Max and Ming perform some measurements that involve time and let us ask what exactly they do. For example, let us try to imagine what Max and Ming do in order to measure the velocity of some object. This may appear a dull problem. But the fact is that when we are interested in a theory of development of events in time, whatever events, the bottom-line question is whether we can explain the rate at which things change in time. A change of position of a body in space is just one example of what may be changing. Here is the way to look at our analysis: It is not about a dull physics problem, it is about how we know, what we think we know, how we learn about the world, what should be taught to our children and how, what all this knowledge is actually based on, and how much our children are going to learn at school about this foundation of knowledge.

The measurement of a steady velocity of some object by a steady observer is performed by designating a well-measured segment in space and by noting the time of two events. The first event occurs when the object enters the segment at its beginning and the second event occurs when the object leaves the segment's end. The length of the segment divided by the time difference gives the velocity. The two events happen at different places (the beginning and the end of the segment), and to measure the time when they occur one has to use two clocks. One clock is located at the beginning of the segment and allows an observer to read the time when the object enters the segment. The other clock is located at the end of the segment and allows the observer to read the time when the object leaves the segment. The clocks should be synchronized in the way that Einstein proposed, to make sure that the clocks display the same time simultaneously. Only then is the difference between their readings equal to the time of travel of the object through the segment.

Let us begin our analysis of what different observers do to measure velocity of some object starting with Max. He measures the velocity of an object with respect to his frame of reference built on the platform. Max has not only marked distances on the platform, but he has also mounted a network of clocks on the platform and he has synchronized all of them with his reference clock. Having done all of this, Max selects a segment on the platform and measures it very well with his ruler. At each end of the segment, there stands a clock from the network that Max built. He uses these two clocks to measure the time of travel of the object. The two clocks, like all other clocks in the Max frame of reference, are set so that they show the same time simultaneously. Max asks a person at the beginning of the segment to take note of the time displayed on the first clock when the object passes by. He also asks another person at the end of the segment to note the time displayed on the second clock when the object arrives there. The length of the segment divided by the difference between the recorded readings of time on the two clocks give Max the velocity. Let us assume that Max obtains this way a velocity v_{Max} for the object. This result has a clear, experimentally well-defined meaning. Everybody could repeat the steps Max makes and check the result.

Now we proceed to the measurement of velocity of the same object by Ming. This seems to pose no problem until we realize that Ming has to build his frame of reference on the train. In order to measure velocity of the object, he should take the same kind of steps as Max did. But Ming should do them on the train instead of the platform.

The problem with time we encounter here is that when Max was building his frame of reference on the platform he was synchronizing all his clocks with the reference clock on the pole that stands on the platform. Ming must now decide how he will build his frame of reference and which clock he will use as his reference clock. He cannot use the Max reference clock because the clocks on the train move with respect to the station platform, and we know that in order for the Einstein synchronization process to work every pair of clocks that are being synchronized must be at rest with respect to each other. Moreover, if Ming would try to use the reference clock of Max, he would be selecting a reference clock for himself differently than Max. Namely, Max used a reference clock that was *at rest from Max's point of view on the platform*. To proceed in a symmetric way, not differently from Max, Ming should introduce a reference clock on the train. So, let us assume that Ming mounts a reference clock on the train at the door of the middle car where his reference point is located. Then Ming mounts other identical clocks along the floor of the train and synchronizes them with his reference clock.

How does he do that? He uses light according to the same Einstein procedure that Max adopted, except that Ming does everything on the train instead of doing it on the platform. Namely, when Ming sets up a new clock, he sends a pulse of light to his reference clock and waits for the reflected pulse to come back. Then he sets the new clock display by applying the required amount of turns on the clock's dial. He finds the required amount of turns using the Einstein procedure for synchronization of his clocks. Ming's procedure is the same as Max's in the sense that Ming carries out steps that look to him exactly the same way as the steps that Max carried out appeared to Max. *Nothing distinguishes one of the observers from the other in how they go about their measurement procedures.* After Ming has mounted and synchronized clocks on the floor of the train, he can find the time of every event by reading the display of the particular clock that is located at the same place on the train where the event occurs.

As a result, we have two sets of coordinates associated with every event. One set is measured by Ming, and he obtains x_{Ming} and t_{Ming}, and another set is measured by Max, who obtains x_{Max} and t_{Max} for the same event. This means that *each and every event has a pair of space and time coordinates assigned by Ming and another pair of space and time coordinates assigned by Max.*

The next problem we encounter is that in order to compare the velocities they obtain, Max and Ming must use rulers of the same length and clocks that have the same period of ticking. This can only be achieved by making sure that Ming has rulers that are made in exactly the same way as the rulers of Max, and that the clocks that Ming uses are made in exactly the same way as the clocks of Max. And in order not to introduce any asymmetry between Max and Ming, we must make sure that each of them builds and handles his instruments in a completely symmetric way. Let us assume that it is so. What comes next?

Let us observe now that there is an intrinsic difficulty involved in an attempt to relate the results of measurements of velocity of some object performed by Max and Ming. *The difficulty is that they use different space and time coordinates for all events, and they know how to measure the velocity of a given object only in terms of their own frames of reference. But they do not know yet how the results of one of them should, in principle, be related to the results of the other.* Strictly speaking, we have found no way yet of deciding whether the results obtained by Ming and Max agree or do not agree with each other. In the pre-Einstein way of thinking, this problem was overlooked and the time coordinates of Ming and Max were arbitrarily assumed to be identical. But what if they are not identical?

When we discussed the measurement of velocity in the previous sections using the pre-Einstein way of thinking, both observers were reading time from the station clock and were obtaining equal readings, assuming that they could read the time instantly from a distance. We have now abandoned this assumption as not quite reasonable because it is neither precisely possible nor precisely correct from the point of view of logic. It is not reasonable because reading of time from a distance takes time. *The problem with the delay in reading time at a distance was ignored in the pre-Einstein reasoning.* In the reasoning that we are carrying out now, the problem of reading time of events at a distance is solved using Einstein's definition of simultaneity and a network of clocks. But this solution applies only to the clocks that are at rest with respect to an observer. We are thus forced to introduce two separate sets of clocks, one for Max and one for Ming. Therefore, we cannot say any more that we know in advance how the time coordinates of Max and Ming should compare and, necessarily, we now have to go through a sequence of steps of guessing, checking, and deducing the right relationship, trying to establish what makes sense logically and what comes out of experiments regarding time and speed. How are the time readings of Ming and Max related to each other for one and the same physical event?

Fortunately, Einstein and other physicists have spent years on studies of the issues involved, and we can take advantage of their results in the discussion that follows. What truly counts in that discussion is that Max knows exactly what he does in his frame of reference in order to measure his coordinates of events, and that Ming knows exactly what he does in his frame of reference in order to measure his coordinates of events. *How the results that they obtain in their frames of reference are connected to each other, how they should be compared with each other, and what conclusions can be drawn can only be analyzed after we understand the* **relationship** *between the coordinates that they measure in their frames of reference for the same events.* We cannot arbitrarily decide how the time coordinates of Ming and Max are related, and we need an explanation.[1]

We know from the constancy of the speed of light that the relationship between space and time coordinates x_{Max} and t_{Max} and coordinates x_{Ming} and t_{Ming} cannot be correctly given by the pre-Einstein theory. The correct relationship can be close to the pre-Einstein Equations 12.1 and 12.2 (see Chapter 12, page 146) only when the velocity v of Ming with respect to Max is **small** in comparison to the speed of light c and when the observers consider only processes that involve small velocities. But when we want to understand the energy and the speed of light absorbed in the matchbox, we are dealing with two kinds of velocities, the small velocity v and the speed of light itself, and we need to explain what to do for all velocities. So, if the correct relationship between the space and time coordinates of events in the Ming and Max frames of reference is not given by Equations 12.1 and 12.2, then what is it?

In order to answer this question, we shall consider some carefully defined events and analyze relationships between the coordinates that Max and Ming obtain for these events. Eventually, we will extrapolate our reasoning to all events and determine the required relationship.

In order to define the first event, let us consider a conductor who rides on the train and always stands at the door in the car where the reference point of Ming is located. Let us assume that the conductor wants to tell the driver of the locomotive that everything is in order and sends him a sign using a pulse of light from his flashlight. Suppose that he sends the pulse at the moment when he is passing the reference point of Max on the platform. This means that the event of producing the pulse in the flashlight has coordinates $x_{Max} = 0$ and $x_{Ming} = 0$. What *time* coordinates does this event have according to Max and according to Ming?

Since the event of producing the pulse coincides with the event in which the reference clocks of Ming and Max are passing by each other, and since Max and Ming have already set their reference clocks in such a way that both these clocks are displaying time 0 when they are passing by each other, the event of producing the pulse of light by the conductor must have the Max time coordinate $t_{Max} = 0$ and the Ming time coordinate $t_{Ming} = 0$. Let us call the event of producing the pulse by the name *Producing*, which is coined to indicate what the event means in physical terms and to help us in further thinking about the event.

Let us now introduce *two other events.* Let the first of these events be that in which the driver of the locomotive is, using a mirror, reflecting the pulse back to the conductor. He does that as a sign of confirmation that everything is fine at the front end of the train. Let us call the event of reflecting the pulse by the driver *Reflecting*. The event *Reflecting* happens in the locomotive, where the driver is.

Let the second of the two events that we are now introducing be the event in which the reflected pulse of light is received back by the conductor. Let us call the event of receiving the reflected pulse by the conductor *Receiving*. The event *Receiving* happens in the middle car of the train at the same place where the reference clock of Ming is located and where the conductor stands. This is the same place, looking from the train, where the event *Producing* initially occurred. For Max on the platform, the train moves and the events *Producing* and *Receiving* happen at different places.

The events *Producing*, *Reflecting*, and *Receiving* can be itemized as follows.

Physical Description of Events
Producing, Reflecting, **and** *Receiving*

Event *Producing* = The conductor is standing at the reference clock of Ming in the middle car on the train, and he is producing a pulse of light.

Event *Reflecting* = The pulse is arriving where the driver is standing in the locomotive, and the driver is reflecting the pulse back toward the conductor.

Event *Receiving* = The reflected pulse is being received by the conductor.

Suppose that Ming stands next to the conductor on the train. What does he see when he observes the sequence of events *Producing, Reflecting,* and *Receiving?*

When the conductor is producing his pulse of light, the reference clock of Ming (this is the clock that Ming uses as his main clock on the train; see Chapter 12) is displaying 0. Ming and the conductor see the pulse going down the corridor toward the locomotive. They know the pulse will be reflected by the driver, and they are waiting for the reflected pulse to come back. The event *Receiving* happens when the reflected pulse arrives back at the reference clock of Ming.

We know that in the real world, Ming finds experimentally that light travels in both directions on his train with the **same speed *c.*** We do not understand yet how it may come about that all observers see light as having always the same speed *c,* but we have to accept the fact that it is so when we describe what happens. And since the light travels from the conductor to the driver and then from the driver to the conductor over the same distance and with the same speed *c,* it takes the light twice longer to go forth and back than it takes the light to go one way. Let us denote the amount of time that the pulse needs to go one way according to Ming by *T.* The total time of waiting by Ming and the conductor for the return of the pulse is *2T.*

Now, let us identify **one more event** as the one in which the reference clock of Ming displays on its face time *T,* which means the time equal to the middle value between the times of the events *Producing* and *Receiving.* Since the display of time *T* appears on the face of Ming's reference clock at the *middle time* between the events *Producing* and *Receiving,* we will name the additional event the *Midtime* event.

For Ming, the event *Midtime* is happening *simultaneously* with the event *Reflecting.* To explain why, we remind the reader that the event *Reflecting* is the act of reflecting the pulse of light by the driver. The event *Midtime* and the event *Reflecting* are simultaneous according to Ming because they both occur at time *T.* The definition of simultaneity of events that we are now using in the case of events *Midtime* and *Reflecting* is exactly the same as the one used in the Einstein procedure for synchronization of clocks that was described in Chapter 13, page 152.

Physical Description of Event *Midtime*

Event *Midtime* = The reference clock of Ming displays time *T.*

We are now prepared to ask the key question, *Can the two events Reflecting and Midtime, which are simultaneous according to Ming, be also seen as simultaneous by Max?* The answer we are heading for is no, Max cannot consider the events *Reflecting* and *Midtime* as simultaneous even though

Ming sees them as simultaneous. But if simultaneity for Max and Ming is not the same, it means that their time coordinates for events cannot be the same. *If they differ, it is tantamount to saying that time is not absolute but changes from one frame of reference to another.*

HOW MAX SEES THE FOUR SELECTED EVENTS

The point to show is that although Ming considers the events *Reflecting* and *Midtime* as simultaneous, Max considers these events as happening at different times. Let us begin to understand why the difference is inevitable. Max sees that pulses of light that physically connect the events always move with the speed c, exactly the same as for Ming. This fact is verified experimentally. Our imagery of what Max sees will be based on that fact. The reader should bear in mind that what follows concerns how the four events look like only from the point of view of Max.

The event *Producing* happens at the Max time $t_{Max\ Producing} = 0$, which is exactly when the Ming reference clock on the train passes by the reference clock of Max on the platform. The event *Producing* happens where the reference clock of Max is located. Therefore, the event *Producing* must have the Max space coordinate $x_{Max\ Producing} = 0$.

The event *Reflecting* is seen by Max in a way that is easiest to imagine in relationship to the event *Producing*. That is to say, Max determines time and space coordinates for the event *Reflecting* by tracing the pulse that was produced by the conductor over its entire path of travel. Suppose there are carefully mounted light-sensitive devices along the platform, and Max can see from their displays where the pulse is at any given moment during its travel. After being produced, the pulse travels along the moving train. Max sees that the pulse travels not only the length of the train between the conductor and the driver, but also an additional distance by which the locomotive has moved forward in the meantime. Unlike the conductor, who always sees himself as standing still at his reference point on the train and the driver as standing always at a *fixed* distance from that reference point, Max sees both of them as moving. The conductor is moving away from Max's reference point on the platform where the event *Producing* occurs, and the driver is also moving forward. Therefore, the pulse of light must travel over the length of the train *plus* the distance by which the driver and the whole train have moved during the period when the pulse was in flight. *This means that according to Max, the pulse travels for a longer time than the time required for light to travel only over the fixed distance that separates the conductor and driver seen by Max as they ride on the train.* Moreover, the conductor sees the pulse as traveling forth and back over equal distances, independently of how fast the train is moving from the Max point of view. In contrast, Max sees the distance traveled by the pulse as depending on how fast the train is going with respect to the platform. In other words, the observer on the train and the observer on the platform see the events very differently located in space and time that they know how to measure in their own frames of reference.

What Einstein thought and did was to figure out the way in which these two frames of reference could be related. This was only possible when he truly understood that measurements of time by two observers, like our Ming and Max, could be well-defined by each of them, but their definitions did not have to imply that both observers would assign the same time to the same events.

There is an aspect of our description of the event *Reflecting* that deserves special emphasis because of what it says about the concepts of prediction and precision. Since Max tracks the pulse of light from the moment when he sees that it is being produced to the moment when he sees that it is being reflected, he can say that the distance the pulse travels must be equal to the speed of light times the duration of the flight of the pulse. Knowing that the distance the pulse travels is equal to the space coordinate $x_{Max\ Reflecting}$ and that the time of travel is equal to the time coordinate $t_{Max\ Reflecting}$, we must conclude that the space coordinate and the time coordinate of the event *Reflecting* that Max obtains are related to each other by a mathematically precise relationship: distance equals speed times time. All events that we discuss can be analyzed using this type of logically necessary relations, based on the constancy of the speed of light, and this is what enabled Einstein to predict with mathematical precision how the time of the event *Midtime* is related to the time of the event *Reflecting* according to Max. So, let us continue with our analysis.

The event *Receiving* comes next. By tracing the movement of the pulse of light, as we did above for the event *Reflecting*, we can also find a precise relation that connects $t_{Max\ Receiving}$ to $t_{Max\ Reflecting}$. Appendix C explains in detail how one can do this.

The event *Midtime* can now be analyzed using the imagery that we have developed for events *Producing*, *Reflecting*, and *Receiving*. We remind the reader that our key unanswered question is whether the events *Midtime* and *Reflecting* can be considered by Max to be simultaneous. Remember that Ming considers these two events to be simultaneous. For him, the time difference between the event *Producing* and the event *Receiving* is 2*T*. Therefore, half of that time, which is *T*, is the same for the events *Midtime* and *Reflecting*, according to Ming.

How can Max obtain his time reading for the event *Midtime?* From his point of view, the reference clock of Ming is always moving with a steady velocity *v* and the midtime *T* must be displayed on its face in the middle of the clock's travel between the events *Producing* and *Receiving*. Since the event *Producing* happens at $t_{Max\ Producing} = 0$, the event *Midtime* must occur, from Max's point of view, at the time equal to the half of $t_{Max\ Receiving}$. Since we know that the Max time coordinates of the events *Receiving* and *Reflecting* are precisely related to each other (Appendix C shows this explicitly in Equation C.1), we can now also precisely predict how $t_{Max\ Midtime}$ is related to $t_{Max\ Reflecting}$ by dividing $t_{Max\ Receiving}$ by 2.

SIMULTANEITY DEPENDS ON THE OBSERVER

In order for the events *Midtime* and *Reflecting* to be simultaneous for Max, he would have to obtain that $t_{Max\ Midtime}$ is equal to $t_{Max\ Reflecting}$. But the exact relation that he finds (see Appendix C) is

$$t_{Max\ Midtime} = \frac{c}{c + v} t_{Max\ Reflecting}. \qquad [14.1]$$

In this relation, there is a coefficient of proportionality between the time coordinates of events *Midtime* and *Reflecting*, which is equal to $\frac{c}{c+v}$.

If v is zero, which means that the train does not move with respect to Max, the velocity v in the denominator of the coefficient is zero and the coefficient equals $\frac{c}{c}$, which is 1. And in this case, the time coordinates $t_{Max\ Midtime}$ and $t_{Max\ Reflecting}$ will coincide. It should be so when the train does not move with respect to Max and the Einstein definition of simultaneity for Max is the same as for Ming.

In contrast, when Ming and Max are in motion with respect to each other, the velocity v in the denominator is not zero and it adds to the speed of light c. The denominator is greater than the numerator. The coefficient $\frac{c}{c+v}$ in Equation 14.1 is smaller than 1, and $t_{Max\ Midtime}$ will be different from $t_{Max\ Reflecting}$. Thus, the Max time coordinate of the event *Midtime* is smaller than we would expect it to be assuming it should be equal to the Max time coordinate of the event *Reflecting*. The time it takes the pulse of light produced by the conductor to catch up with the moving locomotive is longer than the time needed by the pulse to go just over the length of the train, from Max's point of view. The time of the reflected pulse going back to meet the conductor is shorter than the time needed to travel just over the length of the train, as seen by Max. The net effect turns out to be (and this is described in detail in Appendix C) that $t_{Max\ Receiving}$ is less than 2 times $t_{Max\ Reflecting}$, and the half of $t_{Max\ Receiving}$ ends up to be shorter than $t_{Max\ Reflecting}$. The bottom line is that the time readings that Max obtains for the two events, *Reflecting* and *Midtime*, are not the same, while Ming obtains the same readings of time for these two events.

Two events that are separated by a distance and occur simultaneously for Ming do not occur simultaneously for Max if Ming moves with respect to Max. This major result destroys thousands of years of belief by all people that time is absolute.

Since our discussion is not at all specific to the example of Max and Ming, we must conclude that the same holds for all events separated by a distance and all observers who move with respect to each other. If two events are separated by some distance, any two events by any distance at any place in the universe, and if they occur at the same time according to one observer, they do not occur at the same time according to another observer who moves with respect to the first. The experimental discovery of the constancy of the speed of light, which we have built into our reasoning, implies that these observers measure time differently.

The absolute concept of time that was the building block in our education about the world is not valid. The concept of absolute time is approximate and works for us only because the velocities of all material objects we deal with on Earth are very small in comparison to the speed of light, and we need not care about the small corrections that could be made. But, for example, the energy stored in the atomic nucleus, which is made useable in nuclear power plants, is governed by the laws of Nature that take into account that time is not absolute. And in France, over 70% of electric power is drawn from that source, about which only very few people understand how it became possible. And it is impossible to understand how our Sun shines without understanding the Einstein concept of time.

15

Einstein's Theory of Relativity

We have seen in the previous chapter that events simultaneous according to Ming cannot be simultaneous according to Max if the observers move with respect to each other and we know that both of them measure the speed of light to be the same. Assuming the result that the simultaneity of events depends on the observer, we must conclude that time coordinates of events in the frames of reference of Max and Ming cannot be plainly equal as it was taken for granted in the pre-Einstein worldview. But what is the right relation?

We had a glimpse of what change might be required regarding time coordinates (we have not discussed what change might be involved regarding space coordinates) when we discussed the concepts of simultaneity and discovered that they are not the same for Max and Ming. We were focusing on two events, *Reflecting* and *Midtime*, and we looked at them first from the point of view of Ming and then from the point of view of Max. According to the Einstein definition, these two events were simultaneous for Ming. But when we studied what Max would see, we concluded that the two events had time coordinates $t_{Max\ Reflecting}$ and $t_{Max\ Midtime}$, *both measured by Max independently of what Ming was obtaining for his time coordinates of these events*, which had to be different when the velocity v was not zero. The greater the velocity v, the more $t_{Max\ Reflecting}$ and $t_{Max\ Midtime}$ differ from each other because the coefficient $\frac{c}{c+v}$ becomes smaller (see Equation 14.1 on page 162) and smaller when v gets larger. But if the velocity v tends toward zero, this coefficient becomes indistinguishable from 1. Thus, when the velocity v is zero and Ming and Max do not move with respect to each other, their concepts of simultaneity coincide. In this case, Max says that the two events that are simultaneous to Ming are also simultaneous to him.

So, if we are asking now how the time coordinates t_{Max} and t_{Ming} for the same events are related, we may think that they should be practically equal when the velocity v is very small and they may begin to differ considerably when v increases. In the case of velocity v that is very small in comparison to c, but not zero, we may expect that t_{Max} is almost equal to t_{Ming}. There may be a coefficient of proportionality between them that is very near to 1. For Earthly velocities v, it is so near to 1 that we think that the equation $t_{Max} = t_{Ming}$ is exact. But it may be that there is some other truth in here that could be expressed by saying that instead of the relationship $t_{Max} = t_{Ming}$ we have $t_{Max} = At_{Ming}$, where the number A hardly differs from 1 when v is small. But when v increases, A may be increasingly different from 1, and we should figure out how this number A depends on the velocity v with which Ming moves with respect to Max.

The issue of what the number A (dependent on v) stands for is different here from the issue that we discussed in the previous chapter, where we were only concerned with the Max time coordinates of the events $t_{Max\ Reflecting}$ and $t_{Max\ Midtime}$. Nevertheless, the idea that the tiny differences between how Max and Ming measure time in our example can be expressed by saying that $t_{Max} = At_{Max}$ and asking, What number does the symbol A stand for? We need to figure that out in order to understand how $E = mc^2$ comes about.

Einstein was pondering the problem of finding what such A might be. He imagined different bodies and pulses of light as seen by two observers in motion. He considered many examples of events in which pulses of light met with material objects or traveled between them, as in the case of the events *Producing, Reflecting, Receiving,* and *Midtime* in our story. All these material bodies and pulses of light always moved with some steady velocities. The times of their travel were always given by the distances of their travel divided by the velocities. And the distances they traveled were given by their velocities multiplied by time. Thus, the relationships between the coordinates of the events that he was analyzing could only be of the form in which a space coordinate of some event according to one observer was a combination of the time and space coordinates of the same event according to another observer, with some specific coefficients. Also, the time coordinate of the event found by one observer could only be a combination of the time and space coordinates of the same event according to the other observer of the same event. Having concluded that the relationships he was looking for should be just combinations with some unknown coefficients, Einstein focused on the question whether it was possible that a logically consistent set of coefficients could be determined.

He assumed that such coefficients existed, and he studied the implications of the concept of simultaneity that he defined precisely for all observers using pulses of light that traveled forth and back between the events he considered. He observed that there indeed existed a consistent way to describe the relationship between the coordinates of two observers like our Max and Ming using a small set of coefficients such as our hypothetical number A.[1]

When one tries to find the number A, it is useful to observe that A depends only on the velocity v of motion of Ming with respect to Max and on the speed of light c. *There is only one and the same coefficient A for coordinates of all events that Max and Ming can consider.* Therefore, one can find A by considering some selected events for which one knows exactly the time coordinates that both Max and Ming should obtain. The idea is that if we can find an event for which we know precisely by how much we should *multiply* the time coordinate of Ming to obtain the time coordinate of Max for that particular event, we know that A must be equal to that factor.

DERIVATION OF A FROM A MODEL FOR CLOCKS

We can find A by answering the following question: How much time passes from the point of view of Max between the event *Producing* and the event in which Ming's reference clock displays time T_0? We will define the value of T_0 in such a way that we will be able to unambiguously deduce how much time must pass from the point of view of Max.

First, we construct the reference clock of Max. The clock stands on the platform. Imagine a solid stand fixed on the platform next to the tracks. The stand holds a mirror at height H above its base, as shown in Figure 15.1. There is a bulb and a counter mounted at the base of the stand. The bulb is lit for a moment, and a pulse of light goes up to the mirror where it is reflected back to the counter. The counter displays a new value of time for every pulse of light it receives. When the counter receives a pulse of light, it sends a pulse of current to the bulb and the bulb flashes again. A new pulse of light goes up to the mirror, it gets reflected, comes back to the counter, triggers the counter to display another count, and the bulb is lit again. The time interval in which the pulse of light is going up from the bulb to the mirror is equal to the time interval in which the pulse goes down from the mirror to the counter. Each of these intervals is equal to half of the total time that the pulse needs to make a full cycle of going up and down. Let us arrange that the total amount of time that the pulse of light needs to pass from the bulb to the mirror and back to the counter is precisely the time T_0 that we need in our reasoning to find the coefficient A (it will not matter how long the time interval T_0 is in terms of seconds for determination of the coefficient A). Thus, we define the time T_0 as the duration of one full cycle of our model clock. Every time the pulse of light

Figure 15.1   A model of a clock on the platform

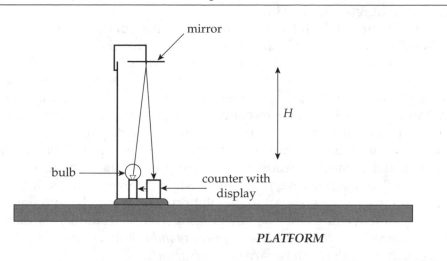

reaches the counter, the counter changes display to a new value that says that another period T_0 has just passed. This periodic process constitutes the mechanism of our model clock.

Since the pulses of light produced by the bulb travel at the speed of light c up and down over the distance H, the height H is translated into time of how long it takes light to fly up and down that height. We observe that the height H of the clock is equal to half of the path of the pulse when it goes up and down. Therefore, H *is equal to the speed of light c times half of the time T_0.*

Typical wristwatches tick once every second, which is a unit of time. A computer clock may tick once in about one billionth part of a second, which is a much shorter unit of time. Our model clock ticks once during every interval of T_0, and T_0 is the unit with which it measures time.

After Max sets up his reference clock this way, he builds and places identical clocks along the platform. Then he synchronizes all of his clocks with his reference clock. The unit of time on all clocks of Max is T_0 and they all simultaneously display numbers $1T_0$, $2T_0$, $3T_0$, and so on, in the frame of reference of Max.

Ming carries out an identical procedure on the train. His reference clock has the same height H. Since the speed of light for Ming is also c, Ming's clocks have the same unit of time T_0 in Ming's frame of reference as Max's clocks have in Max's reference frame. Note that we say that the units of time are the same even though we have not compared them with each other. We can do so on the basis of our assumption that Max and Ming build their clocks using identical procedures in their frames of reference. Ming distributes his clocks on the train and synchronizes them so that they all simultaneously display numbers $1T_0$, $2T_0$, $3T_0$, and so on, in the frame of reference of Ming.

The event in which the Ming reference clock displays time T_0 is now defined as the event in which the pulse of light that traveled from the bulb to the mirror and back to the counter in the Ming reference clock reaches the counter. The same event can be identified by Max who looks at the Ming clock from his (Max's) frame of reference on the platform. We know that in the Einstein theory of relativity, the time reading of Max (read on Max's clocks) for every event that happens on the display of Ming's reference clock that moves with the train is related by multiplication by the coefficient A to the time reading for the same event that is being displayed on the face of the Ming reference clock when the event occurs. If the train was not moving with respect to the platform, we would have A equal to 1 and the time readings for one tick of Ming's clock would be the same for both observers. *In this case we do not need to think about A. But when the train moves with velocity v, that coefficient differs from 1.*

In order to proceed, let us now analyze Figure 15.2. This figure shows the reference clock of Ming from the point of view of Max. The clock is riding on the train (the train is not drawn) to the right with the velocity v. Four successive positions of the clock in motion are shown in Figure 15.2. *These are not four clocks but one clock at four different moments as seen by Max.* At the time $t_{Max} = 0$, a pulse of light is sent from the bulb and it is seen by Max moving diagonally upward to meet the mirror at time $t_{Max} = \frac{1}{2}T$, where T is the time of a full cycle of the moving clock from Max's point of view. The pulse is reflected diagonally downward by the mirror to meet the counter at time $t_{Max} = T$. In the meantime, the clock moves with the train and changes its position with the constant velocity v. At every moment, the distance over which the clock has moved along the platform is given by its velocity times the time of its travel, both measured by Max in his frame of reference. The clock moves from $x_{Max} = 0$ at time $t_{Max} = 0$, to $x_{Max} = \frac{1}{2}vT$ at time $t_{Max} = \frac{1}{2}T$, and to $x_{Max} = vT$ at time $t_{Max} = T$. The last (fourth) image of the clock on the right-hand side of the figure depicts the situation in the middle of the second cycle of the Ming reference clock. For readers who are interested in the details of the path of light in the moving clock, the distances that characterize the path are shown in Figure F.1 in Appendix F.

During the first half of the time period T, the pulse of light that travels only up inside the reference clock of Ming must, according to Max, move over the diagonal path from the bulb position at the moment of sending the pulse to the position of the mirror at the height H at the moment of reflection of the pulse. The mirror moves horizontally and *when the pulse catches up to the mirror the latter has already moved by half of the segment vT* that the moving clock moves over with velocity v in the entire period T. After the pulse of light is reflected from the mirror at the height H, it continues its flight diagonally downward, aiming at the counter that moves in the meantime over the entire distance vT to the new position where the

Figure 15.2   Snapshots of Ming's reference clock in motion as seen by Max.

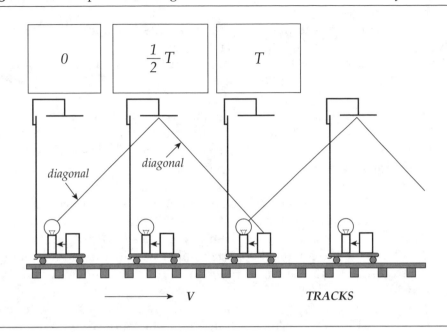

pulse and counter meet each other, completing one cycle of Ming's clock as seen by Max. Remember, the train is always moving with the velocity v with respect to Max. The diagonal path downward has the same length as the diagonal path upward. Each of them is longer than the height H itself because of the horizontal motion of Ming's clock from the point of view of Max.

The total length of the path of the pulse of light in the moving clock is twice the diagonal path. The diagonal path extends to the height H vertically and over half of the distance vT horizontally. The diagonal path in Ming's clock is seen by Max, and it is to be compared with the only-vertical path of the pulse of light in Max's clock that stands on the platform. In the clock standing on the platform, the path of light that Max sees is only vertical, no diagonals, and the total path is twice the height H.

Remember, now, that Ming's clock is moving only from Max's point of view. *It is always at rest from Ming's point of view.* Thus, the path that the pulse of light moves across from Max's point of view is longer than the path that the same pulse moves from Ming's point of view. Ming sees only H up and down, no diagonal, and Max sees the full diagonal path. *But when we realize that we have to accept the fact that the pulse of light moves with the same speed c according to each observer, we have to conclude that Ming's clock must appear to Max as having a longer period of ticking than the identical Max's clock has standing on the platform.* Namely, the longer distance traveled by the pulse divided by the same speed c gives a longer period of flight. Appendix F shows how the length of the diagonal path can be calculated in terms of the height H and the horizontal extension, vT, of the path traveled by the clock.

One can compare the diagonal distance passed by light in the clock moving with the train to the height H of a clock. It needs to be done with mathematical precision. This is an important step for quantitative determination of the coefficient A. When *we divide the length of H by the speed of light c*, we get half of T_0. Similarly, when *we divide the length of the diagonal segment by the same speed of light c*, we get half of T. Therefore, a precise relation between the height H and the length of the diagonal segment in the moving clock tells us how the period T is related to the period T_0, and thus will determine A. What should we expect about how A will depend on the velocity v?

The relationship between the height H and the length of the diagonal segment depends on the velocity v of Ming with respect to Max because the length of the horizontal path of the moving clock depends on the velocity v. The larger v, the longer the horizontal shift and the longer the diagonal path, and, using the same speed of light, the longer period T in comparison to T_0.

When the velocity v is zero, there is no horizontal stretch to take into account and $T = T_0$. This means that when Max and Ming do not move with respect to each other their clocks run the same, and $A = 1$. For puny Earthly velocities v, the horizontal stretch is so tiny in comparison to the height H that the correction is practically invisible. However, if Ming travels with respect to Max with velocity near the speed of light c itself, it takes the pulse of light almost forever to catch up to the mirror, and then to the counter, to complete just one tick of the Ming clock. This means that when the velocity v is near the speed of light, the Ming counting of time appears to Max as slower by a giant factor, and we expect that A will be huge when the velocity v is near c, a situation we never encounter in our daily lives. In such a strange situation, our Figure 15.2 could not be drawn on a page in a book because it would have to extend very, very far horizontally on the paper.

But one can always calculate how T is related to T_0, depending on the ratio of the velocity v to the speed of light c. The result is that T and T_0 are proportional to each other so that T is equal to some number greater than or equal to 1 times T_0. Let us call this number "gamma." Physicists are used to denoting this number with the Greek letter γ and the name has a long tradition. Thus, we have $T = \gamma T_0$ in our model of clocks. For readers who are interested in how to derive the coefficient gamma, it is calculated in Appendix F. We show a plot of the coefficient gamma as a function of the velocity v of Ming with respect to Max in Figure 15.3. We see that when the velocity v is very small in comparison to the speed of light, the factor gamma is nearly 1. When the velocity v is near the speed of light, the factor gamma can be very large.

But the value of our comparison of the two clocks, one standing on the platform and one in motion with respect to the platform, lies not just in the

Figure 15.3   The Einstein factor gamma is plotted as a function of the velocity v of one observer with respect to the other. The velocity may be anywhere in the range between 0 and the speed of light c. The factor gamma ranges from 1 when v is zero to infinity when v approaches c.

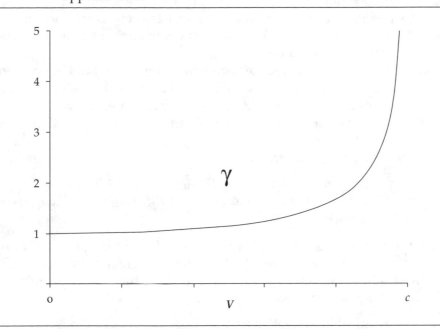

fact that the moving clock has period gamma times longer for Max than the period of the clock standing on the platform. *The great value and the true meaning of the example of two clocks is that in the Einstein theory of time, expressed in the mathematically precise relation* $t_{Max} = A t_{Ming}$, *the number A that relates readings of time by Max,* t_{Max}, *with readings of time by Ming,* t_{Ming}, *for all events, is equal to gamma. And gamma depends on the relative velocity v of the observers in a way that can be calculated with mathematical precision. Therefore, the coefficient A = γ is a known function of the velocity v and the speed of light c.*

Since we know exactly how gamma depends on the velocity v of Ming in motion with respect to Max, and since the relationship between time readings t_{Max} and t_{Ming} for all events involves one and the same coefficient $A = \gamma$, we conclude that the coefficient A in Einstein's theory of time is completely predictable and no longer constitutes an unknown. There exist other ways to find the value of the coefficient A. One is given by a mathematical procedure described in Appendix E. We mention that alternative mathematical procedure because it *predicts* the possibility of existence of a universal speed c for all observers. The factor gamma of unique value for every velocity v is required as a logical implication of **the principle of relativity**[2] that says that *all observers in steady motion are equally valid observers of the world,* none is privileged, none is better or worse an observer of the world than others.[3]

At this point, the authors of this book believe that the reader can accept and become a mental owner of the fact that exact mathematical expressions can be found for coefficients such as A, and that one can find the equations that relate the time and space coordinates of Max and Ming in Einstein's theory[4] and replace the pre-Einstein Equations 12.1 and 12.2. Einstein's precise theory of the relationship between the frames of reference of two observers who move with respect to each other with a steady velocity v has many consequences.

One of the main consequences concerns the paradox of the constancy of the speed of light.[5] One can carefully trace step by step what Max does on the platform and what Ming does on the train when they measure the velocity of some object. In the pre-Einstein theory,[6] one thinks that

1. Max and Ming have the same time coordinates.

2. They have different space coordinates because Ming is on the train and Max is on the station platform, and the train moves with respect to the platform.

3. If Mary[7] moves forward on the train with velocity v_{Ming}, Max sees her as moving with velocity v_{Max}, which is greater than v_{Ming} by the addition of the velocity v of the train. Thus, the velocities are added: v_{Max} is equal to v_{Ming} plus v.

4. The result that velocities add implies that in principle there is no limit to how large a velocity of an object can be. Physical objects can move faster than light.

In the Einstein theory, one concludes[8] that

1. Max and Ming inevitably have **different** time coordinates when they move with respect to each other because simultaneity for one of them is not the same as for the other. The factor gamma reflects the difference in counting time by the two observers.

2. They have different space coordinates because Ming is on the train and Max is on the station platform, and the train moves with respect to the platform.

3. If Mary moves on the train with velocity v_{Ming}, Max sees her as moving with velocity v_{Max}. But v_{Max} is **not** related to v_{Ming} only by addition because the factor gamma gets involved. The involvement of gamma implies a change in the relationship between the velocities. Thus, the rule of adding velocities, which says that v_{Max} is equal to v_{Ming} plus v, is now changed to a new rule, which says that the sum is multiplied by a factor that originates from gamma. This extra factor is known exactly in Einstein's theory.[9] And the extra

factor implies that when Ming sees a pulse of light moving with the velocity v_{Ming} equal to the speed of light c, Max also sees the same pulse of light as moving with the speed c. There is no addition of v to the speed of light.

4. The fact that the velocities v_{Ming} and v combine to produce v_{Max} not by plain addition but also by multiplication with the extra factor that originates in gamma implies for all observers that no object can move faster than light.

When the velocities v or v_{Ming} are very small in comparison to c, the new extra factor is again so close to 1 that the rule of adding velocities works almost perfectly well. For example, *when we consider a person running with a jogging velocity of about 4 meters per second on a train that rides 100 km per hour, the factor we are talking about is greater than 1 only by about one-millionth of one-millionth (one trillionth) of one-tenth of 1 percent.* But when Ming observes a pulse of light, he gets the result that v_{Ming} for the pulse is equal to c and Max obtains v_{Max} of the same pulse also equal to c.

The existence of the factor gamma introduces extremely small corrections to how we see events in moving frames of our daily life. But when the effects of velocity v of relative motion of observers are investigated with great precision, the factor gamma becomes visible, the concepts of time of the observers are no longer identical, and the speed of light does not change from observer to observer at all. This result explains the paradox of the constancy of the speed of light in terms of the theory of the relationship between observers.

The reader may now be rightfully puzzled because the fact that Max obtains the same speed of light as Ming was built into our assumptions about how Max and Ming construct their frames of reference from the beginning. One may wonder whether there is anything new coming out from the reasoning other than what we put in our reasoning at the start. We said at the start that we should accept the constancy of the speed of light and we arrive at the conclusion that it, indeed, is so. Are we not just running in circles? What is the big deal?

The big deal is the discovery that when two observers in relative motion measure time coordinates of the same events, they do not obtain the same results. Two separate events that are simultaneous for one observer are not simultaneous for the other. By deriving and applying gamma to the relationship between their frames of reference, Einstein explained how it may happen that the speed of light is always constant and time is not. A logically built theory of the relationship between the frames of reference of two observers, based on facts, produced a consistent picture, a different one than people had before Einstein.

Even though we did assume in the course of our reasoning that Max and Ming obtain the same speed of light, we did not know initially that the time would come out as not absolute and that this is the way out of the paradox of the speed of light. Thus, we are not running in circles but discover the meaning and consequences of the relativity of time. Einstein broke the circle that existed in the pre-Einstein theory. And in breaking it, he found that the concept of time is different than everybody thought.

But that meant a huge change in thinking about all phenomena. Einstein was asking himself what implications the new understanding of time would have if he now carefully re-analyzed the foundations of pre-Einstein physics. Two basic concepts in physics are energy and mass, and they were considered different and unrelated to each other. When Einstein grappled with questions concerning conservation of energy in processes in which light interacted with matter, thinking about time in his new way, he discovered that energy and mass are related to each other by the speed of light. This is what we take up in the next chapter.

16

How E = mc²
Comes About

The formula $E = mc^2$ is valid for all material objects we know in the universe. The beauty of the Einstein argument for the validity of the formula is that it can be made for any material body of any mass m. One needs to imagine how the body interacts with light, just as we have illustrated using a matchbox on the table in front of Max.[1] The next step is to imagine how another observer, who is moving with respect to Max and whom we call Ming, sees the same process. But instead of the matchbox, we could also employ a star, a moon, a comet, and so on.

In order to facilitate the reader's understanding of the derivation of the formula $E = mc^2$, it will be helpful if the reader knows from the outset that the formula represents one of the most profound conclusions in the history of human thought and understanding of the world: No longer can energy, mass, and the speed of light be considered as independent concepts because they belong in one and the same interactive process of Nature. In other words, you cannot talk about energy as one variable, mass as another variable, and speed of light as a still another one. They exist only together and the formula $E = mc^2$ says how.

So, what we attempt to do in this final section is to demonstrate how several variables, apparently unrelated in the pre-Einstein approach, are brought together in the formula $E = mc^2$. We refer specifically to the energy of motion, energy of light, conservation of energy, and the factor gamma (γ) in the relationship between time coordinates of different observers. In what follows, the reader should keep in mind that in our example *the phrase "energy of motion" always refers to the energy that the matchbox has from Ming's point of view.*

We know from previous chapters that the energy of a photon of frequency f is given by the Planck constant h times the frequency f. According to Max, the right photon has the same frequency f as the left photon. The combined energy of the photons that Max sees is equal to the sum of hf plus hf, so that the sum equals $2hf$. Thus, Max sees that the matchbox absorbs the two photons with combined energy $\Delta_{Max} = 2hf$.

The law of conservation of energy in the Max frame of reference says that the energy of the matchbox *at rest* changes as a result of absorbing light. The matchbox is at rest only from Max's point of view. The amount of energy that the two photons bring into the matchbox according to Max, Δ_{Max}, carries the name of Max because the amount of energy depends on the observer. Thus, Max sees that the energy of the matchbox at rest before absorption, E_{before}, is increased, as a result of the absorption, by the amount Δ_{Max}, to the energy E_{after} that the matchbox has at rest after absorption.

Max concludes that the matchbox at rest has energy E_{after} as a result of an internal change caused by the absorbed light. Irrespective of the details of this internal change, the law of conservation of energy tells Max how to evaluate the amount of E_{after}: by adding the energy of the absorbed light to the energy that the matchbox had before absorption. But from Max's point of view, there is no connection between the increase of the internal energy of the matchbox and its mass. The idea that the increase of internal energy is related to a change in mass does not appear in the Max frame of reference. And it does not occur to Max that the mass may be changing. One needs to consider the matchbox in motion in order to see what happens with its mass, and for that we need Ming, an observer in whose frame of reference the matchbox is moving.

The mass of any object, including the matchbox, is a measure of the amount of effort required to change the velocity of the object. We have discussed the meaning of the notion of mass in the section "What Is Mass?" in Chapter 10 on page 113. But we have not seen yet how, or in what way, the change of energy due to the absorption of light might be related to the mass of the matchbox. The fact that Ming sees the matchbox as moving will tell us something new because the energy of motion that the matchbox has from Ming's point of view depends on the mass of the matchbox and its velocity. Light will change the energy of the matchbox from Ming's point of view, and this change will also influence the energy of motion of the matchbox. This latter change will tell us what happens with the mass of the matchbox.

We have to be very precise because the amount of change in mass that we are going to discover is related to the factor gamma. This factor would be equal to 1 if Ming did not move with respect to Max because in that case

Ming's time coordinate would be the same as Max's for all events. However, as soon as we consider that Ming is moving, the time coordinates of Ming and Max are not the same and the factor gamma is different from 1. We have to be very precise because the difference between gamma and 1 is incredibly small for the Earthly velocities of Ming.

The possibility to see the change in mass comes from the fact that gamma is not equal to 1 when the velocity v of Ming with respect to Max is not zero. In the pre-Einstein theory the factor gamma was absent, which means it was treated as if it was always equal to 1 and thus could not depend on the velocity v. In Earthly circumstances, the difference between gamma and 1 can be overlooked because it is incredibly small. *If v is about 10 miles per hour, the difference is about one billionth part of one billionth part of 1.* We have to stay focused and think carefully about the meaning of the statements we can make concerning what happens with the matchbox because we want to grasp the effect that is extremely small in daily life. The actual size of the change of mass that we want to identify in our reasoning is unimaginably small for a real matchbox absorbing just two photons. But we can make an experiment in our imagination and find out what happens with energy from the point of view of Ming. As a result, we will infer that $E = mc^2$.

Suppose that Max sees Ming moving from left to right with velocity v. When we change the frame of reference from Max over to Ming, we will see the matchbox (which as always is with Max) as moving toward Ming with the velocity v from right to left. Since the matchbox is moving with velocity v from Ming's point of view, it has the energy equal to the sum E_{before} plus the energy of motion that the matchbox has when it moves with the velocity v. We know from the previous chapters, and in particular from the discussion that starts on page 117 in Chapter 10, that the matchbox has the energy of motion in the eye of the observer only because it moves with respect to the observer. The energy of motion of the matchbox that Ming sees is denoted by E_{motion}. This energy can be calculated in terms of the matchbox mass m and its velocity v. Namely, E_{motion} is proportional to the mass m and to the velocity v squared in a mathematically determinable way (see Chapter 10 page 119 and Appendix A). Ming sees the energy of the matchbox before absorption as equal to the sum of the same internal energy that Max sees, E_{before}, plus the energy E_{motion} that the matchbox possesses in the Ming frame of reference because it is moving in that frame. *The energy of motion brings in the concept of mass m into the picture.*

So, how would Ming see the energy of the matchbox in the absorption process in comparison to Max? Would he find the energy conserved or would the new understanding of time imply that energy cannot be conserved for both observers? And, actually, how should one describe the energy of material bodies if time is not absolute? These and other questions like these could not be answered without further study, and Einstein was digging into the unknown, trying to find out the changes in the picture of the world that would be implied by his new theory of relationship between two frames of reference, if it was true.

In order to understand how the energy of the matchbox increases as a result of the process of absorption, we have to turn our attention to the energy of photons as seen by Ming. *We can describe the energies of the photons by multiplying their frequencies by the Planck constant h. The Planck constant is the same for all observers. But the photon frequencies are different for two observers who move with respect to each other, and this is why the energies of the individual photons are not the same for Ming as they are for Max.* We have some imagery of the energy of light and we can use this imagery to deduce what happens according to Ming. The detailed reasoning is given in Appendix H. The result is that the combined energy of the two photons as seen by Ming, Δ_{Ming}, is related to the combined energy of the same two photons as seen by Max, Δ_{Max}, by the factor gamma. In the pre-Einstein theory we had these energies equal, as if gamma was strictly 1. But gamma is not 1 and we can see the situation anew.

1. The combined energy of the two photons entering the matchbox as seen by Ming is gamma times larger than the combined energy of the two photons as seen by Max.

2. The relation described above concerns the energy of light as seen by two observers. It involves the same factor gamma that we have found earlier in the relationship between time coordinates for Max and Ming.

3. Energy is a different concept than space and time coordinates. We have not seen any reason yet for a connection between how energies are related for different observers and how coordinates are related for different observers.

4. The possibility of relating energies for two observers and finding that the energies can be and are related by the same factor gamma that relates coordinates of Max and Ming comes from the fact that we consider here the energy of photons.

5. The energy of a photon is related by the Planck constant to its *frequency* and the frequency is related to the *time interval* between signals that arrive in the observer's eye.

6. But we know that the time intervals change from observer to observer according to the factor gamma. Thus, knowing how the coordinates change with observers, one can deduce how the frequencies change and then how the energies of photons change from observer to observer. The details of this deduction are given in Appendix H.

7. Not only the energy of photons begins to involve the factor gamma, which emerges from the Einstein theory of frames of reference.

When one considers absorption of light by material bodies, the factor gamma enters the analysis of how the energies of the material bodies change. The factor gamma begins to show up in many ways and in many places in relation to different concepts that were unrelated in the pre-Einstein way of thinking. When one observer moves with respect to another, the factor gamma depends on the velocity v and begins to open our eyes to new features that we were unable to even contemplate when we were thinking that gamma was absent and when we were not able to think about consequences of the difference between gamma and 1.

There was no reason in the pre-Einstein worldview to think that the mass of the matchbox could increase when the matchbox absorbed light because the energy of the absorbed light as seen by Ming was equal to the energy of the absorbed light as seen by Max. Now, Δ_{Ming} differs from Δ_{Max} by the factor gamma. The factor gamma follows from understanding that time is not absolute. This is why it is so hard to understand how $E = mc^2$ comes about and what it means. This difficulty is the reason why we had to write such a long and complex sequence of chapters in order to come to the point where the origin and content of the formula $E = mc^2$ are within our reach.

We have two images of the same absorption process as seen from the point of view of two observers, Ming and Max, who move with respect to each other with velocity v. These are the kinds of images that Einstein was considering for the purpose of understanding what happens with the law of conservation of energy when one abandons the pre-Einstein way of thinking about time and takes into account the factor gamma in the relationship between the frames of reference.

Why would Einstein be curious about what happens with energy of light, and why would he consider the case of two observers like our Max and Ming to investigate the difference between their points of view regarding energy? The way to think about this question is to imagine how you would feel if you discovered a new way of counting time. The pre-Einstein way of understanding time, used and developed by Newton and many other physicists, was very successful in description of Nature. Planets would follow laws that Newton and his followers described with ever-increasing accuracy. The big picture worked with the concept of absolute time, and this concept of time was playing a central role in every lecture you could hear. And now imagine yourself coming to the idea that time is different. What are you going to say to the people who know that things have to fit together and that one cannot just play with crazy ideas and destroy the order already found in Nature? Well, you may try to figure out as quickly as possible whether the fundamental laws that you expect to be valid may still hold if you take your idea seriously. One of those laws, basic to everything people know, is the law of conservation of energy.

So, Einstein asked the question, Is the law of conservation of energy valid for all observers when I adopt my theory for the relationship between frames of reference of different observers in relative motion? If I assume that energy *is* conserved, what will this law imply now if time is different?

Ming sees the initial energy of the matchbox as equal to the sum of the internal energy that the matchbox has before the absorption, E_{before}, plus the energy of motion, E_{motion}, that the matchbox carries before the absorption because it moves with velocity v according to Ming. The total initial energy of the matchbox is increased in the absorption process by the combined energy of the two photons, Δ_{Ming}. Therefore, according to Ming, *if the energy is conserved,* after the absorption process is completed, the matchbox must have its energy equal to the sum of three contributions: E_{before} plus E_{motion} plus Δ_{Ming}.

The critical insight that Einstein had at this point was that Δ_{Ming} is equal to gamma times Δ_{Max} and gamma depends on the relative motion of the two observers. Therefore, if energy is to be conserved according to Ming, the absorption of light must contribute a piece to the final energy of the matchbox that depends on how fast the matchbox moves. The piece comes from the difference between gamma and 1 when the velocity v differs from 0. This means that the absorption of light may increase the energy of motion of the matchbox. Since the energy of motion is proportional to the *mass* of the matchbox, and since the velocity of the matchbox does not change in the absorption process, the increase in the energy of motion may only appear as an increase in the mass. *The possibility that there must exist a relationship between the change of energy of an object and the change of its mass when the object interacts with light was noticed by Einstein for the first time in human history.*

Having this insight, one can trace step by step how the energy of the matchbox changes in the process of absorption of two photons in the Ming frame of reference. These steps are described in Appendix I.

The key point is that the amount of change in the energy of motion of the matchbox that the absorption of light causes comes from the difference between gamma and 1. The factor gamma differs from 1 by an extremely small number. This number is extremely small because v^2 in it is *divided* by the square of the huge speed of light, c^2. (Readers interested in the details of the factor gamma can find them in Appendix G.) The c^2 in the denominator is also the reason why the discovery of the relativity of time, hidden in the smallness of the difference between gamma and 1 in Earthly circumstances, was so difficult to make. But this means also that when the factor gamma multiplies the energy of light, the resulting correction in the final energy of the matchbox due to the difference between gamma and 1 is given by v^2 times the energy of light *divided* by c^2.

As we have emphasized several times in this book, we are assuming that many readers have either forgotten their algebra if they took it, or they never took a course at all. That is why we are not presenting the algebra of a problem and instead we refer the interested reader to the Appendices, in this case Appendix I. We can assure the reader who commands basic algebra that she or he will see that the statements we are making are not a matter of our personal opinion, sloppy thinking, or lack of clear argument, but only a consequence of mathematically precise reasoning.

Thus, when gamma times the energy of light is accounted for in the total final energy of the matchbox, the part of that total final energy that is proportional to v^2, and, therefore, corresponds to motion, contains two contributions. One contribution comes from the initial energy of motion with the mass m. The other contribution comes with the energy of light divided by c^2, because the square of the velocity of the matchbox, v^2, in the difference between gamma and 1 is divided by c^2 (see Appendix I). Therefore, after absorption, the piece of the final energy of the matchbox that is proportional to v^2, the piece that corresponds to motion, can be described as a new energy of motion in which the mass m is increased by the energy of light (let us denote the energy of the light by E) divided by c^2. *The change in mass of a body is equal to the change of energy of the body divided by c^2.* The change of energy that counts here is Δ_{Max} observed by Max, for whom the matchbox is at rest.

Finally, if the mass of a body may be increased by absorbing light, we can imagine that in principle the entire mass m could be built up from scratch by light. The resulting mass of the body would be equal to the total energy of light; let us denote it now by E, divided by c^2. But if the energy is conserved, the resulting body must have the same energy E as the absorbed light. Therefore, the mass m of the body must be equal to the energy E of the body at rest divided by c^2. By the same token, the energy E of the body must be equal to its mass m times c^2. This conclusion is usually written as a formula $E = mc^2$.

Nobody in 1905, including Einstein, had the slightest idea whether this suggestion for a relationship between the energy of a body at rest and its mass did or did not make sense in the real world. All arguments based on the factor gamma sounded plausible from the point of view of the whole theory of observers and the resolution of the paradox of the speed of light. But would the energy really work this way? This was entirely uncertain in 1905. Nevertheless, the word was out and could not be taken back. History only confirmed the magnitude of the energy predicted by the formula $E = mc^2$.

In order to understand the magnitudes involved, let us assume that 1% of the energy of mass of a body is released in the form of energy of motion. How much of motion will it be? In order to imagine what may happen in concrete terms, let us think about a nucleus of Uranium or Plutonium. Such a nucleus contains about 100 protons and about 200 neutrons. Protons have electric charge. Two protons powerfully repel each other by electric force when they approach each other. Neutrons do not have electric charge and stay together easier than protons do. In addition, a proton and a neutron can strongly attract each other when they are very close. Thus, the nucleus is made from protons and neutrons that stay together nearly touching each other, except that the protons are, in addition, pushing themselves outward while neutrons provide a glue that keeps the nucleus intact. In nuclei of heavy elements, such as Uranium, there are so many protons that many more neutrons are needed to keep the electric repulsive forces between protons in check by the strong attractive forces at short distance between neutrons and protons. The balance is so barely intact that from time to time some nuclei break in half. But when one sends a single neutron toward the nucleus, and this additional neutron knocks out some neutrons from the nucleus, the balance is gone because there are no longer enough neutrons to hold the nucleus together. With two neutrons knocked out, the nucleus splits in half very quickly, the protons tearing it by the repulsive force that can be no longer counterbalanced by the remaining neutrons. The electric energy that was initially kept in check by the neutrons is suddenly released in an act of fission. We can now use the formula $E = mc^2$ to estimate how fast the emerging halves of the nucleus will move apart.

Suppose that a half of 1% of the energy $E = mc^2$ is released in the form of the energy of motion of the two equal fragments. The energy of motion is proportional to the mass and the velocity squared of the fragments. The energy conservation law says that the half of 1% of mc^2 is turning into the half of mv^2. Therefore, v^2 is equal to 1% of c^2. This means that the velocity v is one tenth of the speed of light c. This is an enormous velocity: about 30 thousand km per second. It is 100,000 times larger velocity than commercial jets can muster. With such velocity, the emerging fragments need only about a second to travel around the entire Earth!

The last bit of reasoning, which the readers were promised earlier in this chapter but which was not delivered yet, concerns the question of *why no material object can move with the speed of light*. Let us observe that if the energy absorbed by the matchbox at rest is Δ_{Max}, the energy absorbed by the matchbox seen in motion with velocity v is gamma times Δ_{Max}. If the energy of the body was actually built from scratch by a giant number of absorbed photons, the total energy of the emerging body would be equal to the total energy of light, and the latter would be equal for Ming to gamma times that for Max. Thus, one can conceive the idea that if the energy of a body of mass m *at rest* is $E = mc^2$, then the energy of a body *in motion* with velocity v is gamma times larger. This idea turns out to be correct in Nature.

The factor gamma depends on the velocity v as shown in Chapter 15, Figure 15.3 on page 171.[2] In particular, gamma tends to infinity when the velocity v approaches the speed of light c. Therefore, *the energy of a material object with mass m tends to infinity when its velocity approaches the speed of light.* In order to do the work required to accelerate a material body to the speed of light, one would have to consume an infinite amount of energy, and this never happens.

How can light move with the velocity c? The current view is that photons do not have any mass, or their mass is zero. They can never slow down or stop like material bodies can. So what are they? The answer we have here is the following: The more one learns the more one needs and wants to learn. Nobody really knows how photons are made.

Another example of the rule that says that the more one has learned the more one needs and wants to learn is provided by Einstein's own path of research subsequent to his discovery of $E = mc^2$ in 1905. In all we have discussed so far, Ming and Max always move with a steady velocity with respect to each other. But they could accelerate and change the motion of one with respect to the other. How would their frames of reference be related in such cases? The theory that includes acceleration of observers is an order of magnitude more difficult to study than the theory we have discussed so far without acceleration. It took Einstein more than 10 years to come up with an answer. Moreover, the answer meant that what we feel as our weight, or gravity of our bodies on the surface of the Earth, is related to the feeling that we have when we accelerate in a car or a plane and experience a force pressing us to the back of the seat, and this resemblance is not accidental but a reflection of a fundamental property of space and time in which our lives unfold. The theory that includes effects of acceleration turns out to describe gravity of all material bodies and how light moves in a gravitational field around stars and planets. Einstein's theory of 1905 that deals only with steady relative motion of two observers is called the special theory of relativity, special because the motion is restricted to steady velocity. This was sufficient to deduce the formula $E = mc^2$. The theory that includes acceleration is called the general theory of relativity. The general theory is a major achievement that allowed Einstein to speak about the structure of the universe as a whole. For obvious reasons, we do not have anything more to say about it here. We mention the general theory of relativity only to convey to the reader that Einstein has the status he does not only for his discoveries in 1905, but also and to a large extent for what he discovered following his curiosity afterwards. Productive learning is an engine of desire to learn more.

17

Toward a Conception of Learning

We remind the reader that there were three major reasons we wrote this book. The first is that 100 years have passed since Einstein published his theory of relativity of time in 1905. If we restrict ourselves only to the United States, it is fair to say that of the people who graduate from high school and then spend four years in college, only a very, very small percentage of them have any understanding of why Einstein's work was no less than a revolutionary change in our conception of the universe and why and how it works as it does. One way to put it is to say that we have been socialized to believe that what he did is so abstract, complex, and mathematical that it requires a special kind of mind to grasp its content and its consequences. So, they perform an act of faith in accepting the message that what he did cannot be understood by ordinary mortals. We disagree with that sweeping conclusion. And in doing so, we are in no way implying that we expect them to be able to understand the contents and ramifications of relativity the way someone who majors or pursues a career in physics would understand. What we do assert is that most people can grasp his basic concepts at a meaningful level for them at the same time as they know that there is more to the story. It was never our intention to convey an impression that we were to cover the whole story.

The second reason we wrote this book derives from the fact that we have spent decades trying to understand why educational reform has been, for all practical purposes, a failure. We hasten to add that one can find a classroom here and a classroom there, a school here and a school there, where reform has been demonstrated to be possible and has produced credible data in support of what was done. Please note that these exceptions refer to single classrooms or to single schools but never to a whole school system. In any event, the number of exceptions is piddling and they do not spread either to other classrooms or to the system as a whole. One of us endeavored to show in previous publications that this discouraging state of affairs has no simple explanation but could have been and actually was predicted by him in 1965. A part of a comprehensive explanation is that the model American classroom reflects a conception of learning that is self-defeating to the goals of reform. As long as we continue to lack clarity about the differences between contexts of productive and unproductive learning, reform is doomed. That lack of clarity is reflected in the fact that if you ask people what they mean by learning, they find themselves puzzled because they cannot come up with an answer that is satisfactory to them, despite the fact that the word and concept of learning has the highest word-count frequency in the educational literature.

The third reason is that precisely because so many people consider themselves not to have the cast of mind that would enable them to grasp the basic concepts in Einstein's $E = mc^2$, and because we have no basis whatever to consider them stupid, we decided that the subject matter of this book should demonstrate that there is something wrong with the concept of learning that the system perpetuates. That does not mean that we expect all people to attain the same level of understanding of the subject. It means, however, that most people can or will be able to comprehend a difficult subject when it is taught and learned in a context of productive learning.

What we have attempted to do in this book is not comprehensible without recognition of three facts and one assumption. These facts are not disputable; we do not know anybody in or out of the field of education who disputes what we characterize as facts.

1. By conventional criteria—test scores, dropout rates, graduation rates—educational outcomes are not what they should be as steps to a productive life. Using identical tests, why do American students score significantly lower than students in China, Japan, Taiwan, Korea, and several other countries?

2. Science education in our schools is less than poor. In fact, if you eliminated from the comparison scores of students in *American* schools who come from Chinese, Japanese, and Korean families, American standing among nations would be even lower than it is.

3. Despite cascades of efforts to reform schools in the post-World War II era, in the course of which trillions of dollars were spent by local, state,

federal, private, and nonprofit sources—the end result has been, to say the least, disappointing. It has also been disillusioning to the point that in the presidential campaigns of 2000 and 2004, no Democratic candidate voiced opposition to the form and substance of the "No Child Left Behind" stance of President George W. Bush, even though it represented a comprehensive indictment of reform efforts by Presidents Johnson, Carter, Reagan, George H. W. Bush, and Clinton, and the entire education establishment, including teachers, administrators, and departments and schools of education across the country. Ironically, the one criticism the Democratic candidates voiced in the 2004 campaign was that President George W. Bush was not funding his reform initiative at the level he had promised. That criticism was identical to that voiced by the Democratic party and educational establishment soon after World War II: Society has ignored and neglected the public schools and should feel obliged to dramatically increase funding for school improvement. So, funding steadily increased, especially during the 1960s. But for the next two decades, achievement test scores continued to decline and then plateaued. The MasterCard commercial tells us "There are certain things money can't buy, for everything else there is MasterCard." Improved educational outcomes cannot be bought with money.

The assumption that informed the writing of this book was that the George W. Bush reform initiative will be no more effective than the previous efforts. How could we make any other prediction about an initiative based on an egregiously oversimplified conception of learning? There were no criteria for distinguishing between contexts of productive and unproductive learning. The reform plan actually suffused the atmosphere of classrooms and schools with thoughts of punishment if arbitrary standards of progress were not achieved. The plan viewed teachers as semi-mindless conduits for subject matter. The reform totally ignores the fact that test scores tell you absolutely nothing about the context of learning in the classroom. The initiative came from afar and it was implemented in a way guaranteed to evoke resentment, lower morale, and, yes, the fudging of test scores.

As in the private sector where data are altered to avoid writing the bottom line in red ink (e.g., Enron, MCI, Global Crossing, Adelphia), so has it been in schools and school systems when one's job is threatened because test scores did not increase as demanded. Fudging or cooking up data or plagiarizing is by no means unknown in scientific research. For how many decades did tobacco companies lie about the consequences of smoking? When the future and well-being of individuals and institutions are threatened, stress can trump morality. Cheating by students in schools, colleges, and universities is not a minor phenomenon.

The general point is that the Bush reform program can be characterized as a well-intentioned experiment concerning the consequences of stress in the different groups who "live" in schools. We use the concept of experiment loosely (of course) because no provision has been made to collect data by which one can judge means, ends, and consequences. One thing we already know: Zillions of test scores will be amassed. What those scores mean will not be illuminated in the largest guessing game in human history. We are not being flip here. What the George W. Bush initiative does not recognize or fund is a collection of data from a sample of classrooms and schools that could, so to speak, put meaningful flesh on the bones of literally impersonal test scores. There is a difference between flying in a storm and flying in the same storm with instruments.

The basis of our certitude in the assumption that the George W. Bush reform effort, as well as earlier efforts, would go nowhere near the intended and stated objectives in a finite time was very clearly related in our way of thinking to what Einstein did and what we have to say about the context of productive learning. Let us elaborate on this point.

Einstein demonstrated that two observers, whom we called Max and Ming, can consider the time needed by light to get from one point to another and they can measure it according to *exactly* the same procedure. His demonstration led to the result that the observers will obtain different readings of time. Most important, two separate events that are simultaneous for one of the observers are not simultaneous for the other. What Einstein was demonstrating was that the two observers were making their measurements in different frames of reference, and the time coordinates of the events they considered were not the same in these different frames. We have pointed out in earlier chapters that Einstein was interested, to the degree of obsession, in the way in which time was conventionally understood and measured, and in the reason the that the conventional thinking could not resolve the paradox of the speed of light being the same for different observers no matter how fast they were moving with respect to each other. He decided to go through a step-by-step analysis of what the observers do and how their results should be compared. He had to imagine the two observers and what they were doing in very concrete terms. He was forced to build and incorporate in his reasoning the concept that the relationship between the frames of reference of the two observers was critically important for all conclusions he could draw. He realized that he needed to find the correct relationship in order to resolve the otherwise inexplicable paradoxes in behavior of light.

But the very possibility that Einstein was able to look at the problem he was grappling with the way he did was the consequence of his own point of view and his entire outlook on the issue he was dealing with. He had a conceptual framework in his mind in which he was motivated and could analyze how the two imagined observers would see concrete events. In order to understand what Einstein was thinking, one would have to confront the incredibly complex problem of the human mind, especially one like Einstein's. It is one thing to understand Einstein's relativity. It is quite another thing to understand how a different mind is set and thinks.

Let us now state our provisional definition of the context of productive learning.

> Learning is a process, which takes place in a quintessentially inter-personal context (even if you are alone) and contains features that we label as intellectual, cognitive, attitudinal, emotional, anxiety-ridden, and so on, that are omnipresent, and the strength of each or in combination is never zero.

Note that when we say interpersonal, we are referring both to the learning by the person who is in the role of a student and by the person who is in the role of a teacher. The student and the teacher inevitably begin their relationship with different frames of reference in their minds, and it goes without saying that these frames are dramatically different.

We expect, of course, that both the student and the teacher know that they have different frames of reference in their minds no matter how well they understand the difference. The question that now arises from all this is what obligations this factual state of the matter places on the teacher in regard to understanding of the frame of reference in the mind of the learner. The student feels no similar obligation to the teacher. The student waits for the teacher, looks for the signals that will give him or her information about the teacher's frame of reference, including all the never-zero dimensions. The teacher literally sees the student and she or he is obliged to interpret what is visible in facial expressions and body language in the context of what happens in the internal frame of reference of the student's mind. As teachers very quickly learn, what is going on inside the student is what the teacher needs to know to be effective. The teacher is always going from overt behavior to covert behavior. Unless you believe that the teacher's task is to deal only with what the teacher sees, the task of the teacher is awesomely complex. This explains why John Dewey said that schoolteachers should be paid at the same level as college professors. He in no way was derogating the college professor, but was indicating the complexity of the process of teaching.

In regard to our definition of the context of learning, there are several questions a teacher should ask. The first is, How and in what ways do I go about determining the attitudes, feelings, and so forth the student brings to the context of learning? The second is, How and in what ways does the teacher convey to the student the teacher's obligations to the student and why those obligations derive from how the teacher conceives the process of learning? The third is, How and in what ways does the teacher begin to build a relationship of safety and trust with the student? These questions can be wrapped up in the statement that the obligation of the teacher is to determine from where, psychologically speaking, the student is coming, and that is the identical question the students ask themselves about the teacher.

These questions are easy to ask. They also sound very virtuous. But, predictably, if you ask teachers what these questions mean for interactions with students, it becomes abundantly clear that the teachers by no means have one and the same frame of reference in their minds from which their answers derive. In the definition we provided, the attention of the teacher is directed both to what he or she sees as well as to its possible meanings in the student's experience of the context. When we said before that teaching is an awesomely difficult task, we were taking seriously something every reader knows: When one human being seeks to understand another human being, that pursuit of understanding is beset with a whole host of problems. The problem is inherent in the first five letters of the word "understanding." We seek to go below where the individual is standing to the invisible level of what we see and hear. Unfortunately, the word "understanding" is like the word "democracy" in that people use it as if it has the same meaning for you that it has for them. Another current example concerns the word "terrorism." To us, terrorism is a monumentally cruel, indiscriminate, immoral form of expressing grievances. In the frame of reference in the mind of a terrorist, he or she has engaged in the pursuit of the loftiest, holiest of activities. This extreme example illustrates how the frames of mind can dramatically differ although one cannot tell a terrorist from a peaceful person just by looking. So, when we say that learning takes place in an interpersonal relationship, the statement is obviously true. At the same time, it tells us next to nothing yet about the purposes of the interaction and how we should proceed.

When two people marry, they assume they "understand" each other. It does not take long for each of them to realize the inevitable: Their frames of reference are not identical. They may seek to adapt to each other, to try to understand each other, but as the divorce statistics tell us, many of them give up trying or adapting to each other; love is not enough! In the classroom, good intentions are also not enough.

In the case of the paradox of the constancy of the speed of light for all observers regardless of how fast they were moving with respect to each other, it was not enough to apply the standard way of thinking about time in order to resolve it. On the one hand, when we look on the surface of the problem, the question "What time is it?" is very clear to everybody and does not require much thinking in order to go about getting the answer and following up with action. On the other hand, we know that this very same question had to be answered by Einstein for the purpose of solving the puzzle of the speed of light in a way that seems incomprehensible to most people even a century after his work was published. And it all began when Einstein came to challenge the basic assumption that time was absolute. And his resolution had tremendous practical consequences for what people did later during the century and how incrementally many things changed in our lives. For example, as we have mentioned before, more than 70% of electric power in France is drawn today from burning mass in nuclear reactors.

What we have been emphasizing in these pages is that in the education arena, the cascade of educational reforms resembles attempts to resolve the paradox of the speed of light without recognition that time is not absolute. Similarly, the fact that reform efforts have, for all practical purposes, been a failure should require us to try to identify the source of the failure. We asked the question, Is there one source that is so basic that if we are not clear about what we think that source is, it will in its wake negatively affect secondary sources? So, if you think that the disappointing performance of schools is explained by our failure to adequately fund them, the odds are very high that you will increase the amount of funding only to find out that the result will disappoint you. Similarly, if you believe that the failures are due to inadequate, outmoded curricula, you will most likely continue to produce more new curricula and eventually you will be disappointed again. Today, some people believe that the problem of educational failure will be solved using computers, as if the basic question of what the bottom-line source of the failures is did not require an answer. Finally, there are those people who believe that until teachers have a much better grasp of their subject matter, improvement cannot occur. So, pressure is exerted to require teachers to take more courses in their subject matter. There is no credible evidence that this has had desired consequences. And by credible evidence, we mean what will be appropriate in a supreme court of evidence.

On the basis of our experience, we have concluded that the basic problem that has gone unexamined is the concept and process of learning. More specifically, the fuzziness of the conventional concepts of learning has not led to an understanding of the differences between features of contexts of productive learning and unproductive learning. Unless and until those differences can be described and tested, the fruits of educational reform will be minimal or nil. So let us turn to the criteria of the context of productive learning.

Given our definition of a context of learning, and the purposes of the teacher and student in their interactions, let us consider the criteria by which one can judge whether the context is productive. By way of introduction, let us describe a teacher we had an opportunity to observe, a teacher whose specific action was literally unique among the hundreds of teachers we had the opportunity to observe and came to know.

On the opening day of school, students came in and saw their names in alphabetical order on the blackboard. She explained to the class of 23 students that there would never be time in the days ahead for her to get to know each student as well as she or they would like to know each other. However, it would almost always be the case on each day that she would arrange to have 15 minutes free to meet with one student. These would be meetings for the student. The student would determine what he or she would be talking about, whether it had anything to do with class work or not. It could have something to do with the class work if the student so desired. In other words, the teacher emphasized that the student would determine the subject, not the teacher. So, beginning on the next Monday of school, the name of the person who was to have the 15 minutes with the teacher on that day would be written on the blackboard. She told the students to look at the blackboard and see that their names were arranged in alphabetical order. She expected that when she was talking with a student in an adjoining alcove, the class would continue to do their work quietly and thereby show their respect for the teacher and the student.

It is hard to exaggerate how eagerly students looked forward to the meeting on their day. And it is also hard to exaggerate how valuable the meetings were to the teacher in understanding the individualities of the students. This was a classroom that any parent would pray to God to have their child in. This teacher did not devise the scheme because of theory, research, or her college education. But she was one of those teachers who, for reasons we hardly comprehend, has understood the significance of the interpersonal nature of learning in the classroom. In that classroom, students felt safe to relate personal feelings about themselves and learning.

The first criterion for a context of productive learning is that students *want* to learn, even if the strength of that wanting is not notably high at the beginning. By meeting individually with a student, the teacher sought to reinforce and systematically strengthen the student's wanting to learn. Our example has to do with a teacher and individual students. But it is no less a criterion by which to judge an entire school. It would be a relatively easy task to devise a short questionnaire, in which students in the school would answer in a yes-no fashion questions relevant to wanting to learn. The sheets containing their answers would not, of course, contain their names. Is it not significant that in the course of a year students are given questionnaires having to do with drug and alcohol abuse, smoking, or sex, but never see the point of determining by a simple questionnaire whether they want to learn and why? We pointed out in the first chapter of this book the results of research indicating that as students go from elementary to middle to high school their interest in and respect for school learning steadily decreases.

The second criterion is similar to the first, but it is especially applicable when students are graduating from high school. The focus is on the degree of the strength of their wanting to continue to learn more about themselves, others, and the world they live in. It makes no difference whether students are going on to college or not. What we want to know is whether whatever they are going to do reflects awareness that they know that there is more they need to learn. The design of the questions on the relevant questionnaire does not pose a major difficulty. People generally are unfamiliar with the degree of sophistication psychologists have acquired in the use of questionnaires, which not only elicit clear answers but also reveal when the respondents are echoing what they think authorities want them to say.[1]

A third criterion concerns appreciation of the subject matter. The word "appreciate" means that something has a value higher than it had before. What we hope for when we require that students go through some course is that the outcome will be that students are glad they took the course because they now understand something they did not understand and could not appreciate before, and now they look forward to knowing more rather than avoid and forget the entire experience. In *Mr. Holland's Opus*, the first half of the film, which is a beautiful portrayal of the context of unproductive learning, the students are ready to mutiny against Mr. Holland. But in the second half, for reasons we have discussed in Chapter 3, he realizes how he himself has engendered the sullenness and passivity in the students. And what was a context of unproductive learning was transformed by him into a productive one. What students of Mr. Holland experienced was not only music in the abstract, but in their relationships with each other.

In order to illustrate how important and how far from being satisfied this criterion is in contemporary schools, let us point out the following fact. Almost all teachers we have asked what were the two or three experiences in their adolescence in which they learned something that they did not know before but opened their eyes to its significance gave answers that referred to experiences outside the school they attended. The same teachers did not know whether their students would answer the same question in a similar way. We have no doubt that if we asked these teachers whether, in their school years, there were teachers from whom they felt they learned something significant, they would respond with a couple of examples. But these examples would not, we predict, have the motivating, memorable force of the experiences outside school that they described earlier.

Let us take another example that one of us (Sarason) can describe as follows.

> I had traumatic experiences in high school in algebra and geometry. It all began on the second day of school when the geometry teacher went to the blackboard, drew two lines, and said authoritatively, "That is an obtuse angle." I did not know what the word "obtuse" meant; I did not know what geometry meant; and I did not know why we were required to know either. It became a memory game and I ended up neither understanding nor wanting to play the game. The experiences in both courses were with different teachers. The result of these experiences was that when I got to

college, I wanted absolutely nothing to do with mathematics. But in my last year I needed four credits, and the only course available at the time when I could take it was with Professor Richard Henry in mathematics. I had come to know Professor Henry who, then, was at least 20 years older than I was. We had gotten to know each other outside of a classroom long before I was forced to take his course because of my involvement in student affairs and as editor of the college weekly. This means I knew in advance that Professor Henry was as delightful and sensitive an adult as I had ever met, a judgment shared by almost all students. It was not unusual that he would ask me when I was finally going to take his course, and my standard answer over the years was the equivalent of saying, "When hell freezes over." But in my senior year, I had no alternative to taking his course. It was in the second or third meeting of the class that he started by telling the class that they were going to have to make an important decision. On the first of the month we would have two options. The first was we would be given a penny the first day. Double that would be given the second day. And that amount would be doubled the third day. The doubling would go on until the end of the month. The other option was that we would be paid one million dollars on the first of the month and that was that. We had to decide which alternative we would take. If memory serves me correctly, all the students in the course were ready to accept the million dollars. We had up to half an hour to arrive at our decision. Small groups of students got together with pencil and paper to figure out which alternative we would take. We assumed that Professor Henry did not present us the problem as a joke. When it became clear to us that the first alternative would give us more than a million dollars, our reactions varied from being surprised to being astounded. Professor Henry had found a way to get us to understand the law of compound interest from personal experience, after which he demonstrated the algebraic formula for that law. He did not begin with the formula. He went from the concrete to the abstract. We thoroughly enjoyed the course.

The point of the two examples, the earlier story of the elementary school teacher who wrote the names of her students on the blackboard and the one about Professor Henry, is that the two teachers were sensitive to and took seriously what they thought they knew about the learners they were teaching. The elementary school teacher understood that students needed to feel trust in and safety with the teacher. Professor Henry knew that many of his students were taking the course because they had to, not because they wanted to. Both teachers acted accordingly, and this allowed them to create the classroom in which their students could appreciate the subject.

In the case of the elementary schoolteacher, the one-on-one meetings with students had several goals, and one of them was that these meetings would provide information relevant to the acquisition of subject matter. In the second example, the overarching goal of Professor Henry became obvious to the students; he wanted them not only to know algebra, but to appreciate its meaning and application.

We cannot explain how, why, and where these two teachers learned to adopt the stance they had about beginning with where the learner is coming from and to come up with ways that did justice both to the student and the subject matter. What we can say from our experience is that the number of such teachers is miniscule. And our direct observational experience with teacher training programs leaves us with no doubt that these programs are scandalously inadequate in helping teachers acquire an appropriate stance.

Note also that teachers are not helped to appreciate what may be involved in trying to learn where the students are coming from and become able to help students appreciate what they are to learn. For example, generally speaking, the relationship between teachers and parents is considered by neither of them as productive. Frequently, that relationship is marked by conflict. Teachers are required to meet and talk with parents about their children, regardless of whether their children are problems or not. Each parent and teacher is expected to gain something important from these meetings. Far more often than not, each of them does not look forward to such meetings with eagerness. We know of no teacher training program that attempts in any serious fashion to help their teachers-to-be to learn how to think about and act appropriately in their relationships with parents. In fact, there are many programs in which the issues involved are, for all practical purposes, totally ignored. Unless you believe that talking appropriately with parents is determined by our genes, the inadequacy of teacher training programs cannot be glossed over.

Because of the way we have characterized training programs, it may be helpful to the reader to point out that by the end of the nineteenth century, schooling became compulsory in America in large measure because schooling was considered essential if the children of millions of immigrants were to become Americans; they needed to learn to read, write, and deal with numbers in order to be able to take their place in the workforce. That parents should have some kind of a role in the education of their children was literally inconceivable. It was also inconceivable that students should be understood and treated as individuals. With classrooms that would have between 50 and 75 students, the concept of individuality was, understandably, irrelevant. Education was a form of indoctrination, a filling of empty vessels. Teachers could go from high school to a two-year teacher training program in which they were indoctrinated about teaching and learning. These two-year programs were in "normal schools" unconnected with colleges and universities. This development has been discussed elsewhere.[2]

What was missing in the education of teachers is analogous to what was missing in the education of medical doctors, except that the situation in medical education was worse. You could go from high school to medical school. Most medical schools were unaffiliated with hospitals or universities. With the usual exceptions, they were business enterprises. Their laboratories were at best primitive, if not worse. One medical school spent more money on advertising than on its laboratories. In 1910, Abraham Flexner was commissioned to do a study of all medical schools in the United States and Canada. That meant, in practice, that Flexner checked and reported data on 155 schools of medicine. He was not a physician, but he was one of the two most eminent educators of the time, John Dewey being the other one. What is clear in his report is that he considered the relationship between mentor and student to be the key building block in the educational process. And the process involved one observing the other in real-life situations. Education was not a matter of telling students, or even showing them, but an interpersonal process. You cannot read the report and not be impressed by Flexner's emphasis on the interpersonal relationship between the medical professor and student.

In regard to the training of educators, one has to ask, What should teachers comprehend about students, without which the goals of productive learning are guaranteed to be shortchanged? Flexner was very explicit about what he thought the medical students should know about the human body, biology, chemistry, physics, even mathematics. But he states explicitly that such knowledge is not enough to fulfill the physician's obligations to his patients. He was relatively brief about this issue and expressed the hope and belief that students would seek a career in medicine because they had a "calling" to devote themselves to such a career. The term "calling" today has an antique flavor because of its long-standing implication that higher powers in the universe had, so to speak, engendered in a person a call to devote his or her life to the care of sick people.

So, of all the things we might think teachers should know about human development, is there one that is especially important? Put in another way, what has been learned over the past century about human characteristics a teacher should know well, not only in terms of dry knowledge but also in terms of action? Let us give an example.

No one has ever denied that far more than any other species of animals, humans manifest curiosity from their earliest days of life. There are other animal species that exhibit curiosity, but none of them come anywhere near the strength and range of curiosity that humans possess. Indeed, human development over the millennia is incomprehensible without giving central importance to curiosity. Humans are quintessentially exploring, question-asking creatures. As almost all parents will attest about their preschoolers, their kids can ask questions that drive the parents up the wall. There is a paradox here. Up until they enter school, the curiosity of kids about almost everything is obvious to one and all. So why is it that in classrooms students ask very few questions and teachers ask galactically more? We feel compelled to remind the reader that Einstein was curious about another paradox: Why was the speed of light the same for two observers who moved with respect to each other, no matter how fast they moved? He was dissatisfied with all kinds of "explanations" that did not clearly grasp the essence of the reason for the constancy of the speed of light and looked instead like a patchwork within the same old picture.

So, how does the reader, and people generally, explain the remarkable difference of the question-asking by students before they enter school and after? What we call a paradox inheres in the fact that when the difference is presented to teachers, and people generally, not one has ever said that the difference is "good," something that should exist and requires no explanation. The school should help in asking questions and capitalize on students' curiosity, whatever form it takes. But it appears to quell it. In contrast, as we have tried to make clear in earlier chapters of this book, Einstein found an explanation for the paradox of the constancy of the speed of light following his drive of curiosity. And we know that his results changed our concept of time and had tremendous implications. Moreover, what he did in 1905 only increased his desire to learn more, and his progress toward the general theory of relativity over more than 10 years eventually led him to an image of the dynamics of the whole universe.

Our explanation of the question-asking paradox starts with an assumption that we truly believe to be a fact: Students in the classroom are always asking themselves questions that they do not ask out loud. Note that what we just said appears as if we are talking here about elementary, middle, or high school. But the issue exists at the college level and everywhere else in the system, wherever a question comes to mind and it is not asked.

What is the reason for this paradoxical behavioral regularity in schools?

Our definition of the context of productive learning is one in which the teacher makes clear to the student why asking questions is essential. In fact, one of the first things that a teacher should take up with the class is why questions are essential for her or him and the students. But it cannot be done by simply stating the issue; it has to be reflected in actions and interpersonal interactions at all times. In regard to this, it is fair to say that actions speak louder than any words. The underlying reason for the paradox is that students are afraid to ask, and teachers in their preparatory programs are not made aware of the role of question-asking in human learning. And if you are not made aware of that, you are setting the stage for a context of unproductive learning. In that kind of context, the teacher is robbed of the opportunity to think creatively in terms of what students are thinking about. Both the students and the teacher are robbed of the possibility of meaningfully conveying their thoughts between their frames of reference. This means that the opportunity for productive learning is lost and cannot be recovered when questions cannot be safely asked.

Teachers criticize what we have just said in this paraphrased way. "To do what you have said takes time and we do not have it. I can see myself taking a week at the beginning of the year to discuss and illustrate with examples the significance of question asking. And you are also suggesting, and we agree, that getting students to really believe that they can trust me with their questions, thoughts, and feelings will take time throughout the year. But we are given a curriculum which *must* be covered in a certain amount of time, and what the students learn will be judged by tests, and so will we on the basis of the outcomes of those tests. Spending a lot of time on questions that students may have, and being able to work with them in order to find meaningful answers, endangers them and us. Sometimes I would not know myself how to answer questions that may come up. I think you are grossly underestimating or are insensitive to how much pressure is put upon me to cover the curriculum and be able to demonstrate that I can teach. After all, what would I say if the students do not pass a test, or do not get admitted wherever they go? And I read your book *Parental Involvement and the Political Principle,* and if I took it seriously it would further require time I do not have. What you say makes sense, but it simply does not square with the realities. We know very well that we do not have time to do what we ourselves think and are deeply convinced we should be doing because we have to follow the schedule framed in the calendar-organized curriculum overwhelmed with subject matter, and we have no time for anything meaningful. We know this makes little sense. In fact, every teacher is acutely aware that there are students in the classroom who need more of their time to help them grasp the subject matter than we can give them. One of the hardest things for teachers is not to let the feeling of guilt about not giving the students enough time plague them to the point of despair. But you are not realistic."

What the teachers said is, of course, correct. In our response, we would always say that in explicit terms. What the teachers said described what can only be called an untenable state of affairs contributing to the reinforcement of contexts of unproductive learning. But when teachers were asked to explain how the state of affairs was created and is being maintained, their prepotent response was to blame administrators, boards of education, an insensitive, unsophisticated public, and ignorant political leaders who underfund schools. They do not assign blame to preparatory programs deficient in two respects. The first is not preparing them for the realities of schools as they are; the second is that there is nothing in their preparation to help them experience and understand a rationale that distinguishes between contexts of productive and unproductive learning. No one needs to tell teachers that preparatory programs are not helpful to them because they realize that as soon as they begin independent practice in the classroom. *But teachers do need to be told and understand that distinguishing between contexts of productive and unproductive learning is the starting point, which determines what one considers to be the goals of education and provides the conceptual basis for how a teacher should seek to understand his or her relationship with students, and the starting point comes before one enters the questions related to the curriculum.*

For example, it makes no difference whether the teacher will be teaching elementary, middle, or high school students, or whether the subject matter is math, science, or whatever. What does matter at the start is how seriously teachers truly grasp the role and force of curiosity in human learning and what conditions must be satisfied for the curiosity to grow and develop in the process. The teacher should also be psychologically prepared to engender in students a feeling of safety and trust with the teacher. Teachers are not psychotherapists, but that in no way means that they are absolved from the responsibility for recognizing and dealing with interpersonal factors sensitively and seriously.

We said that teachers' criticism of what we said to them was correct. By that we meant that they come to operate in a situation which is self-defeating of the goals of education. And nothing reflects this more clearly than the time pressures and evaluation criteria they are under. But in their criticism of what we said and in the discussions that followed, teachers had enormous difficulty articulating what they would do if those time pressures were absent. What they said was so general and superficial as to force us to conclude that they had little understanding of the difference between contexts of productive and unproductive learning.

Initially, our goal in this book was a restricted one: We asserted that if we took the differences between contexts of productive and unproductive learning seriously, it should be possible for high school seniors to grasp why Einstein's accomplishments of 1905 were so revolutionary. And by grasp, we meant several things. The first was to understand the history of attempts to measure the speed of light, then the puzzle of its constancy, and then its relationship to the formula that relates energy, mass, and the speed of light. It is an intrinsically fascinating history. The second thing can be put in the form of a question: How can it be that two observers moving with respect to each other will, each in his frame of reference, conclude that the speed of the same beam of light is constant and the same for both of them, no matter how fast one of them moves with respect to the other? The third thing is to gain some understanding of why and how Einstein demonstrated that the conception that time was absolute was both incomplete and wrong and that a fourth "time dimension" accounted for all of the inconsistencies and puzzles of the pre-Einstein way of thinking about light. To Earthlings rooted to the ground by the force of gravity, the conception and measurement of time as absolute "worked" pragmatically; we deal with relatively small velocities, and we think time is absolute because we think that the procedure by which two people agree on what time it is is independent of how fast one is moving with respect to the other. It is a very different story when you seek to explain the motion of huge masses that exist in the universe, or when you try to be very precise when thinking about what happens in a laboratory.

Before Einstein, energy was one phenomenon, mass was another, and speed of light a third one. What $E = mc^2$ signifies is that all three are seamlessly aspects of one process. The amount of energy (E) of any body is equal to its mass (m) times the speed of light squared (c^2). Einstein made a unity of what heretofore were considered as separate concepts. He made a very big conceptual leap, and his formula encodes the underlying relationships that stem from the nature of time and space.

For all practical purposes, Einstein's work is absent from the curriculum of high schools. And when in introductory textbooks and physics courses Einstein's work is mentioned, it is brief, contains distortions or errors, and convinces students it is an impenetrable mystery cloaked in a strange language containing strange concepts and fearsome-looking equations, all of which has no relation to any aspect of their interests or thinking. They regard it as akin to having to take a bitter-tasting medication, foisted upon them by parents (= teachers), for an illness they did not know they had. In brief, it is an extreme example of a context of unproductive learning.

What we are saying about high school textbooks in physics is also true for many introductory textbooks at the college level. And when college teachers discuss the subject, they assume that many, perhaps even half, of the students will not really "get it." In fact, the percentage of those who "do get it" is unknown, and we venture that the majority does not. But the teachers see it mostly as a problem with the students they have rather than with the teaching and the textbook.

That the teaching of science and math is poor is an old story in science education. Back in the 1980s, the *New York Times* published an interview between its science editor and the dean of sciences of the city university. The dean began by reading the usual litany of the abysmal state of science education in the public schools: A large majority of science teachers had no formal credentials to teach science, in the whole state of Connecticut only one teacher certified to teach science had a background in science, test scores were scandalously poor, students were uninterested and turned off, and so on. At one point the editor asked what the university was doing about it. The dean then described a program for poor minority students in which, during the summer, students were placed in the science labs of university scientists conducting research. The students came to life, they blossomed, they ate up the experience, they learned a lot. In a 1983 book, Sarason described a similar program conducted by a professor of physics at the University of Hartford.[3] What gave the professor the greatest kick each summer was that, unbeknown to the students, they had learned calculus, among other things.

How can one explain this state of affairs? A comprehensive answer would require a separate book, but we can identify some of the issues that would need to be covered. However, before doing so, we must point out to the reader a caveat he or she must keep in mind: There are no villains in the story; no one individual or group brought it about or "willed" it; it is not explained by ignorance or stupidity or lack of motivation on the part of the participants in the story (including students). To indulge in the game of blame assignment is to miss the forest for the trees.

1. Until World War II, girls—half of the school population—had no overt interest in science, let alone in a career. They became teachers, secretaries, nurses, and bookkeepers. Science and the professions required a "male mind"—an opinion millennia old. It was different with boys in that a small percentage of them had interests in engineering and applied and basic sciences. On a percentage basis, their numbers were small, in part because of the Great Depression, meaning that for many boys going to college remained only a dream. We are not aware of any data suggesting the science education in the pre-War years was any better than it is now.

2. War, local or world, changes everything and everyone, and that was true in spades for World War II. With the U.S. entry into the War, the military was faced with one short-term and one long-term problem. The short-term problem was that it was by no means clear that Japan could be defeated. The long-term problem derived from the realistic assumption that the War would be a protracted one, and there would be countless deaths and casualties that the country would lack the facilities and personnel to care for, especially for the psychological and medical problems of those casualties. To say "lack" is an understatement. Physicians, surgeons, psychiatrists, psychologists, nurses, and rehabilitation specialists would be needed in unprecedented numbers, not only after the War but already the day after December 7, 1941, when Pearl Harbor was bombed. In addition, the military had learned from World War I that among those eligible for service, a very large number would be rejected because they were, for all practical purposes, illiterate, and even among those accepted by draft there would be many who were illiterate.[4]

More than any other agency in or out of government, the military had good reason to be critical of schooling in America. During the War, the needs of the military for personnel of all kinds developed and the military supported professional training programs in colleges and university. Those programs were shorter in length than they had been before the War. It was only in the wake of victory in 1945 that the military made its case that in light of the crucial role science, basic and applied, had contributed to the victory, the existing differences among schools had to be remedied. The number and quality of scientists, engineers, and mathematicians the United States needed would have to be available. (How many high school students, or, for that matter, members of the educated public know about the vital role of cryptographers, who are basically mathematicians, in winning the War?) It is not happenstance that the earliest post-World War II government-supported curriculum reform was powered by this question: How and on what basis can new curricula be developed in physics, math, and biology that, unlike existing curricula, would engender students' interest instead of turning them off?

The question posed a half-century ago is more pressing and important today because it has become obvious that reform efforts have failed, and as long as that continues to be the case it will have untoward effects on the entire society. It may come as a surprise to many readers to be told that the military has a better gut feeling for the consequences of the continued failure of educational reform than it is given credit for. The military is a galactically huge organization that inevitably is wasteful, inefficient, and comprised of fiefdoms competitive with and adversarial to each other but smart enough to know that they have to be prepared in a volatile, dangerous, unpredictable world for a role that will require a citizenry far better schooled than is now the case.

3. From the beginning of the Great Depression in 1930, through the War years 1939–1945, and for five years thereafter, the physical conditions of schools as teaching facilities deteriorated. It was during this period that a dramatic demographic change was taking place: Populations—white and black, young and old—moved from south to north, east to west, to urban centers in search of employment, fueled most notably by the recognition that the United States could not or should not be neutral in the War that loomed on the horizon and, therefore, would require stimulation and support of a much-enlarged industrial capacity. This led to what came to be called the "urban problem," which referred to the lack of adequate housing, racial and ethnic conflicts, overcrowded schools, juvenile crime, and communities lacking the financial capability to do much about anything. It was not chaos but a confirmation of confusion and impotence from which schools were not exempt. It was not that the public schools were placed on the back burner. They simply languished; they were where they had always been. It is true there were controversies about what should be taught, about racial and economic inequities, and about the role of schools as agents of social change. But those controversies almost exclusively took place in academic circles, with little or no influence or interest on the part of the larger society or the political system. In a period of economic disaster followed by total war, issues of teaching and learning are intellectual luxuries a society cannot afford. It was not until in the early years of the Eisenhower administration that the negative consequences of the urban problem for the public schools were confronted, and for the first time in U.S. national history the federal government entered the educational scene.[5] It took the form of fiscal grants to urban school systems to help them increase and improve their education of disadvantaged children. It was testimony to the explicit belief that what urban schools

needed was a temporary infusion of funds enabling urban communities to get back on their own economic feet and provide the quality of schooling their students required.

Far from being temporary assistance, it was and it is continued with steady yearly increases in funding of reform efforts, of which the George W. Bush initiative is the most intrusively direct. Although the day is past when any knowledgeable individual or group believes that spending more money will produce the desired outcomes of reform, it is more than noteworthy that there is evidence that most people did not learn anything. And that judgment refers to many educational reformers and theorists, teacher unions, and critics from all points in the political spectrum. When Democrats in the Senate and the Congress voted to approve the George W. Bush program and then could only criticize him for not funding it more liberally, they exposed a near-total ignorance of the history of educational reform.

History is not a museum of relics to which you go on a rainy weekend day. History is not bunk. It contains accounts of successes, failures, and ignorance and leaves it to those of us to understand—at least try to understand—what worked, what did not, and why, and for the purpose of controlling the tendency to want to believe that our world was born yesterday. As we endeavored to indicate in previous chapters, Einstein did not arrive at the significances of $E = mc^2$ ignorant of all previous attempts to solve the puzzles of the speed of light, such as its constancy, and more.

4. Shortly before World War II ended, Congress passed legislation that transformed U.S. society and its relevance to educational reform cannot be overestimated, although that relevance, then and now, has been ignored. More correctly, educators and psychologists concerned with teaching and learning were too imprisoned in inadequate theories of learning to see that relevance. The legislation was called the GI Bill of Rights. The GI Bill never, but never, intended to transform society or to be relevant to conceptions of learning or to serve the purpose of engendering the interest of veterans in the basic and applied natural sciences, social sciences, humanities, and so forth. It was expected that only a small fraction of returning veterans would take advantage of the opportunity to pursue any form or level of higher education they desired. Their tuition would be paid, their fees and books would be paid for, a monthly living allowance would be given them, and much more. The veteran had one decision to make: What did he (a few women) want to make of the opportunity? As long as he was accepted in an approved educational institution, he, so to speak, had it made. And if he had a family and wanted to buy a house, the government would be the guarantor of the mortgage. The veteran could become what he wanted to become.

What the reader has to understand is that the Great Depression was something still fresh in their minds. A large number of them had long given up the dream of going to college and resigned themselves to the expectation that after the War they would, maybe, get jobs that were available, not what they desired.

So, instead of the predicted 250,000 veterans who would use the GI Bill, literally millions did. Why? As Michael Bennett makes clear,[6] many veterans deeply and strongly wanted to learn and enter fields that interested and excited them. In other words, they possessed one of the most important features of a context of productive learning: They *wanted* to learn. Most of those veterans were from ethnic, religious, racial-economic backgrounds that, before the War, were minimally represented in the college student population. They did not have a high quality high school education; their families were not sources of intellectual stimulation and support; more than a few had incurred chronic illnesses and injuries; some had been in the War for as long as five years. Whatever study habits they once had, they were never used or refined; the army and war are not noted for the support they give to intellectual pursuits.

Whatever doubts and anxieties they must have had, they came to the university prepared to give their all in order to capitalize on a golden opportunity. They didn't ask for special privileges or a lowering of standards, and they did not rebel at all to an 80-plus hour weekly reading and writing workload. They were there for the sense of growth. One of the authors of this book began teaching in the university in 1945, and it is his opinion that the period 1945–1960 was a kind of heaven for instructors of these veterans, and over the decades he has never known instructors (in many and diverse institutions) who disagreed with this characterization.

There was another thing going for these veterans: Instructors welcomed, admired, and respected them and had an unverbalized understanding of how their lives had been disrupted and what learning had come to mean for them. That is a feature of a context of productive learning: Understanding how the learner sees himself and the world is the key prerequisite to deciding what and how to relate to the learner. Saying it that way may sound corny, but the required kind of understanding is totally absent, and we mean totally, from the rationale of the Bush initiative which, ironically and perversely, has made classrooms have an uncomfortable resemblance to an army boot camp. Namely, the school bell announcing the beginning of the school day means the teacher begins drilling the students and testing their recall of what they have been taught. Never before has an educational reform been justified on the basis of such a conception of teaching and learning for which there is not a shred of evidence of positive outcomes. H. L. Mencken said that it is hard to be completely wrong. President George W. Bush has made it seem easy.

5. What were the consequences of the GI Bill for the traditional sciences? We have painted a picture of the people and period in very broad strokes. We could not do otherwise because literally no one at the time gave any thought to describing and evaluating what the GI Bill meant in the short and long term for returning veterans or, for that matter, higher

education in general. It is safe to assume that in terms of absolute numbers, the enrollment in the sciences increased. But it is also safe to say that on a percentage basis that increase was puny compared to dramatically escalating enrollments in the social sciences, the humanities, philosophy, and divinity schools. The use of atomic bombs to terminate World War II, the beginning of the cold war with the Soviet Union, testing of the more lethal hydrogen bomb, the Berlin blockade—all of this (and more) contributed to a perception in many veteran and non-veteran students: The sciences, especially physics, could be used in ways that endangered human existence. If such a perception was emerging and articulated on campuses by the early 1950s by some veterans and non-veterans, it was unrelated to their experiences in high school science courses, which in any event were boring, mystifying, and irrelevant to their daily existence. By the dawn of the 1960s, requiring all students to take science and math courses was, for all practical purposes, passé, despite numerous federally funded research projects to make science more interesting and understandable to students at all levels of public schooling. Today, the problem is more acute and depressing, although it could have been predicted. The teaching of science, and students' experience of learning science, were and are in a file-and-forget category.

At this point, we should remind the reader that in the course of writing this book we had primarily two groups of potential readers in mind: high school seniors and college-educated people of all ages, including their teachers. Why include high school seniors together with college-educated people of all ages?

One of us taught, over a period of a few months, a small group of high school students in Warsaw about Einstein's $E = mc^2$. He did that once a week for two hours in far from optimal conditions. The results were encouraging, this at a time in our collaboration when he was getting his bearings teaching other than undergraduate and graduate students. He did one other thing: He arranged to teach a science course in a college of education. It was not a morale-boosting experience for him. While the high school students were self-selected volunteers, the future teachers, all of whom had had more than one math course and an introductory course in physics, had as much if not more difficulty and certainly less satisfaction with Einstein's relativity than the high school seniors. Although we are not, of course, justified in drawing firm conclusions from these experiences, there is reason to believe that teaching a small group of self-selected, motivated, intellectually invigorated, curious high school seniors may have more of the features of a context of productive learning than teaching 20 or more students in a required college course in which previous exposure to Einstein was minimal or absent. Put it this way: Future teachers may know they would never be asked to teach relativity to their students at school. We will have more to say about this later.

Over the millennia, there is one thing all parents have observed in very young children even before their offspring are able to walk and talk: The child is curious and question asking. The child may be unable to use language, but you do not have to be a trained observer to observe the facial expression of puzzlement, as if to say, "What is going on here?" For example, at around nine months of age many children exhibit what has been called stranger anxiety: The mother is holding the child; people who have not seen the child come to visit; they acclaim the child's beauty; they coo at him or her from a distance; they approach the mother with extended hands in order to receive and hold the child; and then, so to speak, all hell breaks loose. The child begins to cry, buries his head in the mother's chest, but not before the facial expression of fear and puzzlement stamp its face. That response to the stranger may go on for weeks, to the point where the parent asks visitors not to attempt to come too close to the child.

What do parents observe when the child begins to crawl and walk? They see an organism going into everything and every place, examining objects, manipulating them, an explorer of his or her world, a combination of Columbus, Galileo, Darwin, and Mendel. It is a combination that is a source of anxiety in parents fearful of injury to the child. And what happens when the child can talk? He or she asks questions, in some cases to the point that sends parents up a wall. Parents find that questions beget answers which beget more questions and on and on. Here is a small sample of frequent questions.

- Why is the sky blue?
- Where is the sun at night?
- What is rain or snow and how are they made?
- What keeps an airplane in the sky?
- Who is God? Where does he live?
- How can a bird fly?
- Why does a car need gasoline?

Those are some of the questions children pose in their language; they are by no means the kind of questions posed to schoolteachers. The frequency of question asking depends in large measure on the answers provided by parents. The answers parents give, more often than not, are not satisfactory to or understood by the child, and they arouse new questions in the child, which he or she will answer in some ways fanciful and outlandish by adult standards. That is particularly the case with questions about sex differences, how babies are "made" and by whom.

The above was by way of emphasizing the obvious: From its earliest days, a human is an organism forever curious about its external and internal world, and that is the case until the individual dies. More than any other animal, the human being asks questions and seeks answers. When the answers are not understood or agreed with, the individual concocts his own answers. What is not so obvious is that the question asking-question answering dynamic is the opposite of passive mental and/or physical activity. In the preschool years, curiosity and physical activity are seamlessly related. Although children vary markedly in temperament, it is still the case that the preschooler is the epitome of physical and mental activity: manipulating this or that, examining it, trying to take it apart, spending different amounts of time with toys or other action, or watching cartoons. Why cartoons? Because they are interesting, exciting, full of suspense, food for imagination and fantasy. And, of course, they take delight in *Mr. Rogers' Neighborhood, Sesame Street,* or in earlier years, *Captain Kangaroo.* Although such programs justify themselves as schools of learning, each portrays people in action that feeds fantasy. Mr. Rogers talked with his viewers as much as he talked to them about thoughts and feelings, including sadness, illness, anger, and guilt, in ways no one else did. It is not hell diving to say that he wanted his viewers to feel he understood them. But entertainment was not number one on his priority list of goals. When he died, it was not surprising that the *New York Times* accorded him an obituary the size given to some world figure. And when he died, one of us had just finished his book *And What Do You Mean By Learning?,* and added a postscript about Mr. Rogers and one of his programs, which left no doubt that Mr. Rogers understood the features of a context of productive learning.

Parents of preschoolers are frequently advised to restrict the amount of TV their preschoolers watch, especially cartoons. We have no quarrel with that advice as long as parents are also told that they should provide substitute activities that can compete with TV and that literally stimulate and excite the preschooler's hunger for new experiences. Having said that, let us not forget that parents of preschoolers with modest incomes and living space cannot afford, as the more prosperous can, a seemingly endless supply of children's books and toys, and mini bikes, ice skates, and more. How many parents who can afford it, relatively speaking, take their preschoolers on excursions to interesting places like theme parks, flying trips to national parks, science and children's museums, summer vacations on or near lakes and oceans, zoos? It is as if some parents see themselves as teachers whose obligation it is to stimulate, expand, and sustain the curiosity of their pupils. The logo of a local travel agent is "See the world before you leave it." His clients are not impoverished people. Whether parents are impoverished or not, their preschoolers eat up, digest, and crave new experiences, the more active the better. Someone said that preschoolers have no conception of fatigue; they keep going and going until they collapse.

And then comes the time when the preschooler begins "real" school. It is hard to exaggerate the differences between the classroom learning context and that which the preschooler experienced at home. Here are just a few of the differences.

1. The beginner is in a physical space in which the teacher (parent surrogate) and many classmates are strangers. If that is inevitable, it is also inevitable that the child has loads of questions about what he or she will

experience, is experiencing. Those questions are not articulated, nor are they solicited by the teacher. The parents of most beginners have told the children that they should "mind" the teacher, do what the teacher says, behave themselves. The exceptions aside, they usually do as they are told. They scan the environment but say nothing, although they are constantly scanning what is about them. It is as if they are at their first baseball game; they have their own seat, and their father is telling the child the players and the umpire will soon appear and the game will begin. The child is eager for the action to start.

2. By the end of the first week certain behavioral-interactional regularities that will endure become clear. There are rules, which can be labeled the constitution of the classroom, an implicit document formulated by the teacher and granting the teacher the roles of legislator, executive, and judiciary. The child is not free to leave his seat, talk to another child, or give voice to feelings and questions without raising his or her hand to get the teacher's attention and then permission. Spontaneity in speech or action is frowned upon; "the good classroom is orderly, children do what they are told." And what if it is a teacher who is newly credentialed to teach? It is the rare neophyte whose major concern and prayer is not whether and how she will impose order and, God forbid, she has an obstreperous child or two who do not obey rules. She wants to like and be liked by her students but not at the expense of being seen by the principal and other teachers as not maintaining law and order.

Mention should be made here of the fact that kindergarten and first-grade teachers see each other very differently. For teachers of Grades 1 and beyond, kindergarten teachers have kinship to babysitters who have little or no responsibility for teaching formal subject matter but rather for activities to make things—build, paint, draw—of some personal interest to the kids and that are imaginative in nature. Spontaneity and the rules of behavior are far less explicit and observed above kindergarten. The kindergarten teachers are aware of how they are viewed but resent the judgment that their children are not acquiring habits of thinking, doing, expression, and imagination. Generally speaking, the conception of learning employed by kindergarten teachers bears far more similarity to a context of productive learning than the conception of "real" teachers does. In the many elementary schools we have observed and come to know more than superficially, "real" teachers did not and could not conceive of the possibility that they had anything to learn from the kindergarten teachers. It is not happenstance that we know of no elementary school that has a kindergarten teacher as principal. Gym teachers, yes; kindergarten teachers, no.

3. We know that as children go from elementary to middle to high school their interest in and respect for school learning goes steadily downhill. Why? Answering that question cannot be glossed over or avoided. When a decade or so after World War II the big three automakers saw that

Japanese auto companies were slowly increasing their sale of cars in the United States, the U.S. companies were not concerned; they practically had a monopoly on the U.S. market. It took a decade, during which the sales of Japanese cars increased at a fast rate, for the U.S. companies to realize they had a problem on their hands. And even after taking notice, it required time for them to ask the question, Why do people buy these foreign cars? Why are they not buying U.S. cars? More specifically, why are Americans more satisfied with foreign cars? What are they providing that we are not? There is no one simple answer to these questions, but two aspects of a complicated answer become clear.

The first aspect is encapsulated in what Henry Ford said a century ago: You can have whatever color Ford you want as long as it is black. It was a combination of smugness and arrogance: Henry Ford would decide what kind of car people should buy. The second aspect is that customer satisfaction cannot be ignored as if customers had no criteria for judging whether they are getting their money's worth, as if they had no thoughts and feelings, no interest in the quality of their purchase. They are not passive, mindless reactors.

Students are customers, except of course they are legally mandated customers whose parents are taxed in one form or other to support the schools that will be critical for the future of their children. If parents are dissatisfied with their child's school and/or their child does not like school and complains that school is uninteresting and a waste of time, parents have a few options they never had until two decades ago: Ask to have the child go to another school in the community, or, if they can afford it, place the child in a private or parochial school. It is worthy of emphasis that after all the states enacted compulsory education legislation toward the end of the nineteenth century, only recently have parents been accorded the option to send their child to another school of choice in the school system. The option was a clear example of a response to customer dissatisfaction.

Compulsory education created two kinds of customers: parents and their children. Children start their schooling with eagerness, curiosity, and the expectation that schooling will be stimulating and that what they will learn will make them "grown up," capable of doing the wonderful things their fantasies are all about.

Parents are grown ups. They have opinions and make judgments about the quality of their child's schooling. They have to overcome a good deal of reluctance before they approach school personnel to tell them their dissatisfactions. School personnel are the experts, and like all experts they do not take kindly to implicit and explicit criticism, either from peers or from those they consider lay people. Parents know that, hence their reluctance to give voice to their discontents. Schools do not have any means (e.g., a questionnaire) by which to give parents the opportunity to express "customer satisfaction or dissatisfaction" with their child's schooling. The rhetoric that parents have a vital role to play in matters educational is just that: empty rhetoric. The "good" parent is one who does not invade the school's turf; the "bad" parent is one who does; parents are biased, partisan, subjective, and uninformed; school personnel are objective, rational, fair, intent only on helping students "to realize their potential," employing tried and true theories of pedagogy. It is important that there is one group who comes to know well the interpersonal chasm between parents and teachers: teachers who are parents and are impelled to meet with the teacher of their child and convey their dissatisfaction with how their child is understood and taught. No one has seen fit to study how teachers regard parents who are teachers.

In middle and high school, schools permit researchers to administer questionnaires about students' use of drugs, alcohol, and sexual activity. The school does not administer a questionnaire once or twice a year centering on how students regard their schooling, their teachers, the courses they take, their interest and boredom with this or that subject matter, textbooks, the degree to which what they learn in school has relevance to life out of school, and the degree to which they feel their teachers understand them. From the miniscule number of studies on student attitude, we know two things for sure. The first is that as students traverse the grades, their interest in and respect for school learning goes down. The second is that we have never known a middle or high school teacher who questioned such findings.

The teacher is the common feature in the two problematic relationships we have discussed. That, of course, is not reason enough to serve as a basis for educational reform. That would be premature, myopic, and unfair in that it would be an instance of misplaced emphasis at the expense of trying to see a larger picture containing other problematic relationships, which if glossed over confirm the maxim that the more things change the more they remain the same. Diane Ravitch's justly acclaimed book is titled *Left Back*.[7] If it is an important book, a scholarly historical chronicle of reform failures, it contains suggestions at its end that leave the reader with these questions: So where do we start and why? What are the predictable barriers to change? To what degree and in what ways are these barriers related? What are the minimal conditions that must be obtained for a reform to stand a chance to succeed, and if those conditions are less than minimal you should stay home and avoid contributing to the history of failures? What specific criteria should we employ as measures of degrees of success and failure? Since schools and school systems are very complicated and, like all institutions, do not take kindly to change, what is a realistic time perspective we should employ and make public because we have to assume that there is a difference between a quick fix and a reform that will endure?

So let us pursue scrutiny of the role of a teacher. Teachers are to parents and students as administrators are to teachers. Stated succinctly, in terms of status, power, and participation in formulation of educational policy, administrators are a relatively small group at the top of a mountain from which emanate policies and directives to teachers at the bottom of the mountain. When in the 1950s teacher unions began to grow in size and militancy, on the surface it was primarily about scandalously low salaries. As is usual in all institutions, grievances about salary are a proxy for lack of respect and recognition as well as resentment about being treated as ciphers who are not mature and informed enough to be consulted, let alone be a participant, in policy and decision making of a school system. The experts are "up there" or "downtown"; the teachers are in the trenches at the foot of the mountain. The larger the system, the stronger is the resentment of the peons to their masters. And at no time is this more clear than when a reform effort is proclaimed on high and teachers have to march to the latest hit on the reform hit parade. This gives rise to what older teachers often call the "here we go again" syndrome.

What we have been describing gives rise to the frame of reference problem and its puzzles that are analogous to those that Einstein was trying to unravel and understand in physics. Two observers moving in space with respect to each other and using the same means for measuring time will agree that the speed of light is predictably the same for them. However, if both of them observe the same event, the time they record for the occurrence of that event will not be the same; the difference would be small, even tiny. But in physics, and in science generally, "tiny" has to be explained and the answer can have enormous implications. Einstein's answer was that the frames of reference of the two observers were not the same, for reasons we discussed in the earlier chapters. Einstein demolished the conception of time as absolute and showed it depended on the observer. As Earthlings, Einstein's conception of time as a fourth dimension is of no practical significance to us in our daily lives where we do not have to take into account huge speeds (like that of light), extremely fast atomic events, or enormous distances of millions of miles between stars. But for human understanding of the physical laws of the universe, Einstein's contribution amounted to a major revelation. Unbeknown to most educated people, it has transformed human life on Earth. The core of Einstein's ideas are still unknown to the public because what passes for science education blunts or extinguishes their curiosity about a strange-looking formula containing three letters of the alphabet having no meaning for them.

It goes without saying that the concept of frames of reference was not invented by Einstein. From the dawn of history, humans have known that different people see the same event differently. But the earliest humans knew one other thing: These different perceptions could trigger different actions that could be threats to life and limb; they can defeat the purposes of everyone.

One way of defining educational reform is that its purpose is to effect an institutional change involving four groups: teachers, parents, administrators, and schools of education, whose frames of reference for understanding, accepting, implementing, and judging outcomes are not the same. (There are more groups, but we take that up later.) We regard the above statement as a glimpse of the obvious. You do not have to be a sage or a specialist in organizational development and practices to know that when there are discrete vested interests varying in status, power, and role in decision making, each of these groups will vary distinctively in how they see the reform as an event or process, goal, and so on. For the sake of simplicity, we shall consider educational reform as an event. In his "thought experiments," Einstein had the luxury of being content to restrict himself to two observers in space. That is conceptually and practically a piece of cake compared to the event we call educational reform. Nevertheless, his and our tasks are identical: What can we come up with and do to make the frames of reference of the different vested interests in the educational event better "synchronized"? Einstein did it for physics with a mathematical precision that will always be unattainable in the realm of human-social-interpersonal affairs. But realistic modesty does not explain why, in the history of educational reform, the problem of finding a relationship between different understandings, attitudes, and vested interests has, for all practical purposes, been virtually ignored and never seriously discussed. In fact, we know of no published account of an educational reform that contains a description of how what we call the relationship among different frames of reference was approached before the starting point of the event, and how precious little they knew of the barriers and problems encountered after the starting point of the event: errors of omission and commission, what one reformer called the "dirty laundry of an educational reform." Finally, the number of published accounts of these events is dwarfed by the number of such events that are aborted before they can be implemented. The reasons are several, but the most frequent is emerging divisiveness among the frames of reference of the different groups.

There is one other vested interest we have to discuss because it is the source of the selection and training of all educational personnel: teachers, administrators, and educational researchers. We refer to schools and departments of education in universities and colleges. It would be unfair to give the impression, as some critics have, that these programs are the major source of the failures of educational reform and the sad state of the quality of schools. One of us has discussed this in detail in an earlier book[8] and we cannot do justice to the issue here. But there are several things that can be said briefly. The first is in the form of a question implying a caveat. Before you take dead aim at the target of your criticism, should you not examine to what extent your frame of reference takes into account and is based on some reasonable, firsthand experience with your target, at least to the degree that you feel you understand them and their frame of reference? This is not to say that to understand all is to forgive all. Do you know their frame of reference well enough to know that from time immemorial, the school of education has been looked upon by the rest of the university as composed of unimaginative, intellectual midgets who do not deserve to be in the university? Is your frame of reference informed by the fact that schools of education and the departments of arts and sciences rest on polar-opposite assumptions? The latter assumes it to be self-evident that the more you know your subject matter the better you are as a teacher. The assumption that undergirds the former is that knowing your subject matter does not mean you know how to teach it in ways students can assimilate and understand it.[9] We are not aware of any published data about the number of university faculty—leaving aside those who are in schools of education—who taught in a public school. It is safe to assume their number is tiny. For what it is worth, we have known six very reputable university faculty who started out as classroom schoolteachers. None of them were even in doubt that teaching grade school students requires knowing much more than subject matter.

The point here is not that each group sees teaching from a different frame of reference. To say more is to labor the obvious. The point is that they not only do not understand each other, but they also are not motivated to try to understand each other or to seek ways and experiences that could serve as a basis of testing and reconciling their differences. It comes with ill grace for a critic who pillories the school of education when his knowledge and experience in the culture of the systems (plural) in which the school is embedded is, to be magnanimous, not much above zero. But it also comes with ill grace for educational faculty to respond to the outside critics as if those critics, as concerned citizens, are unjustified in concluding or hypothesizing that schools of education must be a contributing factor to the level and quality of educational outcomes.

Einstein discovered and unraveled why the frames of reference of two observers of the same events led to puzzles, inconsistencies, and imprecise measurements. Each was unreflectively assuming that his or her measurements were identical and gave absolute results for time. By illuminating a heretofore ignored factor (gamma) in the relationship between frames of reference, Einstein pointed out the required change in the concept of time that eventually changed our understanding of the physical universe. But Einstein did not have to be concerned with whether observers were white or black, rich or poor, urban or suburban, motivated or disinterested, or whether their institutional affiliations, history, and traditions were similar or in conflict.

It is a very different story in the realm of human affairs and institutions. We have discussed the frames of reference of a handful of groups with a vested interest in schooling and educational reform. We did not discuss other major groups whose frames of reference are consequential for educational reform: local, state, and federal governments; churches; and teacher unions. If we had discussed these groups, we would have come to the same conclusion we offered before: They have different frames of reference, which engender and sustain adversarial relationships.

Our aim has been to indicate what should be obvious but is not: Educational reform is overwhelmingly complicated in terms of conceptualization and implementation, a conclusion clearly ignored over the past century of the failures of educational reform. Reforms have been conceived and implemented as if these conflicting frames of reference can be diluted by statements of good intentions, good will, visions of a better future, as if these differences can be diluted by the requirements of a predetermined schedule so unrealistic as to justifiably assign them to the category of quick fixes. Einstein agonized about how physicists define and measure time. So let us listen to how some reformers look back at their reform efforts, and what they say about what were the most important things they learned from their reform efforts.

They will say, "That is easy to answer. I vastly overestimated our theory and underestimated another, the brittleness of verbal agreements on the part of the different groups in the reform effort—verbal agreements before you start implementation. When the implementation began, the shit hit the fan and I began to realize that reform is the opposite of an emotionally neutral, passive experience for those who have different frames of reference and who have to unlearn familiar ways of thinking and actions and learn new ones."

It may strike the reader as an extreme overgeneralization when we say that those who conceive and implement a reform are either unaware of or vastly underestimate the role of time perspective in their conception and implementation of educational change. The George W. Bush program for educational change is the clearest example to date of literally ignoring the obvious fact that different groups with vested interests in the goals of reform will respond to a reform as they see it from their different frames of reference.

Because of the importance we attach to the frame of reference of observers, let us present an example illustrating how differences between the frames of reference determine action, appropriately or inappropriately.

For the school year 1963–1964, the New Haven school system made a vigorous effort to attract graduates of prestigious colleges to be teachers in New Haven schools. It was a response to the then-escalating criticism that teachers newly trained in traditional preparatory programs not only had an inadequate liberal arts and science education, but on average were unimaginative and uncreative. It was a "reform" proudly adapted by schools around the country. Recruits could begin teaching in September 1963, and they were required to take one or two courses at a local college whose preparatory program was the major source of teachers for schools in the New Haven metropolitan area. Some recruits took courses there in the summer before school started in September. I (Sarason) was director of the Yale Psycho-Educational Clinic and offered that I and two colleagues would each meet weekly in two-hour sessions with 10 recruits to discuss any problem they were encountering as teachers. There were to be 10 sessions. My colleagues and I were in agreement that the school authorities had attracted bright, lively college graduates who were strongly motivated to do their bit in urban schools trying to improve the quality of the educational experience of racial and ethnic minorities. As was the case in the 1960s in the United States, these middle class recruits saw themselves as agents of change in a society that needed a lot of changing.

I met with my group at the Yale clinic Wednesday afternoons after the close of the school day. The meeting I shall now discuss took place on the Wednesday after the assassination of President Kennedy on the previous Friday. The mood of the country was one of shock and gloom. There were few people on the streets; it seemed as if everyone was glued to the TV screen: Ruby killing Oswald, the funeral, a new president, Jackie Kennedy and her two children, and so on. There was no school until the following Wednesday. When I entered the conference room, the teachers were engaged in discussion more passionate and more audible than in any previous meeting. I shuffled some papers but listened intently to what the teachers were saying to each other. The focus of their remarks was (a) the happenings of the previous four days and (b) that this day had been a wasted one in terms of meeting the objectives of the lesson plans for the day. Teachers had great difficulty keeping students on task; their minds were on Dallas and their grief about a president they had adored and the behavior of the two Kennedy children. That day, the teachers were saying to each other, students learned nothing. Keeping order was a problem for the teachers.

Frankly, I was dumbstruck for several reasons. First, my frame of reference and that of the teachers in regard to understanding the behavior of students could not have been more different. Second, the same could be said about the difference between the frames of reference of the teachers and students. Third, it was a clear instance of how teachers are prepared and are socialized to regard the teaching of subject matter to be sacred, regardless of whether the students' bodies are in the classrooms and their minds in Dallas. Granted that assassinations of presidents are not, thank God, a frequent occurrence, there are other occurrences in the lives of students in relation to their parents and teachers where the differences between frames of reference are very stirring and destabilizing. The point is that if a frame of reference is not to be empty in meaning, it should sensitize us to when a situation means very different things to different observers. Fourth, in a context of productive learning, the teacher and students understand what each thinks and does; they are not in different worlds, although that is a goal that can only be approximately achieved. Alone or in combination, human beings are infinitely more complicated than atoms.

Following that Wednesday meeting, I spent the good part of two days outlining the different ways in which teachers could have exploited the burning interests and questions of students concerning national history, our political institutions and laws, cultural regional differences, religion and pageantry, and the like in a technical age in which verbal and visual communication are, for all practical purposes, instantaneous. It was an event that guaranteed that subject matter would come alive for students as subject matter rarely does.

We are not born with the concepts of frame of reference and learning. In the course of our development over the years, we learn to treat those concepts superficially, as clichés that explain little or nothing, preventing the gaining of insights into their practical and consequential effects. Even in the broad arena of human services, their importance is not taken as seriously as they should be. That is glaringly the case in schools, especially in regard to what we mean by learning. Again, we are reminded of Einstein, who subjected the conventional concept of time to scrutiny, hypotheses, theory, and experiment and demonstrated with mathematical precision that time was not absolute, that time and position coordinates of events had to be considered together and were not independent, absolute variables, common to all observers. We are not Einstein, but we are capable—indeed, we should feel obligated—of suggesting that the failures of the educational reform movement may be due, in large part, to the inability to examine some basic concepts we take for granted as being self-evidently valid. Can it be that the great philosopher Pogo was right: We have met the enemy and it is us?

We feel safe in assuming that by the time the reader has come to this final chapter, he or she is not in doubt that we, at least, believe that the context of productive learning requires a development of interpersonal relationship between students and teachers for the purpose of understanding, assimilating, and utilizing subject matter. But there is another aspect of such a context we believe is no less important; indeed, it inevitably comes up in interactions between students and teachers. This aspect was implied in John Dewey's assertion that school is not a preparation for life, but life itself.

Concretely, all of the problems in human relationships come up in classrooms; they are inevitable, albeit unpredictable. Many examples in our discussion concerning *Mr. Holland's Opus* illustrated this point. They also are the reason we focused earlier in this chapter on how the constitution of the classroom is forged. And by constitution, we clearly meant the rules by which relationships in the classroom will be judged. We also indicated that the constitution is "written" by the teacher, who is the executive, legislator, and judiciary. The net result is that students are expected to conform to a governance regardless of what they internally may think. Generally speaking, students do conform. But as they go from grade to grade and graduate, their unarticulated questions and resentments color their unfavorable reactions to acts of conformity. What we have just said is one of several reasons that over their school years students view classrooms and subject matter as increasingly irrelevant to them.

This fundamental problem arises because of lack of communication between the minds of the students and the mind of the teacher. The rock bottom reason for this lack is that the frames of reference of two people, a teacher and a student, never align and can only diverge. When Mr. Holland asked Ms. Lang what she liked most about herself, and when she said it was her hair, and when asked explained that her father said that her red hair is like a sunset, Holland told her to play "the sunset." This was an example where a student's difficulty with the subject matter (learning to play the clarinet) allowed Mr. Holland to release feelings she had been unable to express before, when she yet had no way to comprehend the value and purpose of music.

Two things happened. First, Mr. Holland reached out and understood what was going on in Ms. Lang's mind. He adjusted his own action to what he found. Second, she experienced what happened as a result of Holland's help and appreciated the opportunity he gave her to become whom she dreamed of being. This process is an example of how the frame of mind of a teacher and the frame of mind of a student can be related in a productive way. We have sat in and observed hundreds of classrooms, enough to allow us to predict that if you observe a classroom over a full year, you will be able to note many instances in which it would be obvious that the frame of reference of a student was not at all aligned with that of the teacher, and in practically none of these instances did the teacher deal with the student in the deeply interpersonal way Mr. Holland did with Ms. Lang. Needless to say, we have observed a teacher here and a teacher there who did the equivalent of what Mr. Holland did.

The number of such teachers is very tiny. But as we have emphasized in previous chapters, advances in science came from taking tiny effects seriously, and that is crystal clear in the case of Einstein and his formula $E = mc^2$. The tiny effect that Holland brings to the picture of education is a door to understanding what educational reform must be about in order to make a difference. It is not happenstance that, as in the case of Mr. Holland, the small number of teachers like him were catalysts for a high level of learning of subject matter by their students. Among this tiny group were several teachers in truly deplorable ghetto schools, all of which were failing schools. In each of these several instances, the teacher we observed was the only teacher in the school whose achievement test scores were above the national average. Our observations were done years ago. For a more contemporary confirmation in two new high schools serving clearly socially at-risk students, the reader should consult the books by Bensman and by Levine.[10]

To some readers, it may appear that we put too much emphasis on psychological factors in teacher-student relationships in comparison to what is traditionally called subject matter. The fact is that our emphasis on the interpersonal is a reflection of our belief or assumption that "in real life" the psychological and the subject matter are inevitably and fatefully in near constant interactions. Both constitute a single process and experience. This characteristic is true long before the student begins schooling, all the time in school, and remains true afterwards over the person's lifetime, being also continuously true for the teacher.

The point is subtle because people do know both elements we just mentioned: the subject matter and the interpersonal relationship. But these two elements are not related in the prevalent conception of learning as they deserve to be because of the facts that we know to be true about learning, how strongly the interpersonal relationship facilitates or interferes in learning and changes its outcome. The situation is similar to Einstein's mass m and energy E that were both well-known to physicists long before Einstein. The connection between them, a connection that changed entirely the way they were treated since they were understood to be related, was discovered in a tiny difference between gamma and 1. Two well-known concepts were considered unrelated until Einstein showed that they were inseparable. The two aspects of education—the subject matter and the interpersonal relationship—are both well-known but are, so far, considered independent of each other. We want to emphasize that they are inseparable. The inseparability is perceptible in obviously emotionally charged instances, such as in Mr. Holland's classroom. Even when such obvious conditions do not seem to exist in the classroom, the relationship between the interpersonal and the subject matter is never zero in strength. In other conditions, such as a physics or math classroom where there is no talking about music as a language of emotion and science is sold only as cold logic and precise measurement, the interpersonal factors are, in fact, also never zero in strength. While the learning process rivets on the subject matter, the interpersonal is quite high. It may be very invisible, kept private, not articulated, but it will always be present. Thus, considering the subject matter and the interpersonal relationship as separate is analogous to considering E and m as separate.

There is another way of posing the issues above. All schools have mission statements, which tell parents and the general public what the goals of the school are. Without exception, the mission statement will implicitly or explicitly state that the goal of education is not only to ensure that students assimilate and enlarge subject matter. The mission statement will, in one or another way, assert that one of the goals of schooling is to educate citizens, by which it is meant that students have to learn, understand, and act on the obligations they should feel in relationship to students and others in regard to the tolerance for different opinions and values, respect for authority, and the laws and traditions of the community and the larger society, especially as all of these are reflected in and derive from the Constitution's Bill of Rights. Over a period of a school year, in every classroom, every one of these obligations will be put to the test. For example, in the past decade, schools have been sensitized to the presence and behavior of bullies who intimidate other students. Such bullies have long been a fact of life in many schools. But today, if only because of parental pressure, schools are expected to deal directly and seriously with the problem. Let us further illustrate what we are saying by returning to *Mr. Holland's Opus.*

> This case example is about how Mr. Holland and Mr. Stadler were in open conflict with each other, which we described earlier on page 47.[11] Stadler was very smart and easily memorized everything. But his outstanding capability did not prevent him from being rude to the rest of the class, who were less gifted. When Stadler once insulted another student and the two almost started to fight at the end of a period, Holland ordered Stadler to stay after the bell rang. Stadler objected that it was improper for Holland to detain him and that Holland could not do anything because he (Stadler) knew everything Holland was supposed to teach in that class, and he did not need Holland's "bullshit."
>
> Holland got mad. He told Stadler that Stadler only appeared so smart and needed to prove that he appreciated music because the title of the class was music appreciation, and Holland did not see Stadler's appreciation of anything. Holland told Stadler that he was an inch from being suspended and ordered him to write a paper on the subject "Music—A Language of Emotion." Stadler objected, "You cannot make me do it," but Holland snapped, "Watch me." He warned Stadler that it was not for an extra credit and promised to flunk him if the report was not on Holland's desk at the end of the term.
>
> That would be all if not that a girl entered the room and handed Holland a note. He read it quickly, looked at Stadler, and ordered him to come to the room next Saturday at 10:00 A.M. Stadler asked, "Why?" Holland responded, "Research" and left the room.
>
> Stadler did not learn "why" until Saturday. He would remember that day his whole life. That day was the day of the burial of Mr. Russ, the drummer. Mr. Russ was killed in Vietnam. When Stadler and Holland arrived at the cemetery, it was still not clear to Stadler why he was there. But he sensed the sorrow in Holland and

other people from the school who also came, and he asked who the dead person was.

Holland was very brief. He told Stadler it was a kid whom he taught to bang a drum, Louis Russ. Russ made the state wrestling finals for three years running. Holland told Stadler, "He was never as smart as you are. He had to work real hard to even graduate. Maybe, it's why it meant so much to him." Holland did not say anything more. Soldiers fired three times. Russ's father was handed the American flag. A boy from Kennedy High played a trumpet, and the ceremony was over. "You can go now," said Mr. Holland, and Stadler went away. He understood how selfish his attitude toward other students was, and why.

When Holland was fired years later and his students arranged a celebration in his honor, there was a moment when Holland entered the auditorium and was walking down the aisle. Students were standing up and greeting him one after another, shaking hands. And one of those students was Mr. Stadler. In the midst of all of this, Stadler weaved his way to Holland, and Stadler's face was saying he was not sure that Holland would recognize him. But as soon as he stood in Holland's way, Glenn immediately said, "Mr. Stadler, you are *also* here?" Stadler responded, "I had to come."

In real life, of course, conflicts do not often have the happy consequences that one finds in Hollywood films. If Hollywood films tend to sugarcoat the unseemly, in the case of *Mr. Holland's Opus* the Stadler episode conveys an important truth.

One aspect is that the interpersonal relationship between Holland and Stadler allowed Holland to facilitate Stadler's appreciation of music in terms far greater than just memorizing the musical scales. The other aspect is that Stadler learned much more than music: He began to appreciate the role of interpersonal relationships between people, what they do and what it means to them. The third aspect is that the frames of reference in which Holland and Stadler were initially thinking about their relationship were dramatically different, and the difference required that Holland understood it and acted accordingly. The fourth aspect is that the subject matter itself was insufficient to ignite and develop Stadler's conception of himself and his path in life.

There is an issue concerning the thrust of our discussion of the context of productive learning we cannot avoid. It is one that has been raised by a number of colleagues with whom we have shared the contents of this book. The issue is that if one took our arguments seriously, it would require drastic changes in our school systems, based on the founding principles of the goals of school education. For example, the selection and training of educational personnel *entering* the field would have to be radically transformed. That is easy to say even if we had credible knowledge and experience about how to select and to train. But that credible knowledge and experience is hardly available. It would have to be obtained through careful research and evaluation of initial efforts and later through continuous re-evaluation of what would follow. That kind of a basis for action will take time to create and a level of funding that would be the opposite to piddling. Put in another way, we have to be realistically humble in the face of a very complex problem if we are ever to go beyond personal opinions and wishful thinking. And we have to be equally realistic that such efforts will predictably and understandably encounter resistance. Atoms do not have personalities, traditions, vested interests. Humans, individually and collectively, do.

In addition, it follows, as night does day, that schools no longer can be as large as they are, especially our middle and high schools, where cipherdom and anonymity are the fate of students and education is identified with the subject matter to the extent unacceptable from the point of view of education of a person. The subject matter is not conducive to education of a person. We would rather say that subject matter is of such crucial importance that the acquisition, understanding, and the utilization of subject matter must not be diluted by ignoring interpersonal factors.

We are writing this concluding chapter precisely at the time when, within a period of a few weeks, two hurricanes made shambles of lives and property of thousands of people. In the case of the first hurricane (Katrina), it was clear five days before it hit the mainland that a disaster was likely to become a reality. And this in a part of a country where hurricanes are standard fare. But that knowledge was vastly underestimated. And then followed weeks in which the name of the game was blame assignment. When a few weeks later the second hurricane (Rita) approached the Gulf states, the preventive efforts to avoid the worst failures of Katrina were an instance of learning from experience. The history of educational reform is one of failure after failure without any evidence that the powers that be learned anything. In fact, the current educational initiative by President George W. Bush focuses on sheer learning of subject matter to such extreme extent as to guarantee still another dismal failure.

What has to happen to change the course of educational reform? Where will the conceptual leadership come from? We refrain from predicting the future. We do not refrain from predicting that if we continue as we have, the social fabric of this country will be weakened.

Finally, one of the criticisms our point of view has met concerns time perspective. Namely, that we are asserting that even under the best circumstances, it will be decades before we see light at the end of the tunnel of educational reform. What, we are asked, do we do in the meantime? Our answer is that we have no alternative but to do the best we can in whatever ways we can to take whatever steps are available to us to fight the good fight. Our point of view is based on the caveat that an ounce of prevention is better than a pound of inadequate repair. But where to begin a systematic effort, and what has to be recognized to begin with?

In this book we have attempted to explain from the standpoint of the concept of productive learning Einstein's formula $E = mc^2$ for that large number of people who, in the past, had to regard themselves as lacking the kind of brain power to understand the formula but never wanted to truly believe that. Whether we succeed or not will be known to the reader. But the true message of this attempt comes not from the subject matter alone, but from the effort that the authors went through to even imagine a path on which the formula could be explained as we desired.

It is ironically fortunate that we can illustrate the difference between productive learning and just subject matter by using an example of two of the most important physicists whose contributions were discussed in this book: Lenard and Einstein.

Lenard received the Nobel Prize in 1905 for his discoveries concerning a photo-electric effect, and Einstein was awarded his Nobel Prize for explanation of the photo-electric effect in 1921. In one of the most acclaimed books on how to teach physics, written by Arnold B. Arons, titled *A Guide to Introductory Physics Teaching*,[12] the author discusses the works of Lenard and Einstein on the photo-electric effect. Many textbooks discuss the photo-electric effect along these lines. But the advice on how to teach about Lenard's experiments and Einstein's theory does not explain the context of Lenard's life, in which his ingenious experimental work on cathode rays was only a part.

How Einstein regarded Lenard's experiments is best given in a letter[13] he wrote to his future first wife, Mileva, in May 1901 (Mileva was pregnant).

> I just read a wonderful paper by Lenard on the generation of cathode rays by ultraviolet light. Under the influence of this beautiful piece, I am filled with such happiness and joy that I absolutely must share some of it with you. Be of good cheer, dear, and don't fret. After all, I am not leaving you, and will bring everything to happy conclusion. One just has to be patient! You'll see that one does not rest badly in my arms, even if things are beginning a little stupidly. How are you, darling? How is the boy?

Let us then review here a fragment from the biography of Lenard, using a quote from the official Web site of the Nobel Foundation.[14]

> Lenard was an experimentalist of genius, but more doubtful as a theorist. Some of his discoveries were great ones and others were very important, but he claimed for them more than their true value. Although he was given many honors (for instance, he received Honorary Doctorates of the Universities of Christiania, now Oslo,

in 1911, Dresden in 1922 and Pressburg in 1942, the Franklin Medal in 1905, the Eagle Shield of the German Reich in 1933, and was elected Freeman of Heidelberg in the same year), he believed that he was disregarded and this probably explains why he attacked other physicists in many countries. He became a convinced member of Hitler's National Socialist Party and maintained unreserved adherence to it. The party responded by making him the Chief of Aryan or German Physics.

Lenard wrote a textbook titled *Deutsche Physik* in four volumes,[15] which served the purpose of elevating German science to the highest level from the point of view of Hitler's government. In that book, Lenard attacked Einstein as not scientific. The textbook is well written in some sections as far as experimental, hands-on physics is concerned, which means the subject matter is handled perfectly. The motto Lenard gave his book in 1937 says "Written for the joy of all people who seek their spiritual peace in the well-grounded knowledge of Nature." It seems that Lenard was taught physics very well, but in an unproductive context. He knew the subject of experimental physics, but he supported a system that was responsible for one of the greatest crimes against humanity. Readers interested in seeking more information concerning Lenard can consult Appendix J.

Our example of how Mr. Holland handled the case of Mr. Stadler suggests that if Lenard was educated in a context of productive learning and had appreciated human values through a suitable personal contact with teachers like Holland, he *might* have avoided mistakes of his life, especially those in which he voluntarily colluded with the Nazis against scientists whose physics he did not appreciate and derogated using the most vitriolic and ad hominem language. When he criticized Einstein, whom he regarded as a typical Jewish scientist who published his thoughts before he verified their agreement with Nature experimentally, he considered himself a defender of German science, in which he saw the great value of first doing the required experiments and only then allowing oneself to publish the findings under the banner of science (Einstein was later writing on epistemological and methodological issues in physics as if he were trying to respond to Lenard's type of thinking). But Lenard did not apply the same standard to his own opinions and beliefs, which he regarded as self-evident facts, and he was blind to the issue.

The dramatic difference between Einstein and Lenard, both versed in the subject matter, illustrates the magnitude of the human, interpersonal dimensions that the subject matter they knew was insufficient to explain. We do not suggest that the school or college classroom can solve all problems, but it is certainly a mistake to reduce productive learning to the subject matter alone. It is no sin to fall short of the mark, but it is sinful not to have the mark. The writers of this book are not Utopians.

Let us elaborate on this by stating five points as a basis for discussion.

1. Attributing unreflectively characteristics you believe members of a group to possess to an individual in that group whom you meet for the first time is not justified.

2. "If I am not for myself, who will be? If I am not for others, what am I? If not now, when?" (from a rabbinic sage of centuries ago[16])

3. Tolerance of opposing points of view and allegiances.

4. Lincoln's Gettysburg Address and Second Inaugural Address.

5. The Declaration of Independence, the U.S. Constitution, the U.S. Bill of Rights.

All of these five points speak to the issue of what should inform the qualities and goals of human, interpersonal relationships, and what they imply is identifiable and applicable in every classroom. There are more points, but the five above are sufficient for our purpose. Our overarching purpose is to assert that the principles illustrated by those five points are applicable and observable many times in any classroom over the period of the school year. We go so far as to say that if you observe a classroom every school day for one year, there would be no day when at least one of these principles would not apply. It makes no difference whether we are talking about the first grade or a classroom of high school seniors. Obviously, applying any one of these principles has to take into account the personal intellectual and emotional maturity of students. When we say applying these principles, we in no way suggest "telling" the students or sermonizing about the principles in terms of abstractions, but rather always in connection with something that happens in the classroom and outside, something concrete, known to everyone in that room. When, on an earlier page, we discussed the constitution of the classroom, the rules that everyone in the classroom is obligated to honor, we pointed out that we have never observed a classroom in the early weeks of the school year in which those principles were discussed rather than handed down to the students. Indeed, each of the five features above is a part of the basis for our emphasis on the forging of the constitution of the classroom. *We should hasten to add that we are not advocating participatory democracy, in which students and teachers alike each have one vote. But students do deserve to have explained, discuss, and understand why the teacher is explicitly given and must honor the responsibility and authority to make final decisions.*

Preparatory programs for teachers in no way select and train teachers how to think about and act appropriately on these principles and how these principles are related to the interpersonal context of the relationship between a student and a teacher irrespective of the subject matter. If what we have said is taken seriously, we should be humble enough to say that how to select and train these teachers will require far more knowledge and experience than we now possess. In embarking on new seas and charting our course, we will be beset by more than one failure. So what else is new? If you think that what we are suggesting is based on pie-in-the-sky thinking and an indulgence of rampant psychologizing, and if you believe that our educational system can be repaired more quickly in less non-cosmetic ways, we predict that you will end up confirming that the more things change the more they remain the same, which is tantamount to saying that you are engaging in a self-defeating approach, albeit with good intentions. In the educational arena, the road to hell has been paved and re-paved many times with good intentions. But just as the paradox of the speed of light could not be resolved without changing the concept of time, with great consequences, the desired reform of education, with consequences that are desperately needed, cannot be initiated without setting straight the principal dimensions in which the learning process becomes productive through an altered relationship between the frames of mind of a teacher and a student.

In the very small number of instances we have observed that approximated such an altered relationship, the level of acquisition of subject matter by students was strikingly high. This result is found even in certain classrooms in ghetto schools in which the level of performance of the students is way beyond other classrooms with similar, at-risk students. We have given references to two books by Bensman and Levine about schools in which such results occurred not only in a single classroom, but in the entire school.

The examples of Holland and Wolters, or Einstein and Lenard, illustrate the point that educators do not have criteria for determining what constitutes a context of productive learning and what does not. Our analogy between the frames of reference of two observers in Einstein's physics and between two frames of reference in the minds of a student and a teacher, like between Mr. Holland and Ms. Lang, or Mr. Holland and Mr. Stadler, says that the context of productive learning may have enormous implications if it is taken seriously by researchers, educators, and leaders of democratic governments. By analogy to the magnitude of implications that Einstein's new understanding of time had for later developments in physics and their technological offspring, the magnitude of consequences that the altered approach to the educational reform may have cannot be fully predicted today. But if our analogy holds, better understanding of the relationship between the minds of a teacher and a student, far beyond the subject matter itself, may lead to currently unimaginable improvement in education.

Also, as in the case of the paradox of the speed of light and Einstein's theory of relationship between frames of reference of two observers that resolved the paradox, if the key relationship between the teacher and student is not understood, no lasting progress will occur, and the problem of starting a meaningful reform will not be solved.

The development of reforms based on the concept of a context of productive learning may resemble the development that followed from the realization that time is not absolute. The idea quickly led Einstein to the formula $E = mc^2$. But it took years for people to trace the consequences, carry out a great number of experiments, and only then arrive at practical implications, including how to generate electricity from nuclear power and understanding of why the Sun and other stars shine.

The question where to begin a systematic effort, and what has to be recognized to begin with, has only one answer when one takes the concept of a context of productive learning seriously. We have to realize that the absolute assumptions about what happens or should happen in the minds of students and teachers are not justified and cannot be limited to the subject matter. A qualitatively new approach is required.

The rationale of productive learning is based on the relationship between a teacher and a student. This relationship is the vehicle that allows the teacher and the student to align their minds and begin a study of the world. And what they learn this way, in the first place, is the respect and admiration for the possibility of understanding others and benefiting from that understanding. But the required theory of relationship between the minds of a student and a teacher is poorly known today and requires advanced studies of the highest caliber. One cannot gain insight into the required theory without going far beyond the subject matter itself. In the real world, the subject matter in the learning process is always intertwined with the relationship between the minds of a teacher and a student. Just as the formula $E = mc^2$ states that energy and mass are an indissoluble unity, so in the classroom the interpersonal and the subject matter are similarly indissolubly two aspects of the same process.

One of us (Głazek) had the opportunity to observe two students in a classroom with whom his relationship was of such depth and quality that he could learn easily what they thought about their experience in a very specific situation. The experience concerned an introductory course of physics for physics teachers, specifically on electric circuits.

The purpose of the course was to enlarge the thinking and pedagogy of high school teachers, an effort that involved them over six weeks in summer, within a much longer program on staff development for these teachers. The physical-spatial context of the experience Głazek can describe in terms of the following items:

1. Everything took place in a large room in a large school.

2. There were seven large round tables in the room.

3. At each table, there were sitting four or five teachers working in a team on a sequence of written instructions concerning electric circuits.[17]

4. There were four roving instructors to help a team, and there were rules designed for the teams to communicate with the roving instructors about the progress and/or problems in a team's work.

5. At each table there were two flags: a red one to be put up on the table when a problem was encountered by a team, and a green one to be put up when a team's solution of a successive problem in a well-designed sequence of problems was ready.

6. I was sitting at a table in the role of a student of the course like all other teachers, with two other people: my daughter Dominika (at that time 17) and my son Kuba (at that time 15).

7. I knew the subject matter very well, and I could focus on observing how my children were faring and, especially, how the instructors interacted with the teams when the latter had either a red or green flag up.

8. My children sometimes raised a red and sometimes a green flag, and different instructors were coming to our table.

9. After a while, at some point when my children completed a task, I said, "It seems to me you are ready to raise a flag," and my hand went for the flag that was lying on the other side of the table. But Dominika halted my hand and said, "Wait a moment. We do not want this instructor to see our flag. Let us wait for Mano." Kuba silently confirmed with a nod of his head.

10. Throughout the experience, I fully cooperated with my children's systematic maneuvering with their flags so that much more often they could talk with Mano than with the other instructors whom they were not so happy to talk with.

11. After the course was completed, my children passed a test as all adults would have to pass and they passed the test well. Mano even told us that they did very well in comparison to adults.

12. Almost 10 years later, I asked Dominika and Kuba about their memories of the course. I asked them what they learned. They did not remember much about the details of the electric circuits that they studied. They did remember vividly that they liked to talk to Mano and not to other instructors. They said that if they remember and understand how the electric currents flow, it is because Mano talked with them in a way that made them far more comfortable and more interested in understanding the subject matter than other instructors did.

What we have described is, on the surface, a relatively simple, unnoteworthy state of affairs. Nevertheless, what we have described is an instance of how, in the minds of two adolescents, the learning of subject matter and interpersonal relationships were intertwined to the point that 10 years later they remembered Mano with fondness and gratitude and other instructors with far less positive feelings. And it is not clear whether they would have learned what they were supposed to about the electric circuits if Mano was not there. In their own unsophisticated and untutored way, they knew that Mano engendered in them feelings of safety, trust, and mutual understanding that the other instructors did not. Over the years, our observations in classrooms contained many instances such as Dominika and Kuba experienced.

The relationship between perception of events by a student and a teacher cannot be understood in as simple ways as the relationship only between the four coordinates of the events in Einstein's theory can be. But when we realize that, it becomes clear that the interpersonal student-teacher relationship cannot be understood by the ways currently employed to initiate meaningful reforms. The necessary insight will not be gained in the foreseeable future unless a national effort exists with resources and capabilities appropriate to the goal. And this goal surpasses in its complexity and intellectual and practical difficulty any previous national effort of institutional change.

It is beyond the purposes of this book to demonstrate that the relationship between frames of reference of two humans is far more complex than the four-dimensional relativity of Einstein. In an earlier draft of this book, we attempted such a demonstration using models, but it soon became apparent that it would require many pages to justify such models. So, when we say that the complexity of Einstein's four-dimensional relativity is, so to speak, a piece of cake in comparison to the daunting task of identifying, analyzing, and understanding the multidimensional nature of the teacher-student or other interpersonal relationships, the humble stance is the only one we can take, even if for no other reason that we know so little about the internal and external ecologies of human social interpersonal behavior. Let us keep in mind that Einstein's four-dimensional theory of relativity is a consequence of more than two millennia of developments in mathematics and sciences.

Einstein was aware that people who attempt to contribute to science often lose track of reality by focusing on associating or combining reproducible elements that they already know, instead of trying to identify and reach understanding of what they need to deal with. The same comment concerns educators and reformers.[18]

Appendices

The following collection of Appendices is provided here for readers who are inclined to study details of arguments used in the chapters concerning the formula $E = mc^2$. The context of productive learning must include options for search of paths to further study. The Appendices provide some opportunities for enquiry concerning elements of reasoning that the authors know are difficult. An additional trouble that the readers may encounter is the difficulty of finding suitable sources of information that directly relate to our story of $E = mc^2$. Instead of directing the readers to hard-to-find or hard-to-access sources, we decided to provide these Appendices. But it is not necessary to read the Appendices in order to grasp the meaning and content of our story of $E = mc^2$.

Appendix A

Energy of Motion of a Body

Why does the energy of motion contain factor $\frac{1}{2}$ in front of mv^2? One of the ways in which this factor can be understood is the following.

As a result of the long studies of Newton and his predecessors and followers, we know today that a body of mass m at height H above the ground has gravitational energy that is larger than the gravitational energy of the same body on the ground by the amount that is proportional to the mass m itself and the height H. Namely, the amount is gmH. The proportionality coefficient g is universal, in the sense that it characterizes the gravity of the Earth, independently of the properties of the small body of mass m that the Earth's gravity acts on. Thus, the factor g is the same for all masses m.

The same constant g tells us how long the body will fly up when we throw it from the ground straight up with velocity v. Namely, it will fly up until its velocity becomes zero. It has been established by experiments that the gravitational factor g represents the rate of change in time with which velocities of all bodies change in a free fall in the Earth's gravity. The change of velocity when a body falls freely toward the ground is given always by the universal g times the time of fall. The same happens when a body is thrown up and slows down. At the beginning, on the ground, the body has velocity v and after some time t the body reaches the maximal height H where its velocity is slowed down to zero. The height H is reached by the body in the time t in a uniformly slowed motion with the factor g playing the role of acceleration. In this case, it is an "acceleration" that amounts to slowing down, and should perhaps be called "deceleration," or "negative acceleration." But people continue to call the steady change of velocity in time an "acceleration" irrespective of whether it is positive, that is, when the velocity grows in time, or negative, that is, when the velocity steadily diminishes in time. In the case of flying up, this means that the velocity v is slowed down to 0 with gravitational acceleration

g over time t. We thus have that the initial velocity v is equal to g times t. Hence, t is equal to v divided by g.

In a uniformly accelerated motion, the distance is a quadratic function of time (see below). When the acceleration is g, we have $H = \frac{1}{2}gt^2$. The factor $\frac{1}{2}$ in this result is the origin of multiplication of mv^2 by $\frac{1}{2}$ in the expression for the energy of motion.

Why is H equal to $\frac{1}{2}gt^2$ and not some other number times gt^2? Suppose that the velocity at the time t is zero (the body slowed down to zero at the height H), and that it was v at the time 0 (when it was thrown from the ground level). If the motion was uniformly slowed down with acceleration (deceleration) g, the final velocity 0 is the result of uniform decrease of the body velocity in time, from v to 0. At the height H reached at the time t, the velocity is zero. The average velocity (average in time) is then $gt + 0$ divided by 2, which gives $\frac{1}{2}gt$. The path of flight straight up in the time t, denoted here by H, equals the average velocity times the time t, or $\frac{1}{2}gt$ times t, which equals $\frac{1}{2}gt^2$.

When we insert the expression $H = \frac{1}{2}gt^2$ into the expression for gravitational energy gmH, we obtain the conclusion that gmH must be equal to $\frac{1}{2}gmgt^2$. We can regroup the factors and see that the gravitational energy is equal $\frac{1}{2}m(gt)^2$. But gt equals v. Hence, we obtain the gravitational energy at the top of flight equal to $\frac{1}{2}mv^2$. Since the energy of motion at the beginning of the way up is equal to the increase of the gravitational energy at the maximal height H, we obtain the conclusion that the energy of motion of mass m with velocity v is given by $\frac{1}{2}mv^2$. The factor $\frac{1}{2}$ is therefore explained by the factor $\frac{1}{2}$ in the expression $H = \frac{1}{2}gt^2$ that characterizes the motion with a constant acceleration g.

Appendix B

Frequencies and Energies of Photons
If Time Is Absolute

This Appendix concerns the difference between the frequencies and energies that Ming and Max see, according to the pre-Einstein way of thinking about the speed of light and time, for the same two photons, which are to be absorbed in the matchbox (see Chapter 11, page 129).

We can make quantitative statements about the energies of the photons because the energies are simply related to the frequencies of the photons (by multiplication by the Planck constant h, as explained starting on page 106). The frequencies that Max and Ming see may be determined from the knowledge of the distance between the signals and the speeds with which the signals are approaching the observers.

We start with the right photon. If the distance between the signals is D and the signals move with speed c toward the observer, as it happens in the case of Max, the time needed for the signals to travel the distance D is obtained when we divide that distance by the speed c. The frequency that Max sees is an inverse of that time interval (the inverse relationship between the frequency and the time interval of arrivals of signals was discussed earlier, beginning on page 110). Thus, the frequency f that Max sees is obtained by dividing the speed c by the distance D.

Now, Ming sees the signals of the right photon as coming with the speed equal to c *plus* v. The reader should not forget that the pre-Einstein reasoning is flawed precisely because it is based on the assumption that velocities add like that. In reality, the speed of photons is the same for Max and Ming, but this paradox cannot be resolved within the pre-Einstein way of thinking, which we apply now and in which time is an absolute concept. In the pre-Einstein approach, the time interval between the Ming eye meeting one signal and the next signal is obtained by dividing the distance D between the signals by the speed of the signals, $c + v$, instead of only c as was done in the Max case. Since the frequency that Ming sees is the inverse of this time interval, the frequency Ming sees is $c + v$ divided by D.

Our quantitative statements about the frequencies that Max and Ming see for the right photon can now be expressed in the following way. According to Max, the right photon has frequency f equal to c divided by D. According to Ming, the right photon has frequency equal to $c + v$ divided by D. The difference between these two frequencies is equal to the velocity v divided by the distance D. Thus, the frequency that Ming sees for the right photon is equal to f that Max sees *plus* the correction equal to v divided by D.

When we now go on to consider the photon that comes from the left side, namely, the photon that moves in the same direction in which Ming moves with respect to the matchbox, the pre-Einstein expectation is that Ming sees the left photon as approaching him from behind with the speed equal to c *minus* v. By the same reasoning as for the right photon, we can conclude that the frequency of the left photon is seen by Ming as smaller than the frequency f that Max sees: One can say that Ming is moving as if he was trying to outrun the left photon (photons are too fast to be outrun), and the signals that constitute the photon catch up with Ming less frequently than they would if Ming was not moving with respect to Max. Quantitatively, the left photon frequency for Ming is equal to the frequency f that Max sees for the left photon *minus* the correction of v divided by D.

At this point, we have determined that Ming sees the frequencies of the right and left photon as different from the frequency f that Max sees, the same for both photons. And if we denote the frequency that Ming sees for the right photon by f_r (subscript r refers to "right") and the frequency that Ming sees for the left photon by f_l (subscript l refers to "left"), our result can be expressed by saying that f_r equals f plus v divided by D and f_l equals f minus v divided by D. *That the same correction is just added in the case of the right photon and subtracted for the left photon is the consequence of the pre-Einstein theory that the time variable is the same for both observers and velocities plainly add or subtract as our daily experience tells us.*

In order to obtain the energies of the right and left photon as seen by Ming, one has to multiply the frequencies f_r and f_l by the Planck constant h.[1] Thus, the left photon energy is $E_l = hf_l$ and the right photon energy is $E_r = hf_r$. The matchbox absorbs both photons and Ming will say that the energy of the matchbox increases by the amount Δ_{Ming}, which is equal to the sum of E_r plus E_l. But the correction due to a non-zero velocity v in E_r is opposite to the correction in E_l because the corrections in the frequencies are opposite. The sum of energies that gives Δ_{Ming} is exactly the same as Δ_{Max} independently of the value of the velocity v. The corrections cancel out and the result of the pre-Einstein approach is that $\Delta_{Ming} = \Delta_{Max}$.

Appendix C

Max's Time Coordinates of Four Events

This Appendix explains the derivation of Equation 14.1 on page 162 in Chapter 14. One has to read the section that contains Equation 14.1 and the section before that one in order to understand the meaning of symbols used here. One can also accept Equation 14.1 on faith and proceed with reading of the main text without working through this Appendix.

Since the pulse of light is produced in the event *Producing*, which means at the Max reference point with $x_{Max} = 0$ at time $t_{Max} = 0$, and it reaches the driver in the event *Reflecting*, Max can tell where the event *Reflecting* occurs if he knows how long the pulse was traveling. Namely, he can multiply the speed of light by the time of travel of the pulse, and he obtains the distance the pulse traveled along the platform starting from the reference point. Max knows that the time of travel of the pulse is equal to the difference in time between the events *Reflecting* and *Producing*. Since the pulse started at the event *Producing*, which has the Max time coordinate 0, the time of travel of the pulse to the driver is equal to the Max time coordinate of the event *Reflecting*. Similarly, since the event *Producing* happens at $x_{Max} = 0$, the distance that the pulse travels is equal to the Max space coordinate of the event *Reflecting*. Therefore, $x_{Max\ Reflecting}$ must be equal to the speed of light c times $t_{Max\ Reflecting}$.

This does not mean that Max needs to make such calculations as the only way to find the coordinates of the event *Reflecting*. Max can measure the position of the event *Reflecting* by tracing the pulse of light and noticing where the point at which the pulse reaches the driver is located on the platform. Max can read the time coordinate of this event on the clock that stands on the platform at the same point. What we have said in the previous paragraph means that there is a necessary relationship between the results that Max obtains from his measurements of $x_{Max\ Reflecting}$ and $t_{Max\ Reflecting}$.

Thus, we have established that $x_{Max\ Reflecting}$ must be equal to c times $t_{Max\ Reflecting}$. We also know that $x_{Max\ Receiving}$ must be equal to v times $t_{Max\ Receiving}$, since the conductor travels with velocity v along the platform. Then, the condition that the events *Receiving* and *Reflecting* are connected by the pulse of light implies an exact necessary relation between the Max time coordinates of these events.

We have

$$x_{Max\ Reflecting} - x_{Max\ Receiving} = c\ (t_{Max\ Receiving} - t_{Max\ Reflecting}).$$

Substituting in this result the two conditions $x_{Max\ Reflecting} = ct_{Max\ Reflecting}$ and $x_{Max\ Receiving} = vt_{Max\ Receiving}$, one obtains

$$ct_{Max\ Reflecting} - vt_{Max\ Receiving} = ct_{Max\ Receiving} - ct_{Max\ Reflecting},$$

and by adding $ct_{Max\ Reflecting}$ and $vt_{Max\ Receiving}$ to both sides equally, one arrives at

$$2ct_{Max\ Reflecting} = (c+v)\ t_{Max\ Receiving},$$

which after division of both sides by the sum $c + v$ implies that

$$t_{Max\ Receiving} = 2\frac{c}{c+v}t_{Max\ Reflecting}. \qquad [\text{C.1}]$$

The velocity v enters here independently of the existence of Ming. It enters because the events *Reflecting* and *Receiving* are defined in terms of physically observable effects, and Max sees the train as moving with the velocity v in his frame of reference no matter what Ming might say.

It is important to look closer at Equation C.1. If the velocity v of the train is zero, factor $\frac{c}{c+v}$ is equal to 1 and $t_{Max\ Receiving}$ is just 2 times longer than $t_{Max\ Reflecting}$. This is what happens when the train does not move: The time needed by the pulse to go forth and back is twice longer than to go one way. But when the train moves and the velocity v is not zero, the factor $\frac{c}{c+v}$ differs from 1 and the time $t_{Max\ Receiving}$ is less than 2 times longer than $t_{Max\ Reflecting}$.

What time reading does Max obtain for the event *Midtime?* The *Midtime* event is that in which the reference clock of Ming displays time T. This must happen when the clock is in the middle of its travel between the events *Producing* and *Receiving*. Max can see that the hands of Ming's clock read T when the clock is at half of its way between the events

Producing and *Receiving*. Therefore, it is logically necessary that the Max time coordinate of the event *Midtime* is equal to half of $t_{Max\ Receiving}$. Therefore, we divide our previous result for $t_{Max\ Receiving}$ in Equation C.1 by 2 and obtain the conclusion that the Max readings of time for the events *Midtime* and *Reflecting* are related by Equation 14.1 on page 162.

Appendix D

Is the Speed of Light Special?

This Appendix is written for readers who are particularly interested in the theory of special relativity and who are familiar with algebra. It shows that the existence of a maximal speed common to all observers in steady motion is a mathematical consequence of the assumption that all of these observers see the world in basically equivalent ways. The existence of the common maximal speed can thus be interpreted as a logical necessity of the leading principle of relativity that no observers are privileged as long as they move with respect to each other with steady velocities. Thus, the conclusions one arrives at according to this logic are independent of any specific mechanism by which any object, including light, can move with this special maximal speed or smaller speeds in the real world. In particular, it is not formally necessary to use the existence of light in the mathematical reasoning, and it is hence also not relevant if one assumes that light moves with a speed exactly equal to the common maximal speed or not.[1]

Suppose that the coordinates t' and x' in the frame of reference that moves with velocity v with respect to the frame of reference with coordinates t and x are related to each other by the linear equations

$$t' = At + Bx,$$
$$x' = Ct + Dx.$$

The linearity of our equations means that we assume that time and space are homogeneous and the coordinates we consider reflect that property. Moreover, when the equations are linear, the equations of the inverse relation are of the same kind—also linear. This means that none of the observers is privileged by the form of the equations that describe the relationship between their coordinates when the equations are linear.[2]

Inhomogeneous linear equations can be made homogeneous by a shift of coordinates, which is allowed by our leading principle of no privileged observers and homogeneity of space and time.

An object that stands at the origin $x' = 0$ in the frame (x', t') must move with velocity v in the frame (x, t). Thus, the events with coordinates $(x', t') = (0, t')$ must have coordinates $(x, t) = (vt, t)$. An object that stands at the origin $x = 0$ in the frame (x, t) must move with velocity $-v$ in the frame (x', t'). So, the events with coordinates $(x, t) = (0, t)$ must have coordinates $(x', t') = (-vt', t')$. Inserting these pairs of coordinates into the linear equations, one obtains that $C = -vD$ and $C = -vA$, and thus also $D = A$. The only unknowns are A and B. One can apply two successive changes of coordinates with coefficients A_1 and B_1 and with A_2 and B_2. The resulting change is expressible in terms of coefficients A_3 and B_3 that describe the combined transformation in terms of the same algebraic structure if and only if

$$\frac{v_1 A_1}{B_1} = \frac{v_2 A_2}{B_2},$$

where the left-hand side depends only on velocity v_1 and the right-hand side depends only on velocity v_2. The only way to satisfy this condition is that

$$vA(v) = -c^2 B(v),$$

where c^2 denotes a universal constant, denoted by c^2 on the basis of hindsight: We know what comes out of the reasoning at the end. Note that $A(v)$ must not depend on the sign of v in order not to distinguish a direction in space, $A(v) = A(-v)$. In summary, one must have

$$\begin{bmatrix} A(v) & B(v) \\ C(v) & D(v) \end{bmatrix} = A(v) \begin{bmatrix} 1 & -\dfrac{v}{c^2} \\ -v & 1 \end{bmatrix},$$

with some unknown constant c. The reciprocal relation is given by the inverse of the above matrix and must be also obtained by changing v to $-v$, whereby one obtains $A(v) = \gamma$ with γ equal to the inverse of

$$\sqrt{1 - \frac{v^2}{c^2}}.$$

Application of two such transformations one after another produces a third one that contains the velocity

$$v_3 = \frac{v_2 + v_1}{1 + \dfrac{v_2 v_1}{c^2}}, \qquad \text{[D.1]}$$

and this rule for combining velocities preserves the speed equal to the constant c. So far, the speed of light in vacuum has not been distinguished experimentally from the absolute constant c that should exist according to the above mathematical argument. The argument ignores the quantum nature of matter and light.

Appendix E

Einstein's Relationship
Between Frames of Reference

This Appendix summarizes details of the equations that relate coordinates of Max and Ming according to the Einstein theory, for readers who are interested in them. These details are not necessary to understand the main text.

We know from Appendix D that $A = \gamma$, $B = -v\gamma/c^2$, $C = -v\gamma$, and $D = \gamma$, where the factor γ is equal to the inverse of $\sqrt{1 - \frac{v^2}{c^2}}$. Therefore, the pre-Einstein Equation 12.1 on page 146 is replaced in Einstein's special theory of relativity by

$$t_{Max} = \gamma\, t_{Ming} + \frac{\gamma v}{c^2}\, x_{Ming}, \qquad\qquad \text{[E.1]}$$

and the pre-Einstein Equation 12.2 on page 146 is replaced in Einstein's special theory of relativity by

$$x_{Max} = \gamma v\, t_{Ming} + \gamma x_{Ming}. \qquad\qquad \text{[E.2]}$$

The word "special" refers to the fact that the velocity of Ming with respect to Max does not vary in time. A "general" theory concerns observers who move with respect to each other with velocities that may change in time. We are not discussing the general theory of relativity in this book.

The two equations, E.1 and E.2, are commonly called *the Lorentz transformation*, after Dutch physicist Hendrik Antoon Lorentz who wrote them earlier than Einstein (in 1904) for different reasons. Lorentz was working on the theory of material media using equations that described the motion of charged particles, changes of currents, and variations of the associated electric and magnetic fields in time. In these equations, Lorentz observed a possibility to consider new variables t' and x' that were connected to the variables t and x by equations identical to E.1 and E.2. The use of new variables t' and x', instead of t and x, allowed Lorentz to carry out his calculations in a convenient way. But Lorentz did not associate his variables with any alteration of the concept of measurement of time because he saw no reason to think that the time of an event could depend on an observer.

Appendix F

Time and the Pythagorean Theorem

Τ his Appendix is for readers interested in obtaining the factor γ from the geometry of a model for clocks that is described in the main text. Understanding of the main idea described in the text does not require knowledge of this Appendix.

Let us look at the distances that characterize the path of light in Ming's reference clock as seen by Max, shown in Figure F.1.

Figure F.1   This is the path of light in the moving clock shown in Figure 15.2. During the time $\frac{1}{2}T$, the light must cover the distance d, which is the length of the hypotenuse in a triangle with height H and base $\frac{1}{2}vT$. During the entire period T, the light pulse covers the distance $2d$, instead of only $2H$ that it covers in time T_0 in a standing clock, in which it goes only straight up and down the height H.

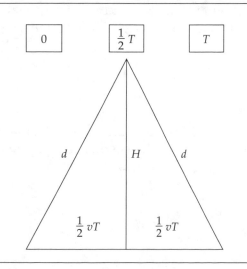

The Pythagorean theorem says that the square of the length of the hypotenuse d in Figure F.1 is equal to the sum of squares of the lengths of the two sides, the vertical H and horizontal $\frac{1}{2}vT$, that form a right angle. This means that d^2 is equal to the sum of $H^2 + (\frac{1}{2}vT)^2$. Since the distance d is traveled by light with speed c in the period $\frac{1}{2}T$ according to Max, Max knows that d must equal $\frac{1}{2}cT$. Max also knows that the height H of the Ming clock is the same as in the Max clock. Hence, the height H that Max inserts into the Pythagorean theorem must be equal to the time of travel upward by the pulse of light according to Ming, $\frac{1}{2}T_0$, times the speed of light c. Remember that T_0 is also the unit of time on the Max clocks.

The Pythagorean theorem for the triangle with sides d, H, and $\frac{1}{2}vT$ states that $d^2 = H^2 + (\frac{1}{2}vT)^2$. Knowing that $d = \frac{1}{2}cT$ and $H = \frac{1}{2}cT_0$, we have

$$\left(\frac{1}{2}cT\right)^2 = \left(\frac{1}{2}vT\right)^2 + \left(\frac{1}{2}cT_0\right)^2.$$

Multiplying both sides by 4 we obtain

$$c^2T^2 = v^2T^2 + c^2T_0^2.$$

Subtracting v^2T^2 from both sides and dividing both sides by the difference $c^2 - v^2$, one obtains

$$T^2 = \frac{c^2}{c^2 - v^2}T_0^2.$$

The coefficient of proportionality between T^2 and T_0^2, the ratio $\frac{c^2}{c^2 - v^2}$ is typically written in the form in which the numerator and denominator are divided by c^2, which renders this coefficient as inverse of $1 - \frac{v^2}{c^2}$. The equation of proportionality of the squares of times is equivalent to the equation of proportionality of times, in which the coefficient is given by a square root,

$$T = \frac{1}{\sqrt{1 - \frac{v^2}{c^2}}}T_0.$$

The ratio of T to T_0 tells us how the unit of time T_0 that Ming uses is seen by Max, and this ratio gives us the coefficient A discussed in Chapter 15 (see page 166),

$$A = \frac{1}{\sqrt{1 - \frac{v^2}{c^2}}}.$$

Traditionally, the inverse of $\sqrt{1 - \frac{v^2}{c^2}}$ is called γ, and we have $A = \gamma$.

Appendix G

How γ Depends on v

The factor γ depends on the velocity v of two observers with respect to each other. In our example, it is the velocity of Ming with respect to Max. The dependence on v has many consequences. One of them is the formula $E = mc^2$ itself: Einstein derived this formula for the first time using the dependence of γ on the velocity v. In this Appendix, we explain the graph given in Figure 15.3 on page 171, which illustrates how γ depends on v.

The formula for γ is

$$\gamma = \frac{1}{\sqrt{1 - \dfrac{v^2}{c^2}}}.$$

When the velocity v is much smaller than the speed of light c, the number $\frac{v}{c}$ is very small; its square is doubly small, in the sense that it is a $\frac{v}{c}$ fraction of $\frac{v}{c}$ itself. For example, if

$$\frac{v}{c} = \frac{1}{1,000}, \text{ then } \frac{v^2}{c^2} = \frac{1}{1,000,000},$$

and so on. Therefore, for velocities v much smaller than c, we have a number very close to 1 under the square root. The square root of that number is even closer to 1, and γ for small velocities, as an inverse of a number very close to 1, is also very close to 1. It is equal to 1 when v is zero.

When the velocity v grows toward c, the ratio $\frac{v}{c}$ approaches 1. When one subtracts a number close to 1 from 1, under the square root, one obtains a very small number. The square root of a small number is a larger but still small number, and this small number is in the denominator in γ. Therefore, when v grows, γ increases. When v tends to c, γ tends to infinity because it is an inverse of the square root of the difference between

1 and $\frac{v^2}{c^2}$ and that difference tends to 0. An inverse of a very small number is a very large number.

Einstein's derivation of the formula $E = mc^2$ was based on the behavior of the factor γ as function of v when v is very close to 0, so small that the deviation of γ from 1 is as tiny as one wishes it to be. We need to describe this deviation as a function of v in order to explain the origin of the formula $E = mc^2$.

Since γ is an inverse of a square root of $1 - \frac{v^2}{c^2}$, γ times the square root of $1 - \frac{v^2}{c^2}$ gives 1. This is written as

$$\gamma \sqrt{1 - \frac{v^2}{c^2}} = 1.$$

Squaring both sides of this equation, we have

$$\gamma^2 \left(1 - \frac{v^2}{c^2}\right) = 1.$$

For very small v, the ratio $\frac{v^2}{c^2}$ is very small in comparison to 1 and γ must be very close to 1. Let us write γ as 1 plus a very small number s and let us find s as a function of v when v tends to 0. We have $\gamma = 1 + s$ and γ^2 equal to $1 + s$ times $1 + s$, or $1 + 2s + s^2$, and

$$(1 + 2s + s^2) \left(1 - \frac{v^2}{c^2}\right) = 1.$$

Multiplying the brackets we get

$$1 + 2s - \frac{v^2}{c^2} + s^2 - 2s\frac{v^2}{c^2} - s^2\frac{v^2}{c^2} = 1.$$

The number 1 can be removed from both sides. Keeping only $2s$ on the left-hand side and moving all other terms to the right-hand side, we have

$$2s = \frac{v^2}{c^2} - s^2 + 2s\frac{v^2}{c^2} + s^2\frac{v^2}{c^2}.$$

The first term on the right-hand side, $\frac{v^2}{c^2}$ is very small. The terms s^2 and $2s\frac{v^2}{c^2}$ are doubly small, and the last term, $s^2\frac{v^2}{c^2}$, is triply small when s is of the order of the first term, $\frac{v^2}{c^2}$. When the doubly and triply small corrections are neglected, which is an increasingly accurate approximation when v tends to 0, we have

$$s = \frac{1}{2}\frac{v^2}{c^2}.$$

This means that when v tends to 0 the behavior of the Einstein factor γ as function of v is given by $1 + s$ and this is the following function:

$$\gamma = 1 + \frac{1}{2}\frac{v^2}{c^2}.$$

Appendix H

Energy of Photons According to Ming

Ming travels head on toward the right photon. His eye meets the signals in the right photon more often than Max's eye does, and Ming sees the frequency of the right photon as larger than f seen by Max, by some small amount. The left photon comes to Ming from behind and the signals of the left photon come to Ming's eye less often than to Max's eye. Ming sees the frequency of the left photon as lower than Max by some small amount. In the pre-Einstein analysis on pages 130–131, the correction to the left photon frequency has equal size and opposite sign to the correction to the right photon frequency. So, when one multiplies the frequencies by the Planck constant h to obtain the energies of the photons according to Ming (in the pre-Einstein approach), and when one adds these energies, the corrections cancel out. This is why, in the pre-Einstein analysis, the combined energy of the two photons according to Ming, which we denote by Δ_{Ming}, is the same as the combined energy of the photons that Max sees, denoted by Δ_{Max}. In the Einstein theory, the situation is different because Ming counts time differently from Max and we have to include the factor γ in the improved analysis.

We recall that the frequency of a photon seen by an observer is the inverse of the time interval between arrivals in the observer's eye of successive signals that constitute the photon. This inverse relationship was used in our discussion of the pre-Einstein description of the absorption process on pages 128–131. We must now include the fact that Ming counts the time intervals differently from Max. No matter how small is the velocity v, as long as it is not zero, there always is a factor γ different from 1. The tiny deviation of γ from 1 is full of consequence, and we are now going to include this tiny deviation in our analysis of the photon frequencies. *The new element in the analysis that follows in comparison to the pre-Einstein analysis is that the "time of Ming" is not the same as "time of Max."* All other elements of the pre-Einstein analysis remain the same. But the change due to the new understanding of time is essential.

Namely, we have to realize that the view of the absorption process shown in Figure 11.1 on page 129 is seen in the Max frame of reference. Max sees that Ming moves and that Ming's eye is met by the right photon signals more often than Max's eye is. Max also sees that Ming's eye is met by the left photon signals less often than Max's eye is. But when one wants to find how the same intervals appear to Ming, to obtain the frequencies that Ming sees, one has to take into account the factor γ. The time intervals that we were considering before in the pre-Einstein analysis were actually obtained in the Max frame of reference, and there was no consideration whatever that Ming would see time differently than Max and that there was a correction to be made for that effect. It was known that the pre-Einstein analysis had a problem with the speed of light being the same for Max and Ming, but the solution was absent.

We now know that $t_{Max} = \gamma t_{Ming}$ for the events in which successive signals meet with Ming's eye. If these events are separated by some interval of time according to Max, say T_{Max}, this interval will be equal to γ times the interval seen by Ming, say T_{Ming}. Thus, we have $T_{Max} = \gamma T_{Ming}$. But if T_{Max} is γ times T_{Ming}, then T_{Ming} is T_{Max} divided by γ.

In order to find the frequency seen by Ming, recall Equation 9.2 on page 110, which says that the frequency is an inverse of the interval. So we have to find the inverse of T_{Ming}, or $\frac{1}{T_{Ming}}$. Since T_{Ming} is T_{Max} divided by γ, the inverse of T_{Ming} is equal to γ times the inverse of T_{Max}. And this means that the frequency seen by Ming is equal to γ times the frequency seen by Max. Thus, the changes necessary in the pre-Einstein reasoning can be described as follows.

First we look at the situation from the point of view of Max and proceed in exactly the same way as in the case of the pre-Einstein reasoning. There is no reason to change anything in that picture except for one thing: The time intervals between arrivals of signals in Ming's eye that we obtain in the pre-Einstein way of thinking are the intervals between the events as seen by Max. The distance between Ming's eye and the right photon decreases according to Max with velocity $c + v$, and the distance between Ming's eye and the left photon decreases according to Max with velocity $c - v$. These facts do not contradict the finding that Ming sees all photons as having speed c. Instead, Ming's time is different. Still, Max sees that the eye of Ming meets with successive signals and he can calculate how often this happens. The unconscious error in the pre-Einstein thinking was to assume that Ming was seeing those time intervals as the same as Max.

Now, to obtain the frequency of the right photon as seen by Ming, we have to take the result of the pre-Einstein reasoning and multiply it by γ. So, we first increase the frequency f by the same amount as in the pre-Einstein theory and then multiply this answer by γ. To obtain the frequency of the left photon, we first decrease the frequency f by the same amount as in the case of the right photon and then we multiply this answer by γ. The resulting frequencies of the right and left photon differ from the pre-Einstein ones only by the multiplication by γ.

When we calculate the energies of the photons, the only thing we do is to multiply the obtained frequencies by the Planck constant. This multiplication comes on top of the factor γ but otherwise preserves the structure of our results. So, when we add the energy of the right photon to the energy of the left photon, the two corrections, one coming from the increase and the other one from the decrease of frequency as in the pre-Einstein theory, still have opposite signs and they cancel out. But the dominant parts, $h\gamma f$ for the right photon and the same $h\gamma f$ for the left photon, are added and produce together our new result for the combined energy of the two photons as seen by Ming, Δ_{Ming}. Instead of just $\Delta_{Max} = 2hf$ obtained in the pre-Einstein theory, we now have γ times more. Thus, the Einstein result is that

$$\Delta_{Ming} = \gamma \Delta_{Max}.$$

Appendix I

How Absorption of Light Changes Mass

1. Ming always moves with respect to Max and the matchbox with a steady velocity v.

2. In Ming's reference frame, the matchbox always moves with velocity v. The velocity before and after the absorption process is the same.

3. Before the absorption process, the matchbox energy is equal to the sum E_{before} plus E_{motion}.

4. The energy of motion of the matchbox according to Ming is proportional to the mass of the matchbox, m, and the velocity v squared. (Details of the formula for E_{motion} are in Appendix A.)

5. In the absorption process, the energy of the matchbox is increased to the new value that, according to the law of conservation of energy, should be equal to the sum E_{before} plus E_{motion} plus Δ_{Ming}, where the last term is the amount of the combined energy of the two absorbed photons as seen by Ming.

6. The amount of energy Δ_{Ming} is gamma times greater than the amount Δ_{Max} of the combined energy of the same two photons as seen by Max.

7. The factor gamma depends on the velocity v of motion of Ming with respect to Max.

8. When the velocity v is not zero but extremely small in comparison to the speed of light, the factor gamma is equal to 1 plus a tiny correction that increases with velocity v. Appendix G discusses how the factor gamma depends on the velocity v when v is extremely small. Namely, the extremely tiny correction to 1 in gamma is equal

to one-half the velocity v squared divided by the speed of light, c, also squared. Since the velocity v is very, very small in comparison to the huge speed of light, squaring v and c and dividing v^2 by c^2 produces a much, much smaller number than the ratio $\frac{v}{c}$ itself. But this very tiny correction is still proportional to v^2. (Readers interested in the relevant mathematical expressions can find them in Appendix G).

9. In the pre-Einstein way of thinking, Ming would see the energy of the absorbed photons, Δ_{Ming}, as equal to their energy as seen by Max, Δ_{Max}. The absorbed energy would be independent of the velocity v. Thus, Ming would add Δ_{Max} to the matchbox's internal energy E_{before} and obtain E_{after} as Max would, entirely independently of the energy of motion of the matchbox, E_{motion}, that would depend on the velocity but would stay unaltered by the absorption of light.

10. But in the Einstein approach, when Max sees the combined energy of the two absorbed photons as equal to Δ_{Max}, Ming sees their combined energy as equal to Δ_{Ming}, which is gamma times larger than Δ_{Max}.

11. Moreover, the tiny correction in the factor gamma by which this factor differs from 1 depends on the velocity v. And on top of that, the dependence is of the same type as in the energy of motion. Namely, the tiny correction to 1 in gamma is proportional to v^2 and the energy of motion is also proportional to v^2.

12. When we multiply Δ_{Max} by gamma in order to obtain Δ_{Ming}, we use the fact that gamma is equal to 1 plus a very tiny number.

13. When we multiply the energy Δ_{Max} by the sum of 1 plus a very tiny number, the answer is equal to the energy Δ_{Max} itself plus the very tiny number times the energy Δ_{Max}.

14. Thus, the energy Δ_{Ming} is equal to the sum of two parts.

15. There is a part that is equal to Δ_{Max}. This part comes from 1 in the factor gamma and it does not depend on the velocity v.

16. There is also an extremely small part equal to Δ_{Max} times the half of the ratio of v^2 to c^2. This part comes from the very tiny difference between gamma and 1. The new, very tiny amount of energy depends on the velocity v because the very tiny correction to 1 in gamma depends on v.

17. The law of conservation of energy says that when the light is absorbed in the matchbox, the latter gains the energy of the former.

18. After absorption, the part of energy of the matchbox in Ming's frame of reference that is independent of the velocity of the

matchbox is equal to the sum of E_{before} plus the energy of light Δ_{Max}, as in the Max frame of reference. This part is the same as in the pre-Einstein way of thinking where γ is not distinguished from 1.

19. After absorption, the part of energy of the matchbox in Ming's frame of reference that depends on the velocity of the matchbox is equal to the sum of the energy of motion the matchbox had before absorption, E_{motion}, plus the very tiny part that is equal to the energy of light Δ_{Max} times the half of the ratio of v^2 to c^2.

20. The formula that describes this part of the energy of the matchbox after absorption, that is, the part that depends on the velocity v, is

$$\frac{1}{2}mv^2 + \frac{1}{2}\Delta_{Max}\frac{v^2}{c^2}.$$

21. The energy of motion of the matchbox before absorption and the very tiny correction that is added due to gamma being different from 1 are both proportional to the same one-half of v^2.

22. In the initial energy of motion of the matchbox, E_{motion}, the same half of v^2 is multiplied by the mass m of the matchbox.

23. In the tiny correction due to gamma being different from 1, the same half of v^2 is multiplied by the energy of the absorbed light, Δ_{Max}, divided by c^2.

24. The entire part of the energy of the matchbox after absorption that depends on the velocity v can be now looked upon as the new energy of motion of the matchbox after absorption because this entire part is proportional to the half of v^2 as the energy of motion of a body should be. But instead of only the mass m, we now have the sum of the mass m plus the combined energy of photons, Δ_{Max}, divided by the square of the speed of light, c^2.

25. Together, the part of the final energy of the matchbox that depends on the velocity v appears to be the same as the energy of motion of a matchbox with a new mass, which we denote by m_{after}.

26. The new mass m_{after} is equal to the sum of the initial mass m plus the combined energy of photons, Δ_{Max}, divided by the square of the speed of light, c^2.

27. The formula for the new mass is

$$m_{after} = m + \frac{\Delta_{Max}}{c^2}.$$

28. If one assumes that energy is conserved, the absorption of light produces a gain in mass that is equal to the gain in energy at rest divided by the square of the speed of light.

Appendix J

Lenard and Einstein

W e do not have a full picture of the relationship between Lenard and Einstein, but we indicate below some sources that may help the interested reader in seeking more information.

Lenard dedicated his *Deutsche Physik* to the Minister of Internal Affairs in Hitler's government, and he addressed the minister with honorable respect as a leader of great research in the Third Reich.[1]

Lenard's anti-Semitic stance has been mentioned by A. I. Miller in his book *Albert Einstein's Special Theory of Relativity: Emergence* (1905) *and Early Interpretation* (1905–1911).[2] Miller writes about an article by Einstein, "Dialog über Einwände gegen die Relativitätstheorie,"[3] that "one of Einstein's goals was to give a lesson in epistemology to such opponents of the relativity theory as Phillip Lenard."[4] Miller continues by saying,

> Mostly owing to Germany's defeat in World War I, Lenard's anti-Semitism and extreme nationalism came into the open. He was an early supporter of Hitler, subsequently becoming Hitler's authority in science. Many of Lenard's former students joined him in reorganizing science under National Socialism, among them was August Becker. . . . Stark too had early espoused the cause of National Socialism but a courageous stand by Max von Laue, in particular, forced Stark into retirement prior to World War II. During the first decade of the 20th century Lenard and Stark had been among the leaders in German science: Lenard was the Nobel laureate in 1905; Stark was awarded the Nobel Prize in 1919 for having discovered the Doppler effect in fast moving hydrogen ions (canal rays) and the splitting of spectral lines in an electric field (Stark effect). Their correspondence reveals that both men had been early supporters of Einstein. For example, we recall the Einstein-Stark correspondence of 1907. Stark considered the transverse

Doppler effect of the radiation from canal rays to have been proof of the relativity theory.[5]

But we know that Lenard and Stark later changed their minds about Einstein (the biography of Stark on the official Web site of the Nobel Foundation does not indicate that Stark adopted the cause of National Socialism in Germany before World War II). Lenard's *Deutsche Physik* of 1937 did not mention the name Einstein in its index, although names such as Lorentz did appear in the index. Lenard's foreword attacked Einstein as a primary example of a misleading Jewish scientist who attempted to replace solid German science rooted in "experimentally verified knowledge" with unproven hypotheses, and who presented "the hypotheses" as viable ideas to the public, while they were, according to Lenard, no more than wishful thinking rather than experimentally verified truth.

Lenard opposed characterization of science as international and considered "the German way of thinking" as superior to the way of thinking of members of other nations. He wrote that "Das heutige deutsche wissenschaftliche Schrifttum fäalt noch mehr durch undeutsches Denken auf als durch undeutsche Wörter" ("Today's German scientific writing misses more through non-German thinking than through non-German words").[6] An extensive source of information on the subject of German science in Hitler's times is the 2004 book by J. Cornwell, *Hitler's Scientists, Science, War, and the Devil's Pact*.[7] It is clear that Lenard's learning was very limited and unproductive outside his specialty.

Notes

CHAPTER 1

1. S. B. Sarason, *The Predictable Failure of Educational Reform,* Jossey-Bass, San Francisco, 1990.

CHAPTER 4

1. The texts are available in English, translated by C. G. Wallis, published in *Great Books of the Western World*, Ed. M. J. Adler, Vol. 15, pp. 845 and 1,006, Encyclopædia Britannica, Chicago, 1993. In particular, see page 1,034 in this publication, above the heading of Chapter 5, for the sentence that we quote here.

2. Readers interested in Einstein and music may find it helpful to read an essay by A. I. Miller (2006, January 31), Genius finds inspiration in the music of another. *The New York Times*, p. F3.

CHAPTER 6

1. The precise meanings of the concepts of energy and mass are not easy to grasp. We will discuss these concepts at length. At this point, we merely use the common words "energy" and "mass" to introduce the subject of our story.

CHAPTER 7

1. See http://www.stargazing.net/astropc for interactive maps of the sky. The image we present in Figure 7.1 was produced using an early version of the computer program that is available for free as Sky Charts—Cartes du Ciel, Version 2.76 2004-11-21, created by Patrick Chevalley (http://www.astrosurf.com/astropc/).

2. Americans use miles as units of distance and Europeans use kilometers (km) as units of distance. One mile equals about 1.609 km. We shall use both units, depending on the context. For example, a speed limit may be given in mph, while the diameter of Earth's orbit may be given in km.

3. In the southern hemisphere, the beacon stars could be Rigel, Canopus, and four stars of the constellation Crux, or the Southern Cross.

4. We know that there exists a record of Römer's work published under the title *Demonstration touchant le mouvement de la lumiere trouvé par Römer de l'Academie Royale des Sciences* in *Journal des Scavans*, pp. 233–236, on Decembre 7, 1676. An English translation is available as *A Demonstration concerning the Motion of Light, communicated from Paris, in the Journal des Scavans, and here made English*, published in *Philosophical Transactions of the Royal Society*, No. 136; pp. 893–894, on June 25, 1677.

5. R. J. MacKay and R. W. Oldford, "Scientific Method, Statistical Method and the Speed of Light," *Statistical Science 15*(3), 254, 2000. This reference is mainly about measurements of the speed of light made much later by A. A. Michelson, but it also mentions Römer.

CHAPTER 8

1. The narrow band is characteristic of water: The light of frequencies in that narrow band penetrates water down to about 50 meters, while all other kinds of light with frequencies outside the narrow band are quickly absorbed in water and do not get beyond a thin surface layer. Our vision organ suggests we evolved from water.

2. See A. A. Michelson and E. W. Morley, "On the Relative Motion of the Earth and the Luminiferous Ether," *American Journal of Science, 34*, 333, 1887. One can find an electronic copy of this article on the American Institute of Physics Web site www.aip.org/history/gap.

3. Nicolai Copernici Torunensis, *De Revolutionibus Orbium Coelestium, Libri VI*, Nurnberg, 1543. A contemporary English translation is available as Nicolaus Copernicus, *On the Revolutions of Heavenly Spheres*, translated by C. G. Wallis, in *Great Books of the Western World*, Ed., M. J. Adler, Vol. 15, p. 505, Encyclopædia Britannica, Chicago, 1993.

4. In the second paragraph of *De Revoltionibus* (see Note 3 in Chapter 8), Copernicus quoted Plato as making "an extremely good point, . . . that this study [of heavenly bodies] should be pursued in especial, that through it the orderly arrangement of days into months and years and the determination of the times for solemnities and sacrifices should keep the state alive and watchful." In the third paragraph, Copernicus says, "Now to take the year itself as my example, I believe it is well known how many different opinions there are about it; so that many people have given up hope of making an exact determination of it." See also *Nicolaus Copernicus Heritage, On the 500th Anniversary of Copernicus* by the National Organizing Committee in Australia, Eds., M. J. W. B. Bialowieyski, K. Bieda, M. A. Hons, Melbourne, 1973, Polpress Pty. Ltd., Richmond, Vic. 3121, ISBN 0-9598265-0-5, pp. 6, 7.

5. The issues considered by astronomers and the church were more complex and different from the simplified examples in our story, but the way we put the question catches some flavor of the problem. The literature concerning the "right" date of Easter is enormous. A useful overview can be found at http://aa.usno.navy.mil/faq/docs/easter.html, and one can consult the Explanatory Supplement to the *Astronomical Almanac*, edited by P. K. Seidelmann, U.S. Naval

Observatory, especially the article by L. E. Doggett, "Calendars," available at http://astro.nmsu.edu/lhuber/leaphist.html.

6. See *The New Encyclopædia Britannica*, Vol. 4, p. 333, Micropedia, 15th edition, Chicago, 1994.

7. The old word *epact* originates from Greek and Latin and means here a period added to harmonize the lunar calendar with the solar calendar.

CHAPTER 9

1. We follow here advice on how to describe Lenard's experiments given in Arnold B. Arons, *A Guide to Introductory Physics Teaching*, John Wiley, New York, pp. 245–250, 1990.

2. Einstein's prediction that the energy of "particles of light" should be equal to the Planck constant h times the frequency of light f was not easy to check experimentally. The first solid evidence for the validity of the formula was provided by R. A. Millikan 11 years after Einstein postulated existence of the "particles of light." Millikan tried to disprove Einstein's relation and found instead that it was too good to be questioned. See R. A. Millikan, "A direct photoelectric determination of Planck's constant h," *Physical Review 7*, 355–388, 1916. An insightful source of historical information about Einstein's work concerning the photoelectric effect can be found in A. K. Wróblewski, "Einstein and physics a hundred years ago," *Acta Physica Polonica B37*, 11–30, 2006, available at http://th-www.if.uj.edu.pl/acta.

3. The wide use of the name "photon" began perhaps with publication of the short article by G. N. Lewis in *Nature 118*, 874, 1926. In his Nobel lecture from 1927, A. H. Compton speaks of "light corpuscles, quanta, or, as we may call them, photons." Subsequently, Compton uses the name "photon" in his lecture with ease, 14 times.

4. In order to show the reader that such processes of learning through discovery are by no means unique to physics, let us point out that for millennia, up until relatively recently in human history, human blood could not be conceived as containing numerous discrete particles called blood cells and that, in addition, these cells are composed of scores of molecules and perform very complex functions.

5. A. Pais, *Einstein Lived Here*, Oxford University Press, New York, pp. 63–78, 1994, reprinted from *American Scientist*, 70, 4, July/August, 1982, pp. 358–365. The story of Einstein's Nobel Prize describes how judgment is passed on scientific work by people who award the prize and how the process was carried out in the case of Einstein's contribution to physics.

6. A. Einstein, "Über einen die Erzeugung und Verwandlung des Lichtes betreffenden heuristischen Gesichtspunkt," *Annalen der Physik 17*, 132, 1905; or *Annalen der Physik 14*, 164, 2005. See also www.ann-phys.org.

7. A. Einstein, "Zur Elektrodynamik bewegter Körper," *Annalen der Physik 17*, 891, 1905; or *Annalen der Physik 14*, 194, 2005. See also http://www.ann-phys.org.

8. A. Einstein, "Ist die Trägheit eines Körpers von seinem Energieinhalt abhängig?" *Annalen der Physik 18*, 639, 1905; reprinted in *Annalen der Physik 14*, 225, 2005. See also http://www.ann-phys.org.

9. It is not clear why Einstein entirely ignored the concept of particles of light, or light quanta, introduced in the paper of March 1905, when he wrote his paper of June 1905. He limited himself in the second paper to a comment that it was interesting that the energy of an electromagnetic field as seen by one observer is related to the energy of the same field as seen by another observer, who moves with respect to the first one, as the frequency of the field seen by the first observer is related to the frequency of the same field seen by the second observer. Einstein did not draw the conclusion in his second article that if the field of frequency f was made of quanta, with every quantum having energy E_f equal to hf, and if the energy of a wave of electromagnetic field was the sum of the energies of the quanta that comprised the wave, then the energy of the wave of the field had to depend on the observer exactly as the frequency of the wave did. It would be natural for Einstein to refer to his March article if he believed that his ideas had been absolutely correct. But he did not think so. The title he gave his March paper about the picture of light as made of "particles" contained the word "heuristic." In fact, the discussion about the nature of light among physicists continued for years. In 1925, 20 years after publication of the March, 1905, article and four years after he was awarded the Nobel Prize for his services to theoretical physics, and especially for his discovery of the law of the photo-electric effect (in his Nobel lecture, Einstein wrote about the theory of relativity and did not discuss the photoelectric effect at all), Einstein wrote a letter to the Brazilian Academy of Sciences in Rio de Janeiro in which he discussed ambiguities in the understanding of the nature of light and options to resolve them experimentally (see A. Einstein, "Remarks on the Present Situation of the Theory of Light," a letter written on May 7, 1925 to the Brazilian Academy of Sciences in Rio de Janeiro, English translation made available by Richard A. Campos, http://arxiv.org/abs/physics/0401044). Regarding the nature of photons, and the quantum theory in general, a public discussion between Einstein and Niels Bohr, another Nobel laureate from 1922 for the quantum theory of atoms and light, continued for more than a quarter of a century, see N. Bohr, "Discussions With Einstein on Epistemological Problems in Atomic Physics," in *Albert Einstein: Philosopher-Scientist*, Cambridge University Press, 1949.

10. Note that the Planck formula $E_f = hf$, which Planck discovered for *the energy of vibrations of atoms*, looks identical to the Einstein formula $E_f = hf$ for *the energy of photons*. But even though they look identical, they refer to completely different objects. Planck's formula refers to the energy of vibrations of atoms. The frequency of vibration of an atom is equal to the inverse of the duration of one cycle of the oscillatory motion that the atom is involved in. Einstein's formula refers to the energy of photons. The frequency of a photon is defined as the inverse of the time period that passes between arrivals of successive signals in the eye of an observer of the photon.

CHAPTER 10

1. There is another concept of mass that is defined as a measure of how strongly a body is gravitationally attracted by the Earth, or other masses. This other concept of mass is called the gravitational mass. A priori, the inertial mass, m, which we talk about in this chapter, and the gravitational mass have no reason to

be equal to each other. But in the real world they are equal, and so precisely, that Einstein postulated that their equality must have a fundamental origin. The theory based on the equality of the inertial mass and gravitational mass is called general relativity and describes masses moving under the influence of gravitational forces. Our story says nothing about gravity, but Note 2 in this chapter does.

2. It is not germane to our present purposes, but it may be interesting to the reader that the gravitational mass, the one that we mentioned in Note 1, has also been investigated in the context of the energy formula $E = mc^2$. Nature is such that the inertial mass and the gravitational mass are numerically identical as far as we can check. Einstein was very intrigued by the equality of the inertial and gravitational masses. This equality was inexplicable in Newton's theory of gravity and found its first explanation in Einstein's general theory of relativity, which he completed many years after he discovered the formula $E = mc^2$ with inertial mass m in it. He then struggled with the question of whether the energy was also related in the same way to the gravitational mass, and in particular, whether gravity attracted energy like gravitational masses, independently of the nature of the energy. His general theory of relativity confirmed this hypothesis and became one of the triumphs of human insight into the structure of the universe. The laws of gravity and energy conservation in all forms became the basis for ways of imagining how the entire universe is held together.

3. We are not very precise here, since, for example, the stone and our hand are warmed up a bit where they touch each other, and we know that our muscles quickly warm up when we do work, the air is moving also, and some energy is dispersed in small amounts in tiny sparks of radiation that are triggered by the pushing and colliding of atoms. But the amounts are tiny and/or not as directly perceptible by us as the motion of the stone is. All these detailed, complex processes obey the rule of conservation of energy in total.

CHAPTER 11

1. See Chapter 8: What Came Out From the Search for Ether?, where we discussed studies carried out by Copernicus, starting on page 94.

2. See the discussion of Römer's studies of the movements of Io around Jupiter in Chapter 7, starting on page 82.

3. Dirac, who was the first to provide a quantum theory of electrons in agreement with Einstein's concept of time and predicted the existence of antimatter (he received a Nobel Prize in Physics for his work in 1933), attached great value to a mathematically sound formulation of ideas. He expressed his point of view in a beautifully succinct lecture: P. A. M. Dirac, "The Mathematical Foundations of Quantum Theory," in A. R. Marlow, Ed., *Mathematical Foundations of Quantum Theory*. New York: Academic Press, 1978.

CHAPTER 12

1. In practice, no observer knows any position or time coordinate of any event exactly because all measurements are made with some error. But the classical theory of relativity says that if we knew the exact coordinates for an event

according to one observer, we would also know the coordinates that another observer has to obtain for the same event.

2. Major historical importance is attached to the experiments carried out by A. A. Michelson and E. W. Morley, especially to their work published in 1887 in which they tried to find a dependence of the speed of light on the direction of its motion, measured with respect to the direction of the velocity of the Earth in the orbit around the Sun. Michelson and Morley tried this way to obtain new information about the hypothetical ether that was believed to be omnipresent in the space through which the Earth travels in the solar system (see A. A. Michelson and E. W. Morley, "On the Relative Motion of the Earth and the Luminiferous Ether," *American Journal of Science 34*, 333–345, 1887; an electronic copy of this article is available at http://www.aip.org/history/gap.) The expected effect of dependence of the speed of light on the motion of the Earth with respect to the hypothetical ether was not found. (Albert Michelson received the Nobel Prize in Physics in 1907 "for his optical precision instruments and the spectroscopic and metrological investigations carried out with their aid." It is interesting that in his Nobel lecture Michelson did not attach any special significance to his now-famous measurements of the speed of light published in 1887. His Nobel lecture was about recent advances in spectroscopy and did not mention Morley.) The concept of a medium in which light had speed c, as if it was like a wave in a sea and as if the sea formed a distinct frame of reference, could not be sustained.

In an analogy to the Michelson and Morley experiment, we can say that Ming cannot discover his velocity with respect to a hypothetical ether by measuring the speed of light that he produces and detects on the train because he always obtains the same speed c no matter how fast and in what direction he travels according to Max. There is also no a priori reason to consider one of the observers (Max or Ming) as more important than the other. And Max sees pulses of light that he produces and detects himself as having also the speed c. But what speed of a pulse of light will Max see if the pulse is produced by Ming? In other words, does the speed of light depend on the velocity of the source?

No, if the observers are equally valid and neither is more important than the other, the speed of light should not depend on the source. Namely, if light appears to behave like a wave of ether for Ming, it should also appear to behave like a wave of ether for Max. This argument is valid even if the ether does not exist. The only aspect that counts is how light behaves. Apparently, light exists and behaves in many ways like a wave. But if it behaves that way for one observer and no observer is in a privileged position, it should also appear to behave in the same way for other observers. Regarding waves, the velocity of a wave in water does not depend on the velocity of a boat that makes the wave. Thus, the speed of a pulse of light made by Ming should, according to Max, have the same speed c that a pulse of light made by Max himself has.

3. See Note 2 for this chapter.

CHAPTER 13

1. P. Galison, *Einstein's Clocks, Poincaré's Maps, Empires of Time.* New York, Norton, 2003.

2. Galison (2003) writes that "during the time that Einstein served as a patent inspector . . . coordinated clocks began playing an ever-increasing role in both

public and private sites. The numbers: 1901, eight patents; 1902, ten; 1903, six; and then in 1904 (the peak year from 1889 to 1910) fourteen patents on electric clocks overcame the hurdles of the patent office. . . . Einstein was . . . chiefly charged with the evaluation of electromechanical patents" (p. 248).

CHAPTER 14

1. What we have just said means that the observers need to know how their frames of reference are related if they want to take advantage of coordinates when they talk about events. They can also communicate about the events in terms of physical characteristics that allow the observers to identify events no matter what coordinates they use and what is the relationship between their frames of reference. But the latter way of communication about events is not efficient. It is awkward because it always requires elaborate description of what one means, as if there was no dictionary between different languages they know—like using gestures or drawings instead of a common language. The more efficient way is to find the relationship between the frames of reference once, like a dictionary between two different languages, and communicate quickly, gaining ability to clearly express abstract thoughts.

CHAPTER 15

1. Einstein found that there should be four coefficients relating t_{Max} and x_{Max} to t_{Ming} and x_{Ming}. Namely, t_{Max} could be a combination of t_{Ming} and x_{Ming} with two coefficients, and x_{Max} could be a combination of t_{Ming} and x_{Ming} with some other two coefficients. Appendix D explains an interesting example of how one can find these coefficients (there also exist other ways of finding them), and Appendix E describes the result.

2. In his original article of June 1905, Einstein used two principles. One was "daß dem Begriffe der absoluten Ruhe nicht nur in der Mechanik, sondern auch in der Elektrodynamik keine Eigenschaften der Erscheinungen entsprechen, sondern daß vielmehr für alle Koordinatensysteme, für welche die mechanishen Gleichungen gelten, auch die gleichen elektrodynamischen und optischen Gesetze gelten." Trying to translate this statement into English most closely to the German version, one can say "that no features of phenomena correspond to the concept of absolute rest not only in mechanics, but also in electrodynamics, and that moreover for all systems of coordinates [frames of reference], in which the mechanical equations are valid, also the same electrodynamical and optical laws are valid." The second principle was "daßsich das Licht im leeren Raume stets mit einer bestimmten, von Bewegungszustande des emittierenden Körpers unabhängigen Geschwindigkeit V fortpflanze." In English, "that light in empty space always propagates itself with a definite speed V, which is independent of the state of motion of the emitting body." Einstein was using the letter V for the speed of light instead of c (in his paper about $E = mc^2$, he also used only the letter V and never c). Einstein also assumed that the relationship between coordinates of the same events in two frames of reference that move with respect to each other with a steady velocity must be linear (combinations with some coefficients) because of the "property of homogeneity that we attribute to space and time." Appendix D

shows that the principle of relativity stated in the text implies the existence of a speed c that is the same for all observers.

3. When a student follows a path of interest and rediscovers the principle of relativity, it is a remarkable point on his or her learning path. A student's arrival at this point creates an opportunity for the teacher to mention that the path to a discovery is not purely inductive but also significantly deductive. This is discussed in A. Einstein, "Physics and Reality," *Journal of the Franklin Institute 221*, 349–382, 1936. The art of teaching students about physics is to help them understand the inductive part of the path to discovery, which leads from special hands-on examples to general ideas, and the role of the deductive part of the path that involves conceiving and adopting general ideas and checking their detailed implications by logical inference, when a specific question is asked or a special example is considered. The student should also appreciate that it is entirely unclear how it happens that we are capable of making discoveries using both inductive and deductive ways of thinking, what and why happens in between. The phenomenon of creativity is well-known to exist but not even remotely understood.

4. Appendix D describes one way in which one can find the Einstein equations, and the result is given in Appendix E.

5. There exists a direct mathematical argument for the existence of a special speed c that must be the same for all observers in steady motion. For readers who know algebra, the argument is described in Appendix E.

6. See Chapter 12, page 146.

7. See the discussion in Chapter 12, starting on page 144.

8. The relationship between Max's and Ming's *space* coordinates, mentioned in point 2, is also changed by the presence of the factor gamma. We have not discussed that change in order to simplify our discussion in the main text. Readers interested in the Einstein relation for space coordinates can find it in Appendices D and E. The extra factor mentioned in point 3 is displayed in Equation D.1 on page 237 in Appendix D.

9. This factor can be found in many ways, and one (not the easiest) is given in Appendix D, with the result given in Equation D.1 on page 237.

CHAPTER 16

1. Einstein described the formula $E = mc^2$ for the first time in 1905 using the process of emission of light, rather than absorption. We use absorption instead, in order to explain how the energy of a body may build up by absorbing the energy of light and in order to remain faithful to the morning scene at the beginning of our story of $E = mc^2$, in which our skin absorbs sunlight and we feel how the energy of the sunlight warms up our skin.

2. The dependence of gamma on the velocity v is described in Appendix G.

CHAPTER 17

1. The readers interested in details of such questionnaires and their outcomes can find the relevant information in two monographs, including a "lie scale." See S. B. Sarason, K. T. Hill, P. G. Zimbardo, "A Longitudinal Study of the Relation of Test Anxiety to Performance on Intelligence and Achievement Tests,"

Monographs of the Society for Research in Child Development, Serial No. 98, Vol. 29, No. 7, 1964, and the second part of the study, K. T. Hill, S. B. Sarason, "The Relation of Test Anxiety and Defensiveness to Test and School Performance over the Elementary School Years, a further longitudinal study," Series No. 104, Vol. 31, No. 2, 1966.

2. S. B. Sarason, *The Case for Change, Rethinking the Preparation of Educators,* Jossey-Bass Publishers, San Francisco, 1993.

3. S. B. Sarason, *Schooling in America: Scapegoat and Salvation,* Free Press, New York, 1983.

4. E. Ginzberg and D. Bray, *The Uneducated,* Columbia University Press, New York, 1953.

5. S. B. Sarason, *Revisiting "The Culture of School and The Problem of Change,"* Teachers College Press, New York, 1996, see page 92.

6. M. J. Bennett, *When Dreams Come True,* Brasey, Washington DC, 1996.

7. D. Ravitch, *Left Back: A Century of Failed School Reforms,* Simon & Schuster, New York, 2000.

8. S. B. Sarason, *American Psychology and Schools: A Critique,* Teachers College Press, New York, 2001.

9. See Note 8.

10. D. Bensman, *Central Park East and Its Graduates,* Teachers College Press, New York, 2000; and E. Levine, *One Kid at a Time: Big Lessons From a Small School,* Teachers College Press, New York, 2001.

11. In addition to what we repeat here, we add new material from the film.

12. A. B. Arons, *A guide to Introductory Physics Teaching,* John Wiley, New York, 1990, pp. 245–250.

13. G. Holton, *Einstein, History, and Other Passions: The Rebellion Against Science at the End of the Twentieth Century,* Addison-Wesley, Reading, MA, 1997, p. 183.

14. The quotation originates from Nobel Lectures, Physics 1901–1921, Elsevier, Amsterdam, 1967.

15. P. Lenard, *Deutsche Physik, in vier Bander,* I. F. Lehmanns Verlag, Munich Berlin, 1940.

16. Rabbi Hillel, Jewish sage, master of Talmud, flourished during the second half of the first century BC and the first quarter of the first century AD. Stories about Hillel belong to the most popular Talmudic tales in Jewish literature and folklore.

17. L. C. McDermott, P. S. Shaffer, and M. L. Rosenquist, *Physics by Inquiry: An Introduction to Physics and the Physical Sciences,* John Wiley & Sons, New York, 1996. A Polish edition of the book is published by Prószyński i Ska, Warsaw 2000.

18. For readers interested in how scientists may think about educational reform, see the book by K. G. Wilson and B. Daviss, *Redesigning Education, A Nobel Prize Winner Reveals What Must Be Done to Reform American Education.* See also the whole issue of *Daedalus,* Journal of the American Academy of Arts and Sciences, Fall 1998, entitled *Education Yesterday, Education Tomorrow.*

APPENDIX B

1. This general rule has been explained on page 106.

APPENDIX D

1. We have learned how to carry out this reasoning from Professor A. Szymacha, who described it in his book *Szczególna Teoria Względności*, Alfa, Warszawa, 1985.

2. In principle, one can also have nonlinear relations whose form does not distinguish any observer. For example, one can add to the time coordinates an arbitrary function of space coordinates for all observers equally. But such nonlinear relations involve coordinates that do not correspond to the assumed basic property of homogeneity of space and time.

APPENDIX J

1. See Chapter 17, note 15.

2. A. I. Miller, *Albert Einstein's Special Theory of Relativity: Emergence (1905) and Early Interpretation (1905–1911)*, Addison-Wesley, Reading, MA, 1981.

3. A. Einstein, "Dialog über Einwände gegen die Relativitätstheorie," *Naturwissenschaften, 697*, 1918.

4. Miller, 1981, p. 272, note 33.

5. Miller, 1981, p. 378, note 16.

6. Lenard, 1937, *Deutsche Physik*, p. xiv, note 1; see Chapter 17, note 15.

7. J. Cornwell, *Hitler's Scientists, Science, War, and the Devil's Pact*, Penguin, New York, 2004.

Index

CORWIN PRESS

The Corwin Press logo—a raven striding across an open book—represents the union of courage and learning. Corwin Press is committed to improving education for all learners by publishing books and other professional development resources for those serving the field of PreK–12 education. By providing practical, hands-on materials, Corwin Press continues to carry out the promise of its motto: **"Helping Educators Do Their Work Better."**